Chopin's Poland

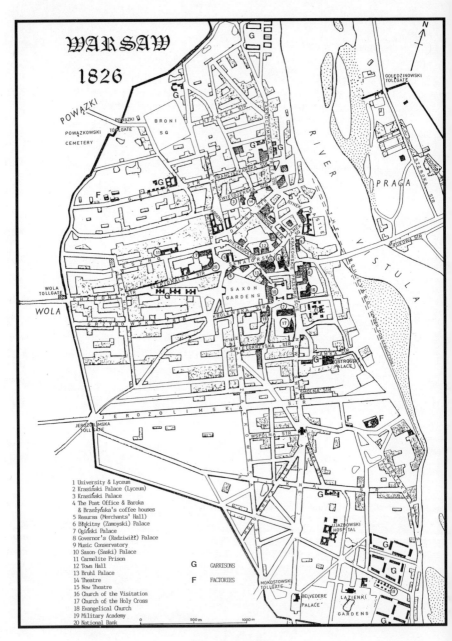

Warsaw in 1826

Iwo and Pamela
Załuski

Chopin's Poland

Peter Owen Publishers
London & Chester Springs

PETER OWEN PUBLISHERS
73 Kenway Road London SW5 0RE
Peter Owen books are distributed in the USA by
Dufour Editions Inc. Chester Springs PA 19425–0007

First published in Great Britain 1996
© Iwo and Pamela Załuski 1996

ISBN 0–7206–0980–1

A catalogue record for this book is available from
the British Library

Printed and made in Great Britain
by Biddles of Guildford and King's Lynn

ACKNOWLEDGEMENTS

Mieczysław Kłos (Poturzyn)
Henryk Brudło, Ewa Ruszkowska, Leon Okowiński, Ignacy
Zukowski, Franciszek Kułaga (Sulechów)
Revd Konrad Lutyński, Sr. Mgr. Teresa Florczak (Archiwum
Archidiecezjalne Poznań)
Hanna Wróblewska-Straus (Ostrogski Palace Warsaw)
Andrzej Merkur, Ryszard Grzelakowski (Duszniki)
Dr Roman Wytyczak (Ossoliński Library Wrocław)
Barbara Zagajewska, Leszek Nawrocki (Sochaczew)
Marek Sperski (Sopot)
Kazimierz Ziótkowski, Aleksandra Głowacka (Samniki)
Henryk Górecki (Szafarnia)

Contents

Illustrations

ONE
Nicolas Chopin's Poland

About thirty-five kilometres to the south of Nancy, the capital of Lorraine, in the French Department of Vosges, lies the village of Marainville. It is situated on the banks of the River Madon, which joins the Moselle on the southern outskirts of Nancy. In 1732, King Louis XV of France, who married Maria Leszczyńska, made her father, the former King of Poland, the Duke of Lorraine, thus turning the French province into a 'little Poland'. Stanisław Leszczyński, or '*le bon roi Stanislas*', as he was known, was an enlightened ruler, builder, and reformer in education, welfare and agriculture. Among his architectural legacies is Nancy's magnificent centre. His arrival in Lorraine was followed by a series of immigration waves of fellow countrymen, France having been traditionally admired by Poles as a cultural role model. In 1766 the eighty-nine-year-old Duke Stanislas slipped and fell into the fire in his hearth. He died from his burns, and Lorraine mourned a popular administrator. The Polish connection at the head of the hierarchy of Lorraine was gone, but the community remained. Among them was the magnate, Count Pac, whose estate at Marainville was administered by Adam Weydlich, who employed a wheelwright, François Chopin.

On 15 April 1771, the Chopins produced their only son, Nicolas, a bright boy who at sixteen graduated from secondary school. That year, Adam Weydlich left to run a snuff factory in Warsaw, and offered Nicolas a job there. The world was a turbulent place full of

7

new ideas ranging from cultural enlightenment to bloody revolution, but it was Nicolas's oyster for the taking, and this was an opportunity to see it. The idea of life in the Polish capital appealed to him, and he accepted. In autumn 1787 Nicolas Chopin, armed with books by Voltaire, a flute and a violin, accompanied the Weydlichs to Poland. At the factory he was a clerk in the finance department, a boring but secure job. 'Mr Weydlich is very good to me,' he wrote home, 'and I can see very good prospects here.'

Over the next five years, Nicolas learned Polish and assimilated himself into Warsaw life. He saw about him a city of stark contrasts, both physical and intellectual. Warsaw, with its population of 100,000, was in the throes of a spectacular decline; but it was a city that Nicolas found intensely alive. Earlier that year King Stanisław August Poniatowski, met his former lover, Catherine the Great of Russia, to discuss his plans for Poland's future, and a new era of cooperation with her powerful eastern neighbour. The meeting was a political and a personal disaster, and Poland was awash with speculation about an impending war with Russia.

Many wealthy Poles were tuning up to fiddle while Warsaw burned. The arts were flourishing, the theatre was enjoying success, and music was made everywhere. Poets and authors found hungry readers. Corruption was rife and the seething streets spoke volumes about social inequalities. Wealthy Jewish traders, starving beggars, soldiers, foreign adventurers and fortune seekers, many homeless, milled about in disarray – going about their business, looking for some, or merely surviving. The carriages of the fabulously rich magnates, drawn by teams of six plumed stallions, thundered past with little regard for life and safety. Magnificent baroque and rococo palaces, their styles borrowed from Europe's finest sources, with huge gardens in the fashionable English mode, stood among squalid hovels which clung leech-like to the walls of the great estates. At this time there was no bridge to link the capital with the suburb of Praga on the other side of the River Vistula – only a ferry.

Warsaw's main thoroughfare, the Krakowskie Przedmieście, ran parallel to the River Vistula, near the west bank. Here Nicolas saw fine churches, such as the Holy Cross and the Visitation. At the north end stood the Royal Palace, the residence of King Stanisław August. The column of King Zygmunt III in the Castle Square before it, is to this day the most famous landmark in Poland. Beyond the Palace was the city centre, the Stare Miasto.

In some ways, reflected Nicolas, Warsaw must be similar to Paris, where discontent was only just being held down by a regime that was unable to countenance even the idea of revolution. The Polish state was obviously in imminent danger of collapse, but for all that he chose to remain and throw in his lot with this fascinating land. Its peculiar political structure was unique in Europe, and it was only because of the perverse Polish mentality that this structure had survived.

The Polish-Lithuanian Commonwealth was an enormous feudal land with no aristocracy and no hereditary sovereign. Titles did not exist until the Napoleonic era, and the Commonwealth was ruled by an elected king; the philosophy was to prevent a single royal dynasty becoming too powerful. The elected kings were not necessarily Polish. Many pan-European political entrepreneurs sought a Polish kingship for their own ends, while the Poles would buy security by electing a foreign warrior, on the understanding that he would not then invade Poland. The elections were run by the Seym (Parliament). This consisted of the real rulers of Poland, the magnates, who were the aristocracy in effect if not in name, the feudal landowners, some of whom were wealthy beyond conception. The Radziwiłł dynasty owned six hundred villages, with a hundred times that figure of peasants in thrall. Yet the magnates did not supply the state with a regular army, as in most feudal systems. In times of war, peasants were hurriedly rounded up, armed with sharp farm equipment, and sent out in their multitudes as cannon fodder. Poland's territorial security was left to chance by a cavalier attitude that trusted everything to turn out right in the end.

The system was propagated through the use of the *liberum veto*, whereby one magnate could negate any decision by exercising his veto, virtually ensuring that no new laws were passed for years at a time, to preserve the *status quo*. This suited the magnates, to whom new decisions might bring an unwelcome change of fortune; but in the final analysis it turned out to be the downward road to stagnation and disaster.

The Commonwealth, in its closing stages, had honed organized anarchy almost to perfection. Its sheer size, corruption and quirks were viewed with suspicion, even alarm, by the major European powers. The concept of an elected government and an elected king was radical, and smacked of revolution. An hereditary monarchy with its attendant aristocracy was the norm, and Europe needed to keep it that way.

Another factor in Poland's formation was nationhood, often a nebulous concept in eighteenth-century Europe. The Germans were a people with the same language and same culture who occupied the broad swathe of central Europe, yet they were dispersed throughout a patchwork quilt of city states, kingdoms and electorates, partly enclosed within the complex and seemingly illogical borders of the Holy Roman Empire.

On the other hand there were lands where mixed populations lived together in varying states of harmony. Such a state was Poland, where not only Polish, but also Lithuanian, Belorussian, Volhynian, Ruthenian, Ukrainian, Slovakian, Yiddish and German were spoken. Four scripts, Roman, Cyrillic, Gothic and Hebrew represented the four religions; Roman and Orthodox Catholicism, Protestantism and Judaism. Often twin – or even triplet – villages would co-exist in a state of apartheid, one Catholic Polish, the other Jewish, the third possibly Orthodox Volhynian. The magnates owed their allegiance to the German aristocracy, to French or Austrian interests, or to the Russian throne. They lived on a different plane to the ordinary people, and even spoke the language of their respective spheres of influence. Polish was strictly for the peasants.

It has been said of Poles, paradoxically, that collaboration was a good career move. It was certainly true in 1772, when the Polish system came close to collapse. Russia, Prussia and Austria saw their chance to cut the Commonwealth down to size. With the collaboration of their tame magnates, the three powers annexed large chunks of Poland. The rump was left to cope with the continuing recession as best it could.

This was the Poland that Nicolas Chopin had chosen to live and work in, a Poland that he grew to love as his own.

The nightmare scenario of revolutions came to pass. The first, across the Atlantic in 1776, was distant and remote from Europe. Yet the American War of Independence was a breeding ground for radical ideas, notably those of the Jacobins of France, the first left-wing socialist agitators of modern history. Great numbers of

Fryderyk Chopin, in a pencil sketch by Princess Eliza Radziwiłł (1829). Chopin often stayed with the Radziwiłł family at Antonin, their hunting lodge. Eliza kept a sketch-book in which she drew members of her family and friends, including the composer. The sketch-book survived World War II.

Europeans fired with the Jacobin revolution ethic crossed the Atlantic to join this war against imperialism.

In 1789, two years after Nicolas's arrival in Warsaw, news came from France that Paris was in flames and the Bastille had been stormed. Revolution in Europe had begun, and a heady atmosphere heralded the threshold of a new era. It represented hope for millions of common Europeans and cold sweat for the hereditary ruling establishments. In Warsaw it was a harbinger of change and a journey into the unknown. Nicolas shelved all thoughts about returning to France when he heard that all youths over the age of eighteen were being press-ganged into the army.

'As we heard that France is not yet calm after the revolutions that have erupted,' he wrote home, 'I put off my trip, but now I am considering leaving. . . . But finding ourselves in a foreign country where I can get on bit by bit, I would regret leaving here only to become a soldier, even in my own country.'

His letters home drew no response. There was no way of knowing whether letters had reached their destinations as communications with Marainville were cut. Nicolas and Weydlich, anxious for any news, drew a blank on all fronts. A big question mark hung over Count Pac's estates, and Weydlich, who had interests in the Strasbourg region, had no way of finding out what had befallen them. Nicolas Chopin lost all contact with his family, and never regained it.

Poland lurched on in a morass of chaos, until things came to a head in the spring of 1791. Warsaw was a hive of uncertainty as the King, throne-weariness now added to his weakness, and the magnates tried to thrash out a new constitution in the Seym. The Castle Square was packed with Varsovians waiting to hear the outcome, but the meetings went on endlessly. Nicolas often went to the high gallery overlooking the Chamber to listen to the debates. Finally, on May 3, the eagerly awaited announcement of a new Constitution for Poland was made. A procession, led by the King, with representatives of all Poles who would participate in the new Poland – the Court, the clergy, the magnates, the trade guilds – made its way to St John's Cathedral for the inauguration and blessing. The May 3 Constitution was an enlightened document which became the basis for the very existence of the Polish state to this day, and the date is one of the most important in the Polish calendar. It embraced the best of the progressive ideas of the time. The abolition of the election of the King would free Poland from foreign domination, and the scrapping of the *liberum veto* would lead to a functioning Seym where new laws and policy could be implemented; the granting of rights to the middle classes would ensure the creation of wealth; and the emancipation of the serfs meant freedom for millions.

It looked to Nicolas like the beginning of a new era of nationhood, hope and progress. But the euphoria was short-lived. Catherine of Russia, who looked upon Stanisław August with utter disdain, was alarmed at the bloodless creation of a progressive state on her borders. The Prussians were of similar mind. It became evident that the reinvented Polish state would not be allowed to function. A group of pro-Russian magnates known as the Targowicians, who were opposed to the Constitution, invited their foreign allies to intervene militarily. Within weeks the soil of Poland thundered to the boots of the invaders, and Poland was partitioned for the second time. This time Catherine seized nearly half of Poland's territories to the east, while the Prussians took the Poznań and Baltic regions in the west, along with the cities of Toruń and Gdańsk.

What was left of Poland could not survive without trade or the fertile lands to the east, with the Vistula thoroughfare split three ways, and surrounded by unfriendly states. Nicolas watched his adopted homeland dying before his eyes. Weydlich's snuff factory went out of business, and Nicolas found himself jobless, with no prospects. He had nothing to lose except some occasional tutoring in French, so he joined Kościuszko's army.

Tadeusz Kościuszko, one of the greatest patriots in Polish history, was born in Mereczowszczyno in 1746. He went to France to study military and naval tactics, passed out as a captain of artillery, and returned to Poland two years after the First Partition of 1772. In 1776 he crossed the Atlantic and joined George Washington in his bid for American independence from Great Britain. With his charismatic personality and natural instinct for tactics he distinguished himself on the battlefield, and was promoted to colonel. By 1783 Kościuszko had become a legend, and the United States Congress honoured him with American citizenship and promotion to brigadier-general. When Poland was invaded in 1791 Kościuszko returned to his homeland to lead the Polish forces in

driving out the invaders and their Targowician allies. He defeated
the Russians at Zieleńce and Dubienka, in western Ukraine.

In the long run, Poland was no match for the Russians. The
Targowicians installed a 40,000-strong Russian army in Warsaw,
which the locals had to feed. The King, a broken man, acceded
to the Targowicians' demands, and Poland's tattered rump dwin-
dled to a shadow of its former state. The Polish leaders fled to
Leipzig and began the tradition of government-in-exile. Poland
was partitioned for the second time, and the economy collapsed.
Thirty thousand Polish soldiers were made redundant, and cast
onto Warsaw's human scrapheap. Kościuszko, banking on Poland's traditional love affair with France, went to Paris to seek
help. Meeting with sympathy but no hard offers, he returned to
Leipzig to ponder the next move.

In 1793 what was left of the Polish resistance begged Kościuszko
to return to Poland as absolute dictator and lead them in the
struggle to restore the constitution. Kościuszko saw flaws in the
idea, not the least of which were 40,000 Russian soldiers in Warsaw
and a further two national armies poised on the crippled state's
western and southern borders, more or less on red alert. After a
winter of deliberation, he agreed, and the following March he
appeared in Kraków's main square, and proclaimed insurrection
to a delirious crowd of peasants with scythes and a force of 4,000
regular Polish soldiers. This ragtag army set off for Warsaw and
defeated a Russian army sent to intercept it at Racławice, just
north of Kraków. News of this victory spread fast, and prompted
Jan Kiliński, a Warsaw cobbler with a gift for whipping up frenzy,
to proclaim insurrection in the capital. His call was heard, and
Warsaw rose with such ferocity that the Russians, fearing the
added prospect of doing battle with the advancing Kościuszko,
abandoned the city after twenty-four hours, leaving behind 4,000
dead and some of their Targowician allies lynched. Nicolas witnessed
Kościuszko's triumphant entry into Warsaw, and re-enlisted.

But Kościuszko's triumph was short lived. The Prussians and
the Austrians invaded, and in the autumn 40,000 Russian troops,
thirsting for revenge, advanced on Warsaw. Nicolas was with
Kościuszko when he marched south to meet them.

On this march he met the handsome and debonair Mateusz
Łączyński, a district governor with his residence in Kiernozia,

about eighty kilometres west of Warsaw, who had joined Kościuszko's triumphant entry into Warsaw. The two fighting men became close, and Mateusz told Nicolas about his family in Kiernozia, his energetic but scatter-brained wife Ewa, and his children: Benedikt, Teodor, Honorata, the extraordinarily pretty blue-eyed and blonde-haired nine-year-old Maria, and baby Katarzyna.

Kościuszko met the Russians at Maciejowice, about eighty kilometres upstream on the Vistula, where the Polish army was defeated. Kościuszko was wounded and taken prisoner by the Russians. Mateusz Łączyński died trying to drag a wounded friend from the path of a Cossack charge. Nicolas was wounded, but made his way back to Warsaw, where he recovered and was stationed on the fortifications in Praga.

As Warsaw's eastern suburb on the other side of the Vistula, Praga's lot was to be the first line of defence against attack from the east. All the soldiers in the unit knew that when the Russians came, they would do so in force, and would not be taking any prisoners. The cold air in Praga was pervaded with a sense of doom and foreboding, as both soldiers and civilians awaited the inevitable. In November, Nicolas and his unit were recalled into the city and replaced. The Russians attacked, took Praga, and with it a terrible revenge on soldier and civilian alike. Crying 'Remember Warsaw!' they massacred everyone they could find.

It was the death rattle of the Polish state, and the three great powers gorged themselves on the carcass. Russia, Austria and Prussia all met at the small town of Brześć Litewski, today on the Belorussian side of the River Bug. Stanisław August abdicated and was taken to St Petersburg – and further humiliation from Catherine. Nicolas Chopin's Poland had ceased to exist; he found himself living in the Prussian city of Warschau, and his King was Friedrich Wilhelm III.

Demoralized and penniless, Nicolas eked out a living teaching French. He contacted Mateusz Łączyński's family in Kiernozia, and was able to describe his heroic death. His own future was bleak, and he began to contemplate returning to France. His deliberation turned to intention, and his preparations to go were complete. At the last minute his battle wounds resurfaced, he fell ill, and was forced to shelve his plans. This happened to him twice, and finally his plans came to nothing. 'Twice I have tried to leave,' he wrote, 'and twice I have nearly died. Now I must bow to providence and stay.'

Next year, in 1795, Ewa Łączyńska employed Nicolas as tutor. Benedikt had gone to study in Paris, which left Teodor, Honorata and Maria. After Mateusz's death, Ewa had let the manor fall into decay; the park was overgrown and unkempt, and bats nested under the eaves; but for all that the post was a new opportunity for Nicolas. He was happy in the Łączyński house, where he was popular with the children, and stayed for six years.

The manor at Kiernozia is still there, recently restored.

During his stay Nicolas observed the momentous events that unfolded in Europe. In France, a Corsican named Napoleon Bonaparte was in meteoric ascendancy; in Russia Catherine died in 1796, and was succeeded by her son, Paul. The new tsar released fifty-year-old Kościuszko, who returned for a while to America before finally settling in France. His warrior days over, he spent his remaining years working peacefully but unsuccessfully for the restoration of Poland until his death in Switzerland in 1817. Tsar Paul was two years into his barbarous reign when Stanisław August died in St Petersburg, closing for ever the epilogue to a monumental chapter in Polish history. Tsar Paul's death by assassination followed in 1801, and he was succeeded by his son, who ascended the Russian throne as Tsar Alexander I.

The following year, in 1802, sixteen-year-old Maria, now a stunning beauty, departed for Warsaw to complete her education at the Convent of Our Lady of the Assumption, and Nicolas's employment ended. He found another post as tutor to the children of Count Kacper Skarbek, who had an estate at Żelazowa Wola, about thirty kilometres away.

The Counts Skarbek had been a wealthy landowning family. Although Count Kacper owned estates in the Kujawy region and in Pomerania, he had chosen to live in Warsaw. Both he and his second wife, Ludwika, were profligate spenders with expensive tastes. The nineteenth century opened with the Skarbeks deeply in debt partially due to prohibitive Prussian property taxes, and one by one, the estates had to be sold off. Furthermore, life in Warsaw was very expensive, and Count Kacper became bankrupt. He fled to Paris and Countess Ludwika took her children, Fryderyk, ten, Anna, eight, and Michał, five, to Żelazowa Wola, their last remaining property.

The estate at Żelazowa Wola was beautifully set on the banks of the River Utrata. The two-storey manor, with its two wings, was considered humble by Count Kacper in comparison with his Warsaw apartment and his former estates. But the neat, white-painted house had some attractive features; a vine-covered pergola, a terrace and simply laid-out grounds leading to a bridge over the river. Countess Ludwika, left to bring up her children on her own, employed on her staff a young girl, a distant relative, by the name of Tekla Justyna Krzyżanowska.

Justyna was born in 1782 in the village of Długie, in Mazovia, the daughter of Jakub and Antonina Krzyżanowski, and was baptized on September 14 of that year. She had two sets of godparents, as befitting a girl of *szlachta*, or petty noble, birth. The first pair were Countess Justyna Skarbek and Mr Mateusz Kornowski of Sarnowo. The second pair were Miss Marcjanna Zaleska from Skarbanowa and Count Eugeniusz Skarbek of Izbica, which was another estate of the Skarbek family in Kujawy. Her parents were not wealthy, and when Justyna grew up she had to find a means of support.

Countess Ludwika took twenty-year-old Justyna in on ambiguous terms. As an educated but poor relative, and a god-daughter of two members of the Skarbek family, she could hardly be employed as a maid-servant, and she was too young to be a house-keeper. Her unwritten brief was as a general mother's help who probably called her employer by her Christian name. She was well read, played the piano and had a beautiful singing voice, and with her blonde hair, blue eyes, good looks and charming personality must have added to the overall ethos in the playrooms and woods of Żelazowa Wola, where she was treated more like an elder sister by the children.

Now that they were settled in the country, the boys needed a more formal home education. When the staff was augmented by a good-looking, equally educated young French veteran of the Kościuszko campaigns, it was only a matter of time before romance blossomed amid the mallows on the banks of the Utrata. Soon the whole village talked of the handsome young couple, frequently seen in the area in the company of the Skarbek children. Their betrothal was greeted with delight by everyone at Żelazowa Wola. For Countess Ludwika, with her husband dodging debtors in Paris, it was particularly good news; she was pleased for them both, and from an economic point of view she knew that the couple would become self-sufficient by the time the children grew up, and she would be able to treat them as family friends, rather than employees.

In 1805 the rural idyll was rocked by the news that Napoleon Bonaparte had defeated the Austrian army at Austerlitz, and entered Vienna. The question of Polish nationhood, dormant for the past ten years, was raised again. Napoleon, riding on the traditional Franco-Polish love affair, appeared vaguely attentive, which was taken by most Poles as being on their side. The Polish forces in exile in Italy and the diplomats and ex-warriors in Paris began to agitate for the liberation of Poland. Napoleon made sympathetic noises, but would not commit himself.

On 28 June 1806, Nicolas (he was thirty-five but gave his age as thirty-seven) and twenty-four-year-old Justyna, were married in the enormous, red-brick Church of St Roch, in Brochów, seven kilometres from Żelazowa Wola. The witnesses were Franciszek Grembicki and Karola Henke. It was a splendid affair, and back at Żelazowa Wola there were traditional garlands of roses and honeysuckle borne by the children, and the arrival of many horse-drawn carriages bedecked with ribbons and flowers as friends and relatives came from all over the county. Żelazowa Wola had a band which turned up at all occasions to play polonaises, polkas, mazurkas and the local speciality, the *kujawiak*. There was a feast of roast pork and chicken, carp from the river, and quantities of poppy-seed cakes, *babka* cakes and sweets for the children. Wine, beer and vodka flowed in abundance. After the feast the young couple were serenaded to their new home, the small, single-storey left wing, which Countess Ludwika had set aside for them.

In the closing days of that summer the Chopins announced that Justyna was pregnant, and the news was greeted with great joy at Żelazowa Wola. The golden autumn was giving way to the cold and damp approaches of winter, when news came that on October 14, Napoleon had defeated the Prussian Army at Jena, and had entered Berlin. This was momentous news for all Poles, especially those living in the Prussian partition under King Friedrich Wilhelm III. A month later the foggy Kujawy countryside, on the direct route from Berlin to Warsaw, resounded to the sound of soldiers on the march. This time they were greeted with joy: they

The Chopin family, from oil paintings by Ambrozy Mieroszewski (1829). The paintings were lost during the destruction of Warsaw in World War II, and these pictures were reconstructed (from illustrations in books) by Jan Zamoyski. Clockwise from top left: Justyna Chopin, Fryderyk's mother; Nicolas Chopin, his father; Izabela Chopin, his second sister; Ludwika Chopin, his eldest sister.

were French troops led by General Joachim Murat and General Dąbrowski, on their way to Warsaw. The capital was bedecked with Napoleonic eagles on the houses and shops, and bonfires of welcome were lit round the Castle. Napoleon slipped unannounced into Warsaw on the night of December 18, after a hard ride from Łowicz.

On 7 January 1807, there was a reception at the Castle, where the Emperor was to meet Warsaw society. A group of ladies, bedecked in their finery, waited nervously for the great man's entrance. When Napoleon finally arrived, accompanied by Talleyrand and Maréchal Duroc, his eyes fell upon a beautiful, twenty-one-year-old girl in the group, with blonde hair and eyes of extraordinary beauty. She was dressed in a narrow, high-waisted blue velvet dress that matched her eyes. Her neck was adorned with a diamond and sapphire necklace. 'Ah, qu'il y a de jolies femmes à Varsovie,' sighed the Emperor, unable to take his eyes off her. Further enquiries revealed that she was the wife of the septuagenarian Count Anastasiusz Colonna-Walewski. Smitten by her charms, he had her brought to him, and that was the beginning of a relationship that held a special interest for Nicolas, who remembered her as a little girl. For Napoleon's future mistress was Maria Łączyńska, who had been married off to a man fifty years her senior.

Meanwhile, King Friedrich Wilhelm, smarting from his defeat at Jena, approached Tsar Alexander I to discuss ways of stopping Napoleon. On February 8 an army of Russians and Prussians met Napoleon's combined French and Polish forces at Eylau (Bagrationovsk), to the south of Königsberg (Kaliningrad) in East Prussia. The battle ended in a bloody draw, and both sides retired to lick their wounds and collect their dead: Napoleon lost 15,000 men, and the Russians and Prussians 18,000. Despite the inconclusive outcome Napoleon was still in charge in Warsaw, and the question was not whether Napoleon would restore the Polish state, but when; yet he was reluctant to give a straight answer. 'I want to see', he said, 'if the Poles deserve to be a nation.' The Polish masses were determined not to disappoint him, and were fanatically behind him, but a number of leaders, including Kościuszko, read between the lines and mistrusted his apparently pro-Polish stance.

Casimir Palace, the site of the Warsaw Lyceum which Chopin attended as a student. The Chopin family lived in the building on the left from 1817 to 1827.

Many landowners in Prussian Poland moved back to Warsaw to be there when the spoils were being distributed. Among them were the Skarbeks, and in a spring bursting with renewed hope, Nicolas again found himself living in the capital which he had left twelve years previously. On 6 April 1807, Justyna presented her husband with their first child. Ludwika, nicknamed Ludka, was named after Countess Skarbek.

That summer East Prussia saw more violent action. On June 14 Napoleon drove a Russian army into the River Alle (Lyna) at Friedland (Pravdinsk), not far from Eylau. The Russians suffered heavy losses, many of them due to drowning – there were no bridges across the river. The defeat resulted in a meeting between Napoleon and Alexander on board a raft, in the middle of the River Niemen, the border, at Tilsit (Sovetsk) near its outlet into the Baltic Sea. Napoleon gave the Tsar his assurance that he would not restore the Polish state.

Napoleon pursued an ambiguous middle ground, half-fulfilling both Russian and Polish aspirations. He proclaimed the Prussian partition of Poland as the Grand Duchy of Warsaw. In deference to the Constitution of May 3, which stipulated Friedrich Augustus of Saxony as King, Napoleon appointed him Grand Duke. He was a titular head, with responsibility for legislative matters, but the real governing was done by the French.

The Constitution of the Duchy was based on the French model, and in spirit it had much in common with the Constitution of May 3; all citizens, landowners and serfs alike, were equal before the law; there was to be religious freedom; there would be devolution to local administration. What Napoleon demanded in return was money and men for his campaigns. It was a high price for a ravaged land, but the Poles paid happily. Crushing war taxes were paid to finance Napoleon's wars, and for the upkeep of the French garrisons stationed in Warsaw. As cannon fodder, idealistically fired young Poles martyred themselves on the battlefields, gaining a reputation for bravery verging on madness.

Warsaw teemed with activity. French soldiers and officials were everywhere, and the following year Countess Ludwika, her children and the Chopins, with their year-old Ludka in Justyna's arms, returned to the tranquillity of Żelazowa Wola. Justyna continued helping Countess Ludwika to run the house, as well as bringing up little Ludka. Nicolas continued to tutor Fryderyk, Anna and Michał, and the atmosphere at Żelazowa Wola was one of love and togetherness. Afternoons were spent in storytelling under the lime trees, and the sound of music was never absent for long. Nicolas's flute playing was by no means noteworthy, but Justyna played the piano well, and the sounds of the polonaise and other dance tunes could be heard wafting over the gardens on summer evenings. Nicolas and Justyna had a way with children, and the children adored them both. Nicolas was highly respected as a tutor, as is evident from Fryderyk Skarbek's *Memoirs*, published in Poznań in 1878:

Nicolas Chopin, this tutor under whose care I lived in a strange house, became my teacher.... He was neither an emigrant nor a spoiled priest, as were most French tutors at that time; they directed the trend of education of our young people into paths so uncharacteristic of the Polish nation.... He was not imbued either with the principles of exaggerated republican liberty, or with the affected bigotry of the French emigrants; neither was he a royalist infused with an idolatrous respect for the throne and the altar, but a moral, honest man who, devoting himself to the upbringing of young Poles, never attempted to turn them into Frenchmen or to inculcate in them the principles then reigning in France. With respect for the Poles, and with gratitude towards the people in whose land he had found a hospitable reception and a suitable way of earning his living, he sincerely repaid his debt of gratitude by the conscientious upbringing of their offspring to be useful citizens. By his sojourn of many years in our country, through his amicable relations with Polish homes, but chiefly through his marriage to a Polish lady, and hence through the bonds of matrimony ... he became a Pole indeed.... Under this revered teacher ... I received my first inclination towards learning ... which rested more on a general development of mental powers than on any training in particular subjects.

On 1 March 1810 Justyna presented her husband with their second child, Fryderyk Franciszek.

TWO
The Duchy of Warsaw

The local band was going from house to house in Żelazowa Wola, to announce a forthcoming marriage; its arrival at the Chopins' cottage coincided with the birth of Fryderyk Chopin, thus giving rise to the legend that the infant was born to the sound of music. On April 23 Fryderyk Chopin was baptized in the Church of St Roch in Brochów, where his parents had married four years previously. His godparents were Fryderyk Skarbek (represented at the font by Franciszek Grembicki, a witness at the Chopins' marriage) and Fryderyk's sister Anna. The infant was christened Fryderyk Franciszek, after Fryderyk Skarbek and Nicolas's father, François.

Confusion surrounds the actual birth date of Fryderyk Chopin. The baptism certificate was written at the time of the ceremony, but the birth certificate was written later. Although Nicolas signed the birth declaration, the positioning of his signature on the document appears incongruous – as though he had signed it first and the priest had written the declaration in later – and the priest may have confused the birth date.

The birth certificate reads:

In the year 1810, on April 23 at three o'clock in the afternoon: Before us, the parish priest of Brochów, district of Sochaczew, department of Warsaw, Nicolas Chopin, father, domiciled in the village of Żelazowa Wola, presented himself and showed us a male child, born in his house on February 22 at six o'clock in the evening this year, declaring that the child was born of him and of Justyna Krzyżanowska his wife, twenty-eight years of age, and that his wishes were to give the child two Christian names, Fryderyk Franciszek. After having made this declaration he showed us the child in the presence of Józef Wyrzychowski, steward, thirty-eight years old, and Fryderyk Geszt, forty years old, both domiciled in the village of Żelazowa Wola. The father and both witnesses, having read the birth certificate which was shown to them, saw fit to sign it. We have signed this document: Fr. Jan Duchnowski, Parish priest of Brochów in the function of civil servant. Signed Nicolas Chopin.

The baptism certificate reads:

23 April 1810. I, the above, [Józef Morawski, vicar of St Roch's Church, Brochów] performed the baptism ceremony on the infant with two names Fryderyk Franciszek, born February 22 of his excellency Nicolas Choppen (*sic*), Frenchman, and Justyna née Krzyżanowska, the married parents. The godparents, his Excellency Franciszek Grembicki from the village of Cieplina with her Excellency Miss Anna Skarbek, Countess of Żelazowa Wola.

Both Fryderyk Chopin and his family insisted that his birthday was March 1, followed by his name day on March 5. The date of February 22 is widely accepted because of the signature of Nicolas, but if he had signed first and never seen the actual entry then the certificate's authenticity might be suspect. Opinion is divided between adherents to written documentation and those who maintain that most people – together with their families – know the dates of their own birthdays.

A few weeks later, on May 8 Justyna herself stood as godparent, together with the steward at the estate, Józef Wyrzychowski, to the illegitimate baby of a local girl. The baby girl was named Justyna Józefa, after them. At the end of May Nicolas also stood as a godparent to a local child. Life at Żelazowa Wola was free and easy, with everyone, from the Skarbeks to the peasants, sharing in everything they did and being involved with one another, all under the umbrella of the Catholic Church. Nicolas was not a religious man, but he considered himself a Catholic.

On May 4 of that same year Nicolas's beautiful ex-pupil Maria

Walewska gave birth to Napoleon's baby boy at the Walewski Castle at Walewice, some fifty kilometres south-west of Żelazowa Wola. The boy was called Count Alexander Walewski.

Later that summer Countess Ludwika received a visit from Professor Samuel Bogumił Linde, a man of letters, and author of a Polish dictionary. He had been appointed Rector of the Warsaw Lyceum, which was founded in 1804 by the Prussian government as a German language school. He later introduced bilingual teaching to attract well-born Polish pupils, such as the Skarbek boys. Fryderyk Skarbek was a pupil at the Lyceum from 1805 until his graduation at the highest level in 1808. Linde had noted in the brilliant young scholar a kindred spirit in the making. With Napoleon's establishment of the Duchy of Warsaw German fell by the wayside, and the German speakers either left or embraced Polish as the official language. Linde considered himself Polish.

After his graduation Fryderyk Skarbek spent a year at Żelazowa Wola before going to Paris to continue his studies, which accounted for his absence from Fryderyk Chopin's baptism.

During this visit Linde met Nicolas and his family. By coincidence he needed a temporary replacement for his sick French teacher, and offered the job to Nicolas, as from October.

It was an opportunity for Nicolas to return to the capital. With Fryderyk Skarbek in Paris and Michał, now thirteen, at the Lyceum, only sixteen-year-old Anna remained. As tutor to the boys Nicolas had become superfluous at Żelazowa Wola, even though he was now a friend of the family. Countess Ludwika also wanted to move back to Warsaw, so Nicolas accepted Linde's offer. As the weeks went by it became clear that the French teacher would not be returning, and Nicolas's job was made permanent.

The last section of the main post road from Poznań to Warsaw was the same then as now. Although little more than a beaten cart track, it was the main thoroughfare to Berlin and western Europe. It passed through Sochachew, south of Żelazowa Wola, where the Chopins joined it. The rutted and pot-holed road continued through the flat countryside till it reached the toll-gate at the outlying village of Wola, now a Warsaw suburb. All coaches stopped here to pay a 'hoof toll', so called because payment was based on the number of horses pulling the coaches. After Wola the road continued into the city and straight to the enormous courtyard of the Saxon Palace.

All that is left of this complex of buildings off the Krakowskie Przedmieście is a short row of ruined columns and arches, now the Grave of the Unknown Soldier, attended by a platoon of guards. The remainder of the site is the expansive Plac Zwycięstwa (Victory Square), which constituted the courtyard. The Saxon Palace changed shape several times during the two hundred and fifty years of its existence until its destruction in World War II. Nicolas Chopin saw a fine, rambling, multi-winged building that occupied the western side of its square. As well as the Lyceum it housed commercial and administrative offices, and residential apartments. Behind the Palace were the Saxon Gardens, the largest park in Warsaw, apart from the Belvedere and Łazienki Gardens at the southern extremes of the city. The Saxon Gardens are still there, albeit shrunken in size, the only part of the complex that retains the name. The orangery, the pheasantry, the decorative pavilions, the bowers and the exotic plants, imported from all over the world in the name of the then fashionable new science of botany, are all gone; only the shady chestnut trees remain among the lawns and walkways of the park.

The Chopins settled into their apartment, and Nicolas renewed acquaintanceship with his old haunts, seeking out Weydlich's snuff factory and the scenes of insurrection as different conquering powers crossed the capital with their varying brands of oppression. Justyna took Ludka and Frycek, as little Fryderyk came to be nicknamed, into the Saxon Gardens to watch them playing on the grass, to mingle with other mothers, to exchange baby talk, to see and be seen.

On 1 October 1810 Nicolas took up his duties as teacher of French at the Lyceum. His salary was meagre, but he supplemented it by taking in boarders from outside Warsaw, including Michał Skarbek. Nicolas was forced to keep careful accounts, which he did meticulously. His balance sheets included, for instance, the information that three *złoty*, the fee for a music lesson, fed the family for one day. The music lesson in question was given by Justyna, a better pianist than Nicolas was a flautist. Legend has it that while Frycek showed signs of pleasure when his mother played the piano, his father's flute playing made him cry. Once he broke the flute, giving rise to jokes about his budding critical faculties.

Soon after their arrival Justyna was again pregnant, and on 9 July 1811 she gave birth to Izabela, fair-haired and blue-eyed,

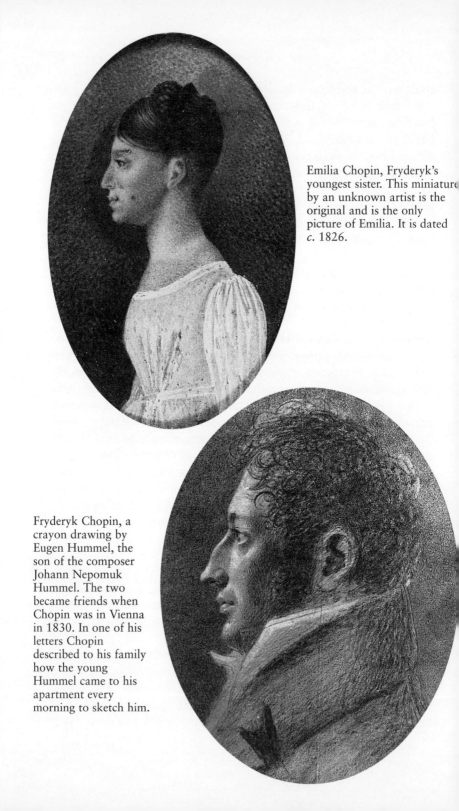

Emilia Chopin, Fryderyk's youngest sister. This miniature by an unknown artist is the original and is the only picture of Emilia. It is dated *c*. 1826.

Fryderyk Chopin, a crayon drawing by Eugen Hummel, the son of the composer Johann Nepomuk Hummel. The two became friends when Chopin was in Vienna in 1830. In one of his letters Chopin described to his family how the young Hummel came to his apartment every morning to sketch him.

like her mother. She made a contrast to Ludka, who had her father's Gallic colouring. Justyna had certain qualities of an earth-mother, and was happiest when surrounded by children, a trait later inherited by Ludka. The Chopins had a fortepiano, and Justyna, who had a lovely voice, played and led sing-songs for the boarders to join in. As she grew out of toddlerhood, Ludka began to show interest in her mother's piano playing. Justyna sat with her at the piano and began to teach her the rudiments.

The first two years of the Chopins' Warsaw experience were not easy. On 1 January 1812 Nicolas took up a part-time post teaching French Literature at the School of Artillery, which supplemented his income. The school was housed in the Arsenal, opposite the Krasiński Palace. It was rebuilt after World War II at the western end of Długa Street, and now houses the Warsaw Archaeological Museum.

The Duchy, crippled from financing Napoleon's endless campaigns, was now filled with French soldiers, signifying yet another campaign in the planning stages. There was talk of an invasion of Russia, and a general call for men of fighting age to join the army yielded volunteers in their tens of thousands, ready and willing to die for their French hero. M. de Pradt, the French Ambassador, described what he saw in Warsaw in 1812:

Nothing could exceed the misery of all classes. The army was not paid, the officers were in rags, the best houses were in ruins, the greatest lords were compelled to leave Warsaw from want of money to provide their tables. No pleasures, no society, no invitations as in Paris or London. I even saw princesses quit Warsaw from the most extreme distress. The Princess Radziwiłł had brought two women from England and France; she wished to send them back, but had to keep them because she was unable to pay their salaries and travelling expenses. I saw in Warsaw two French physicians who informed me that they could not procure their fees even from the greatest lords.

In charge of mobilization was Prince Józef Poniatowski, Commander of the Polish army and Marshal of France. He was born in 1763, the nephew of Stanisław August. As a professional warrior he fought with Kościuszko at the time of the second and third partitions and distinguished himself both on the battlefield and at the tactics table. After careful deliberation – at first he did not trust Napoleon – he joined in the creation and administration of the Duchy of Warsaw, and gave it his total loyalty. In 1809 he scored his first major victory by defeating an Austrian army which had invaded the Duchy and taken Warsaw.

By midsummer Napoleon's Grande Armée was ready and poised to cross into Russian Poland and beyond, with Poniatowski's Fifth (Polish) Corps in the avant-garde, thirsting for Russian blood. Nicolas was not so sure about this turn of events. The patriotism of the common Pole was blind, and seemed unable to take into account the possibility that Emperor Napoleon of France, just like Tsar Alexander of Russia, King Friedrich Wilhelm of Prussia and Emperor Franz of Austria, might just cynically be using Poland for his own ends. When, on June 24, the order to invade was announced on the banks of the River Niemen in Lithuania, Poniatowski's lancers were the first over the river and on to Russian soil. Napoleon had invaded Russia with a great, multinational army of a half a million men, of whom 98,000 were Polish.

Umiński's dragoons were the first in Moscow, but when Napoleon entered the city on September 14, he found it deserted and burnt. The Muscovites had harnessed two mythological giants against their foe: the Russian Winter and the Scorched Earth. Napoleon was to be denied the wherewithal to survive. He stayed in Moscow until October 18, with nothing to do but kick his heels while his troops vandalized the Kremlin. There was no point in staying and starving to death; autumn was progressing, and the rains promised a thousand-mile trek back through freezing mire and devastated landscape with his remaining force of 100,000. Napoleon had no alternative but to fix his eyes on the monochrome plains of the eternal western horizon, and set off back the way he had come, with Prince Józef Poniatowski's men bringing up the rear – the most unenviable position of the whole retreat. Only 18,000 frost-bitten survivors recrossed the icy waters of the River Niemen. Napoleon Bonaparte, unstoppable conqueror of Europe, hero to some, villain to others, was conquered by the forces of nature.

Napoleon's defeat was traumatic for the Poles, and the future looked doubly uncertain at the Saxon Palace. On November 20, as the first French stragglers started appearing from the east,

Justyna Chopin gave birth to Emilia. She was a very sickly baby, and it was doubtful if she would survive. At three weeks she was close to death, and on December 15 Fr. Teodor Borysiewicz was hurriedly called to baptize her with ordinary water. After that Emilka, as she was known, rallied, and her parents knew she would survive. Nicolas wondered how the extra mouth would be fed.

On December 5 Napoleon abandoned his army and made for snow-bound Warsaw. Five days later he was staying at the Hotel Angielski (the irony of staying at the 'English Hotel' may or may not have crossed his mind). Outside, his horse-drawn sled was ready to take him westwards, out of the grip of the terrible Asiatic winter. With him were Potocki and Matusewicz, who bore the brunt of his diatribe against the Duchy and against Poles in general. He then climbed into his sled and headed back to Paris, without a backward glance, to ponder how he, one of the greatest military generals of all time, could fall victim to the greatest military disaster of all time. What was left of the Grande Armée slogged its weary way back to France, and only a small fraction of the French soldiers who had set off made it back to their homeland. The Polish army was in disarray, but Poniatowski's Fifth Corps managed to stay together and regrouped on German soil, to fight another day, their loyalty to Napoleon unimpaired.

Having lost the dubious protection of one of history's greatest conquerors, speculation was rife from the drawing-rooms of the Saxon Palace to the smoky cafés of Długa Street about what would happen next. Inevitably eyes turned eastwards. Tsar Alexander, bitter at the enthusiasm with which Napoleon's Polish contingents had fought on Russian soil, would not be resting on his imperial laurels. But revenge was not on his agenda. He had thought of himself as an enlightened bearer of a grand vision, inspired by God, of a new Europe in which a restored Polish state of his creation would flourish to his design. This new Poland would eventually include the previous Duchy of Lithuania and Ruthenia, broadly today's Lithuania, Belarus and western Ukraine. Polish leaders were divided into two camps on this issue. Some, like Prince Adam Czartoryski – and composer and diplomat Prince Michał Ogiński – went along with Alexander's theories, and advocated burying hatchets and throwing in their lot with the Russians. Poniatowski viewed Alexander's proposals with suspicion;

he knew that as a legend in his own lifetime, he was a potential rallying point for insurrection. He remained loyal to Napoleon, and rejected the conciliatory gestures that the Russians and the Czartoryski faction were making. His policy was reinforced by the fact that he still commanded a highly motivated Polish army, now kicking its heels impatiently in Kraków.

Frycek Chopin was approaching his third birthday and the snows of Napoleon's Russian winter had not yet thawed when Russian troops were once again marching along the Krakowskie Przedmieście past the Saxon Palace. Nicolas entertained feelings of *déjà vu* as his adopted homeland once again faced the prospect of becoming booty to its traditional foes, and talk of a fourth partition was on everybody's lips. What would Warsaw's official language be this time? Certainly not French, as in June 1813 the Duchy of Warsaw was abolished by Russia, Prussia and Austria at the Treaty of Reichenbach, and Grand Duke Friedrich Augustus was deposed.

But Napoleon was not finished. In October Poniatowski was involved in the French Emperor's next adventure, this time near the Saxon city of Leipzig. The scenario was the Battle of the Nations, which promised a definitive outcome for Poland, whichever way it went. The combined forces of Prussia, Austria, Sweden and Russia again did battle with a revived Napoleon seeking, without success, to correct the mistakes of his Russian fiasco. As he retreated westwards across the bridge over the River Elster, the Polish Army made up Napoleon's rearguard. The retreating French, having crossed safely, then blew up the bridge, leaving Poniatowski trapped in a bend of the river with no means of escaping the advancing enemies. Mortally wounded and fired with that despairing and innate Polish rage, Poniatowski spurred his horse into the river in a hail of fire to die with honour. His death, on 19 October 1813, marked the end of Poland's Napoleonic experience. It was back to the Russians, Prussians and Austrians once more. Friedrich Wilhelm and Alexander pursued Napoleon, and entered Paris on the last day of March 1814. On April 11, Napoleon abdicated at Fontainebleau, and was placed under house arrest on the island of Elba, where he was allowed a symbolic personal guard. Half of them were Polish.

A congress established in Vienna by the victorious allies sought to repair the mess that Napoleon had made of Europe. It started with the arrival, in September, of the delegates. The President was the Austrian statesman and diplomat Prince Clemens Metternich, and Russia, Austria, Prussia, France and Britain were respectively represented by Tsar Alexander, Emperor Franz, King Friedrich Wilhelm, Charles de Talleyrand and, jointly, Viscount Castlereagh and the Duke of Wellington. Their deliberations (when the delegates found the time to do so in between bouts of endless socializing verging on debauchery) were interrupted by Napoleon's escape, and his final adventure on the field of Waterloo, just outside Brussels. Here he was defeated by the combined forces of Britain under the Duke of Wellington and – at the eleventh hour – General Blücher's Prussians.

While the deposed Emperor languished on St Helena, the Congress of Vienna became the talking shop of what came to be known as the Holy Alliance. Tsar Alexander took the spiritual mantle and gave the political conference an air of divinely ordained fatalism. Final agreement was reached on 9 June 1815, despite vastly differing interests, and with it a new map of Europe was drawn. The congress made certain concessions to the Poles. The name of Poland was restored to the maps. Kraków was made a republic, albeit in thrall to Vienna. The Duchy of Warsaw, less the Duchy of Poznań, Gdańsk and Toruń, which were given to the Prussians in compensation, was proclaimed the Kingdom of Poland with Tsar Alexander as King. On November 27 Poland was granted a new constitution, drawn up by Czartoryski, based loosely on its Napoleonic predecessor: Roman Catholicism was the official religion; other religions were freely allowed; the press was free; Poland retained its flag, kept its national army, and was united with Russia through the body of the Tsar; the Seym was again to meet.

General Józef Zajączek, forgiven for having fought with Kościuszko and Napoleon, was appointed viceroy and installed at the Castle. The Russian, Count Nicolai Novosiltsov, whose repressive policies and secret police very quickly began to upset the Poles, became commissioner. Alexander's younger brother, Grand Duke Constantine, was placed at the head of the Polish army, still smarting from the loss of Prince Józef Poniatowski – an impossible act for a Russian to follow. It looked as though Europe was in for a period of stability, and the Poles accepted that their 'Congress Kingdom' was all they would get for the moment, and decided to make the best of it.

Among those making the best of it were the Chopins. On 14 June

1815 Emilka, still frail but out of the danger of death, was formally rebaptized by Fr. Marcin Perkowski at the Church of the Holy Cross. Her godparents were Mazovian landowner Count Ksawery Zboiński and Franciszka Dekert. Culture and music played an important part in a loving family atmosphere; the Chopins were gregarious and popular, and their apartment was ever alive with children's laughter, healthy argument and good conversation. Linde and his wife Ludwika were frequent visitors. The sound of music in the making, specifically of flute and fortepiano, was never absent for long, and melodies were often heard being picked out with a finger by one of the children.

Books and sheet music were proliferating as Poland lurched into its new era. The arts were blossoming and the university was inaugurated. New compositions were available in the music shops that were appearing in the city. Names like Buchholtz and Janicki became synonymous with the manufacture of fortepianos and violins respectively. By 1821 Warsaw boasted thirty musical instrument factories. Businesses were sprouting, as were factories and shops. In a few short years, Warsaw changed from a market-town economy based on what peasants brought in from outside, to a sophisticated centre of industry and commerce which attracted international trade. Nicolas saw the population of the city double to 140,000, and there was no shortage of boys from out of town seeking to board with him while attending the Lyceum. Although there was unspeakable poverty in the streets, help was at hand. The Benevolent Society established itself, with its headquarters in the Krakowskie Przedmieście; its brief was to give aid to those in need, and more people were in a position to contribute to its funds. Among these was Nicolas; despite his meagre salary, he was still able to contribute a quota of twenty-four *zloty* per month. The Hospital of the Child Jesus ran a soup kitchen purveying its famous rude but nourishing 'Rumfordzka soup'.

Frycek was already playing the piano. His initial inspiration, apart from sitting under the fortepiano while his mother played, had been watching Ludka being taught by their mother. He often asked Ludka to teach him some of the things that she had learned. Ludka, who adored her little brother, complied, and legend has it that she was Frycek's first teacher. What a seven-year-old's methodology in teaching a five-year-old might be is not clear, but one

A Musical Story by Chopin, young Fryderyk playing to his father's lodgers, by A. C. Gow (1879).
(Reproduced by kind permission of Tate Gallery Publications)

may assume many fun-filled hours of sitting side by side at the fortepiano, messing about. This inevitably led to more serious experimentation, for both were talented and intelligent. Frycek's speciality was to pick tunes out by ear, and then to put harmonies to them. Justyna noticed that there was true music being made; her second child, although no Mozart, showed promise, and she added her weight to these 'lessons'. With her guidance taking over from Ludka's, Frycek began to show more innate talent than his sister.

Nicolas and Justyna were awakened one night by the sound of someone playing the fortepiano. They recognized the tune as a piece that Justyna often played. An investigation revealed that Frycek, unable to sleep, and with the familiar tune churning round his head, had decided to exorcize it by trying it out for himself. The fact that it was the middle of the night seemed irrelevant to the six-year-old boy. It was this occasion which caused Nicolas and Justyna to come to a decision: Frycek must have formal piano lessons.

Woyciech Żywny was a sixty-year-old German-speaking Czech. Primarily a violinist, he had come to Poland as court pianist to Prince Kazimierz Sapieha. With the collapse of the court Żywny found himself unemployed, but his background, rooted in the world of Mozart and the Bohemian classical school, ensured that he soon found employment as a music teacher. Frycek and Ludka saw a tall, clean-shaven man with a long nose and a yellow wig. His clothes were of velvet, and out-of-date, but his waistcoat was curiously different: he had a collection of waistcoats, which he had had made from the auctioned-off trousers of ex-King Stanisław August. He wore a heavy frock coat which he never removed, winter or summer. His teeth, nose, chin, and even his clothes were stained brown, testimony to an addiction to snuff, which he kept in a large pouch featuring portraits of Haydn and Mozart. In his pockets he carried very large pencils, which he always wielded during lessons. He spoke Polish with a strong German accent.

Any initial nervousness the children felt was soon dissipated. Mr Żywny was an inspired teacher who may have wielded his pencils in anger in the past, but with the Chopin children he used them exclusively for marking and writing. He recognized a rare talent in the little boy, and set about teaching him such basic skills as Justyna had so far neglected. He introduced Frycek to good music well played, and acquainted him with Bach and Mozart.

He taught him to read music, and then to copy it out. He taught him the basics of composition and the theories of harmony and counterpoint, using Bach and Mozart as role models. Nicolas and Justyna saw that Mr Żywny's fee was money well spent.

Some of Frycek's other artistic talents were developing. Although he was not going to school, the academic atmosphere of the apartment rubbed off on him as he listened to the boys talking and arguing about their homework. He learned to read and write in the home environment, and spoke both French and Polish from infancy. He enjoyed drawing, a skill that he developed in his childhood, and put to amusing use in later life. On 6 December 1816 he presented his father with an exquisitely decorated name-day card, consisting of a beautifully handwritten poem enclosed in a finely drawn and lightly shaded laurel-leaf horseshoe. In later life Fryderyk Chopin's handwriting was meticulously neat – no doubt the legacy of his father, one of whose disciplines was calligraphy.

Grand Duke Constantine was looking to expand facilities for his Polish army, and set his sights on the Saxon Palace. He was already using the square for parades, and Frycek often stared out of the window as the soldiers marched up and down, until, inspired by the bands that accompanied these parades, a march tune of his own began to germinate in his head. But before he could work it out at the piano everyone had to move out. In March 1817 the Lyceum was rehoused at the Casimir Palace, on the other side of the Krakowskie Przedmieście. Built in the seventeenth century by King Władysław IV, it consisted of a large central building with two detached wings, forming three sides of an open-cornered square, the fourth side giving on to its entrance from the street. The palace stood in its own park, which sloped down towards the River Vistula behind it. The park was planted with rose and lilac bushes, as well as lime and beech trees, and there were fruit trees, with cherries, pears and apples there for the picking. The Chopins were housed on the second floor of the south wing, at the end closest to the main building. Today the Casimir Palace houses the University of Warsaw, which was inaugurated in 1818, one year after the Chopins moved in. The Palace was destroyed in 1944 by the Nazis, and rebuilt in 1948. A plaque commemorates Chopin's stay there.

The Chopins were pleased with their apartment. It was bigger than the one at the Saxon Palace, and there was more room for the boarders, now six in total. Their resources stretched to a Buchholtz fortepiano. The Chopins were in good company. On the first floor lived Samuel and Ludwika Linde, with their daughter also called Ludwika, or Lulu. On the ground floor lived the poet, Kazimierz Brodziński, and the Kolbergs.

Professor Juliusz Kolberg was an engineer and a topographer, and lectured in surveying at the university. He was born in Mecklenburg in 1776, but, like many German immigrants to Warsaw during the years after the partitions, he chose to consider himself Polish. The German language was not used in his home, and his six sons were brought up in Polish. His passion lay in poetry, and translating Polish literature into German. His wife, Karolina, was also of German descent. Of his sons, three played a particular part in the Chopin story: Wilhelm, nicknamed Wiluś, was three years older than Frycek, and became one of his closest friends. Oskar, who was born in 1814, became an ethnographer and author, and devoted his life to collecting Polish songs, dances and legends. The youngest was Antoni, who became an artist. As a family, the Kolbergs were among the closest to the Chopins.

The spring of 1817 brought with it an idyllic academic atmosphere to the Casimir Palace, with the boys, in their Lyceum uniforms of knee-length blue jackets buttoned up to the neck, long trousers and tall caps, mingling with teachers, academics and parents on the lawn among the blossom-clad trees. This ethos of learning and achieving rubbed off on Frycek. When the excitement of the move and his seventh birthday had died down, and the new Buchholtz fortepiano had been installed in its new place, he returned to his lessons with Żywny. The tunes running around in his head, specifically the soldiers' march, came back to tease him. With a little help from Żywny in getting it down on paper, he presented his parents with his first composition, 'Military March'. Although it was published in a journal at the time without the composer's identity noted, this very early 1817 Chopin composition is now lost.

In the closing days of that year Nicolas heard that Maria Walewska had died in Paris on December 11, aged twenty-eight. She had gone to live in the French capital with seven-year-old Alexander, who was already being groomed for a distinguished career in politics. Count Alexander Walewski became Napoleon III's foreign minister, then a senator, and eventually President of the Chamber. He died in 1868.

THREE
Woyciech Żywny

The ensuing year was the first formative period in Frycek's musical development. Żywny used a mixture of disciplined method and inspiration through the joy of music, to which Frycek responded and from which he learned much. The old Bohemian felt at home in the Chopin apartment, and usually stayed to supper. Evenings were spent in making music, and Frycek listened and compared, while his teacher and his mother both showed him different sides to the art of piano playing. The seeds of Frycek's future creativity and methodology were sown at this time. It was Żywny who showed Frycek the value of improving technique and loosening the fingers by playing Bach. It was Żywny who taught him, with the example of Mozart, the art of elegant and delicate playing. And all the while Justyna kept up his love of the simple folk music of Poland.

Frycek never forgot these early lessons; there is much in Bach and Mozart that is easy for a promising beginner to play: the Anna Magdalena Notebook and the very first Prelude of The Well-Tempered Clavier (or 'The Forty-eight'), would have been well within Frycek's reach; Mozart's Variations on 'Ah, vous dirai-je, maman' would have taught him how to mould improvisation into an accepted form. In later life, Frycek always regarded 'The Forty-eight' as his essential practice, and never embarked on a concert without having first worked out on them. That special touch, which Berlioz likened to listening to a concert of elves, flowered from his early association with Mozart.

But one name above all influenced Fryderyk Chopin the composer in these, his earliest formative years – Michał Ogiński.

Prince Michał Kleofas Ogiński was born at Guzów, near Warsaw, in 1765. Although he was a violinist, pianist and composer, he was also a career politician, warrior and adventurer. He fought for Kościuszko on the Lithuanian front, and from Catherine the Great he earned a price on his head for his reckless cavalry raids behind Russian lines. After the collapse of Poland he escaped to Paris disguised as a lady's maid. According to some sources, now largely disproved, he wrote the music to Józef Wybicki's poem, 'Poland has not yet perished while we still live', which became the Song of the Legions, the Polish forces stationed in North Italy, poised to march on Poland. In 1926, this song was adopted as the Polish National Anthem. After a brief diplomatic flirtation with Napoleon, during which he wrote his only opera, *Zelis et Valcour*, which he dedicated to Napoleon, he declined to be involved with the Duchy of Warsaw. Like Kościuszko, he did not trust Napoleon. Instead, he used his resources of diplomacy throughout France, Italy, Britain, Prussia and Turkey in a quest for a restored Polish state. He was granted a pardon by Tsar Alexander for his part in the Kościuszko affair, and made a senator. Ogiński became an adviser on Poland to the Tsar, with Prince Adam Czartoryski. In 1815 the Tsar chose Czartoryski to go with him to the Congress of Vienna. Disillusioned, Ogiński left Russia and spent the remaining years of his life wandering Europe, still seeking support for a free Poland. He eventually settled in Florence, where he died in 1833.

In between fighting and negotiating, Ogiński fitted in music-making, and claimed, in his writings, to have enjoyed playing all the Haydn String Quartets in one sitting – if true, a feat of endurance comparable to some of the military campaigns in which he was involved. But it is as the composer of some twenty polonaises and other dances for the piano that he made a musical name for himself. Technically simple, beautifully melodic, yet varied in feeling from dramatic through exquisitely delicate to whimsical, they lent themselves to amateur performance in drawing rooms and salons. Their Haydnesque elegance flavoured with a Polish feel appealed to a nation facing extinction, and they became mainstays of the Polish musical heritage. Today one of the most frequently performed tunes in Poland is the Polonaise in A minor, 'Farewell to the

Fatherland', which is played by every pianist, dance band, folk group, busker and orchestra in the country.

Frycek was an improviser, and his method of composition reflected this. He would sit at the piano and play, letting the creative process flow. When he chanced on a good tune, or an interesting harmonic progression, he would work on it until he got it absolutely right. In later years this process would take hours of meticulous work to achieve that feeling of spontaneous creation. Like Mozart, he could pick tunes up by ear with total facility, and, again like Mozart, delighted in playing them in different ways, mimicking different styles, and playing about with them. Some teachers might have suppressed this free creativity in favour of a more disciplined approach to form and technique, but Żywny encouraged him, and taught him how to develop and control his ideas, and to modulate into different keys, while never constricting the creative flow. Dances, such as Ogiński's polonaises and Mozart's minuets provided valuable models. Each was in ternary form, which Żywny explained meant inserting a contrasting middle section. Frycek quickly grasped these rules, and continued to test his new-found gift for composition.

Two polonaises followed, in B flat and G minor. The Polonaise in B flat bears a strong similarity in feel to Ogiński's polonaise in the same key. Both have a military flavour and have a contrasting, more melancholy trio section in the minor. The Polonaise in G minor was Frycek's first published composition. He dedicated it to Wiktoria Skarbek, Countess Ludwika's cousin. This time Frycek imitates Ogiński's crossed hands technique: while the left hand plays the simple accompaniment in the middle of the keyboard, the right hand alternates the tune between the treble, and the bass. Because Frycek had not yet mastered how to copy out his music, Żywny helped him with this, especially when the treble and bass clefs were inverted. The music of the Polonaise in G minor was printed by Fr. J.J. Cybulski, Żywny's friend, in November 1817, at his printing workshop in the parish house attached to the Church of the Virgin Mary in the Nowe Miasto. Its publication was mentioned in the *Warsaw Review* the following January.

Also mentioned in the same notice was a set of variations and a set of dances – although their nature or number were not given. Neither the dances nor the variations, which were doubtless modelled on Mozart, have survived.

That year Frycek advanced in his art with lightning speed, and Żywny watched his pupil's growth from week to week. He realized that he bore a heavy responsibility, and he would have to tread carefully so as not to spoil a rare talent. All else was put aside, and his dedication to Frycek was total. Ludka, who may have been forgiven for feelings of jealousy, accepted her brother's achievements with pride: the two had always been close. Soon the whole Casimir Palace noticed the beautiful sounds emanating from the second floor window. The Chopins were invited everywhere, and asked if they would bring Frycek with them. Fryderyk Chopin's first performances, in the drawing-rooms of Warsaw, had begun.

Warsaw's miniature Enlightenment was in full swing. Gone were the days of recession, the oppressive hand of grinding poverty and the total lack of any kind of good life when the whole population, including the aristocracy, were intent only on survival. Now salons, on the old French model, were thriving. Poets, musicians, authors and painters were invited to the better houses, at which it was *de rigueur* to be seen – and heard.

Among the most prominent hostesses was Countess Zofia Zamoyska, the sister of Prince Adam Czartoryski, who established a salon at the Zamoyskis' fabulous residence, the Błękitny (Azure) Palace. This was situated at the north-western corner of the Saxon Gardens, giving on to Senatorska Street. Legend has it that it was linked to the Saxon Palace by a secret underground passage. It was the most opulent palace in Warsaw and housed a superb collection of paintings and an enormous library. The Zamoyskis and the Czartoryskis put on lavish banquets and balls to which the glitterati were invited. Countess Zofia herself was a great philanthropic personage with a finger in most charitable organizations in the city. She was particularly fond of children, and organized teas and dances for them at the palace.

Countess Zofia's attention was drawn to the eight-year-old boy whose skill at the piano in Warsaw's drawing-rooms was such that he was being hailed as the Polish Mozart. Frycek was invited to her children's functions, where he was asked to play. At her salon she entertained the eminent poet Julian Ursyn Niemcewicz. His enormously popular 'Historic Songs', which told of Polish kings and heroes, was published in Warsaw that year, and his own salon was one of Warsaw's most fashionable. At the beginning of 1818 Countess Zofia was planning a grand charity concert, and she asked Niemcewicz to arrange for Frycek to take part. Niemcewicz called on Nicolas personally, to ask him to allow Frycek to perform. Nicolas, whose views on charity were well known, gladly gave his consent. And so it was arranged. The *Warsaw Gazette*, in its supplement of 21 February 1818, announced the details:

Concert for the Poor. On Tuesday next, February 24, a Vocal and Instrumental Concert will be given for the benefit of the poor by the most illustrious amateurs of the city, and visiting artists, in the Theatre at the Radziwiłł Palace, at which Miss Vicini, on violin, Messrs Kaczyński, Arnold, Bryce, Feuillide, Schoppin [*sic*] etc will entertain the esteemed audience. The Music, which through its melodies soothes our feelings and touches our emotions, must surely also bring relief to a suffering populace. Further details of this Concert will be announced on the poster. Tickets at the usual price will be available at the box-office of the French Theatre.

The 'usual price' was a euphemism for very expensive. The Warsaw music scene was lively, and a number of organizations arranged concerts. In 1818 the music questor could count on at least one full-scale concert, with symphony orchestra, singers and soloists, every week. The music of Beethoven, Haydn, Mozart, Cherubini, Spohr and Méhul found a wide audience in the Polish capital. Pianists introduced the concertos of Field, Ries, Dussek and, of course, Beethoven. Poland looked to Italy for its opera, and to Germany for its symphonic intake, but home-grown composers, especially of operas, also enjoyed a revival after two decades of cultural stagnation: Mateusz Kamieński (1734–1821) had written the first opera in the Polish language; Józef Kozłowski (1757–1831), whose output of theatre and choral music was considerable, was well known despite spending most of his career at the Russian court. The prolific Józef Elsner (1769–1854) wrote everything from chamber music to operas. Karol Kurpiński (1785–1857) was making a name for himself with his operas.

But the greatest Polish opera composer of them all, Stanisław Moniuszko, was only conceived that year in the Krakowskie Przedmieście.

For his début public concert, Frycek was dressed up to the nines. The audience saw a slight little boy of eight, with delicate features, blue eyes and curled fair hair. He wore a white collar over a velvet jacket, short trousers, white stockings and black shoes with buckles. He played the Piano Concerto in E minor by Czech composer Adalbert Gyrowetz. Frycek's audience comprised the cream of Warsaw society, and members of the most illustrious families were there. The concert was a great success. Julian Niemcewicz afterwards thanked Frycek in person for his contribution, and congratulated him on his remarkable performance. That night, when his mother asked the excited Frycek which part of the concert the audience liked best, he replied, 'My new white collar, mama!'

Frycek Chopin became the talk of the town overnight, and all the salons vied for his attendance. Niemcewicz even wrote the 'marvellous little boy' into one of his 'dramatic eclogues'. These were small scale dramas, usually social and political commentaries and satires, put on at some of the salons as instant entertainment. It was evident that this boy was destined to become a great musician, whose fame would spread outside the boundaries of his native land.

It is not known how Frycek reacted to performing in public when he was a child, but in later life he loathed it, and suffered from severe stage-fright. 'I am not fit to give concerts,' he wrote, 'crowds intimidate me. I feel poisoned by their breath, paralysed by curious looks, and confused by the sight of strange faces.' Perhaps he felt that way at the Radziwiłł Palace on the night of Tuesday, 24 February 1818. Fryderyk Chopin gave only about twenty concerts in his whole life.

The Błękitny Palace, with the Zamoyski Library, was burnt down in 1944, and rebuilt after World War II. Today it houses Warsaw's Communications Offices. The Radziwiłł Palace was a government building opposite the Saxon Palace, and it housed the hall in which regular concerts were held. The Palace was destroyed in World War II, and has been rebuilt, with the added statue of Prince Józef Poniatowski on horseback in front of it. Today it is the official residence of the President of Poland.

That year there was further disruption at the Casimir Palace, with the establishment of the university in the main building, and the academic atmosphere, as well as the Chopins' social life, intensified accordingly. It increased even further in the October of that year when Warsaw had a visit from the Tsarina Maria Feodorovna, Alexander's mother, who was engaged in a stately tour of her son's Polish kingdom. While inspecting the university and other educational establishments, she called on the Lyceum. Frycek, although not yet nine, was placed in his father's class for the occasion. The Tsarina visited Monsieur Chopin's class, and Frycek presented her with two dances. The Tsarina, who took an interest in children and their achievements, graciously accepted these offerings. The *Correspondents' Gazette* of 6 October 1818 recorded that 'to the details of the visit of her Majesty the mother of the Tsar to the university and the Lyceum must be added the fact that Master Chopin, nine-year-old son of a professor at the Lyceum, already an accomplished musician at such an early age, offered Her Majesty two dances for the fortepiano of his own composition, which the Monarch, praising the talent of so young a boy, and to encourage him to further achievement, graciously accepted from him.'

Nothing is known of these dances, which some sources claim were polonaises. It is possible they were the 'Several Dances' that Frycek is documented to have written in 1817. Like the Variations for Fortepiano, and the Military March, they are now lost, although the story behind the Military March has survived in a mixture of fact and legend through its connection with Grand Duke Constantine.

Constantine Pavlovitch Romanov was born on 27 April 1779 at Tsarskoye Selo. He was the second son of Tsar Paul and Maria Feodorovna, and the younger brother of Tsar Alexander. When he was sixteen, Constantine married Juliana of Coburg, but the marriage soon collapsed, and she returned to Germany. He joined the army and proved himself incompetent on the battlefield and short-tempered in officer circles. A liaison with a French girl, Josephine Friedrichs, resulted in the birth of a boy, named Paul, in 1810, the year of Frycek's birth. Josephine was paid off and married off, but Constantine retained custody of Paul. After the defeat of Napoleon, Constantine took up residence in Warsaw, where he met Countess Joanna Grudzińska, the step-daughter of the Superintendent of the Royal Castle, with whom he fell in love. At the Congress of Vienna his brother appointed him Commander of the Polish Garrison in Warsaw.

Grand Duke Constantine fancied himself as a Pole. He loved

Poles, and everything Polish, even though the feeling was not re-
ciprocated. He had wild, staring eyes and an unattractive face
that verged on the ugly. His moods fluctuated between jovial
buffoonery and a violent temper, none of which endeared him to
a nation which expected at least a modicum of sophistication
from their ruling classes. As Commander of the Garrison he delighted in endless parades and marches in front of the Saxon Palace.
His treatment of the soldiers was unnecessarily high-handed, and
he had no qualms about meting out the most humiliating punishments, including floggings – to which the populace were invited –
for the slightest lapses in military discipline. Within months of his
appointment he managed to enrage most people with whom he
came into contact. He meant well at heart, and tried to do what
he thought was right. He was seen at all the correct places, went
to concerts and the theatre, and was invited to the salons.

Inevitably he heard Frycek playing the piano. This 'Chopinek',
as Frycek was sometimes called in the diminutive, was not only
extraordinarily talented, but was the same age as Paul. He spoke
perfect French, so the Duke invited him to Belvedere Palace, his
official residence, so the two boys could play together and speak
French – the language of the upper classes. What was more, Paul's
French tutor, the Comte de Moriolles, had a young daughter of
the same age, called Alexandrine, so the visit was child-oriented.
Frycek, who knew all about the ugly Grand Duke's temper, was
apprehensive when the carriage, drawn Russian-style by four horses
abreast, with a Cossack mounted on each of the outside horses,
arrived at the Casimir Palace to fetch him – watched wrily by the
combined academic might of the Lyceum and the university.

The carriage turned left into the Krakowskie Przedmieście and
continued in a direct line to the southern end of Warsaw. It drew
up outside the Belvedere Palace, situated on a hill overlooking the
Łazienki Gardens, with its extensive lawns, shrubs, woods and
ornamental lakes. Frycek was introduced to Paul and Alexandrine,
and a good time was consequently had by the three children.
Frycek, Paul and 'Moriolka' managed to hit it off, and the occasion was deemed enough of a success for it to be repeated, until
it became a regular Sunday occurrence. Sometimes the children
would stay indoors, or play in the Łazienki Gardens, or even just
stay in the carriage and go for a ride.

There was a piano at the palace, which Frycek often played. On several occasions the Grand Duke, who usually left the children to their own devices, came to listen. Frycek played his usual repertoire, which the Duke always enjoyed very much. As time went on, he would come more and more often to listen to Frycek playing, always sitting attentively. One day the Duke asked him to play something military, so Frycek launched into the Military March he had composed the previous year. The Grand Duke leapt up in sheer delight, and marched round and round the room, grinning broadly and swinging his arms in time to the music. He liked the march so much that he had it orchestrated and played at his military parades.

Frycek had now graduated to Beethoven and Hummel, and Żywny was beginning to find teaching Frycek increasingly difficult as the boy overtook his teacher's piano technique. Fortunately, teacher and pupil had a remarkable mutual understanding and empathy which transcended such minor problems. Frycek's visits to salons and concerts gave him a taste of the best of European music, and his influences became wider and more varied. He loved the soaring melodies of Italian opera, as sung by the human voice. This love established itself in Frycek's creative psyche towards the end of 1819, with the arrival in the capital of Angelica Catalani.

This remarkable Italian soprano was regarded as the greatest of her day, even though she had a reputation for taking liberties with the music. That year she was touring Poland, and her performance in Warsaw on December 22 was recorded in the *Warsaw Gazette* as 'not only remarkable, it also raised money for charity'. So it should have done; the tickets were so expensive that they inspired a rhyme that did the rounds of Warsaw:

> Oh, dear Lady Catalani
> Can't you sing for cheaper?
> Your Italian tralala should
> Only cost one thaler.

Frycek heard Catalani singing, and she made a deep impression on him. Her name even slipped into Frycek's vocabulary, to mean a singer of considerable lung power. Frycek's love of melody was enforced by Catalani's singing, and his melodic invention at the piano began to take on vocal qualities of phrasing and 'breathing'.

There was a very strong feeling for opera in Warsaw, and Frycek grew to love it passionately. He himself had a very tuneful voice, and sang in church choirs during his youth, as did Ludka. Their singing talents were inherited from their mother, whose beautiful voice is documented.

Frycek met Angelica Catalani at the salon of Konstanty Wolicki, where music reigned supreme. He played the piano, and Catalani presented him with a gold watch, on which were inscribed the words: 'Mme Catalani à Frédéric Chopin agé de 10 ans à VARSOVIE le 3 janvier 1820.' Frycek loved this gift and kept it with him till his dying day.

In 1820 the Belvedere Palace was closed for restoration, and Frycek's visits were suspended. The Grand Duke, seeking to legitimize his affair with Countess Joanna Grudzińska, asked his brother for permission to divorce his German wife, to whom he was still legally married. Alexander gave his consent and the divorce was arranged. Constantine married Countess Joanna, who thenceforward proceeded to exert a pacific influence on her irascible husband; he had become brutal and eccentric. On her marriage she was given the title Princess of Łowicz by the Tsar. The Poles bestowed on her the further title of 'Guardian Angel of Poland', in acknowledgement of her ability to control her husband's antics. When the palace was renovated and the newlyweds had settled in, Frycek was again a regular visitor. This time, apart from playing with Paul and 'Moriolka', he entered an alliance with the newly titled Princess, who recognized the intense power of his music: it was the most effective sedative when the Duke had worked himself up into a rage. Legend has it that she used to send for Frycek to come to the Belvedere Palace to calm the Duke down on such occasions.

The Belvedere Palace, previously the official residence of the President of Poland, is now a government building.

Żywny, unable to teach Frycek anything more, resigned as his piano tutor. Nicolas and Justyna understood, but insisted that his continuing friendship and involvement with Frycek should remain. He continued to come round, listen to the boy playing, pass comments and advice, and stay to supper. Frycek, now eleven, had grown to love the old Bohemian, and was loath to let him go. As a token of this love and gratitude, he wrote and dedicated his next polonaise to him. This Polonaise in A flat, more sophisticated than its predecessors, holds hints of the great tone poems of his future treatment of the form. The Ogiński crossed-hands device is still there, in the second subject, with the clefs inverted for eight bars, but now the straight diatonic harmonies are spiced with chromaticism and flowery runs in the right hand that point to the virtuoso cadenza-style decorations of many of his future works. The dedication runs: 'Dédiée à Monsieur A. Żywny par Son élève Fryderyk Chopin à Varsovie ce 23 Avril 1821.' The dedicatee was touched by this supreme gift.

Frycek's trio of childhood Polonaises, in B flat, G minor and A flat, constitute a telling document of Fryderyk Chopin's musical transition from clever infant to budding composer.

Woyciech Żywny lived from 1837 in the Krakowskie Przedmieście, at today's No. 19. A plaque marks the house, which has been rebuilt.

Frycek entered a period with no piano teacher. Żywny had implanted the basics firmly, and Frycek could sight-read, write down his music and control his improvisations. His technique was kept in trim with Bach, and his touch exercised with Mozart. He accepted nothing less than perfection in his own execution, and he had learned the method, habit and discipline of practice. For the time being he had the power and ability to develop at his own pace. In his enthusiasm to improve his technique, Frycek adopted the habit of sleeping with pieces of wood wedged between his fingers to stretch them. Fortunately the bits of wood kept falling out in the night, and when his horrified mother found out what he had been doing, she put a stop to it. The practice was reputed to have contributed to the permanent damage to Schumann's hands, so she was wise to have done so.

Frycek was still taught at home. His gift for drawing, especially caricatures, was improving. Ludka's admiration for her brother was considerable. She was herself encouraged to emulate his playing – and his composing – even though he now completely overshadowed her. Izabela, who was now ten, was the prettiest of the three girls. She showed no aptitude for music, but rather for writing and language; she was already translating from German into Polish. Nine-year-old Emilka was the brightest of the girls; delicate and not very strong, her great love was poetry, which she wrote, and literature. She had a fertile imagination which she expressed in making up stories; unlike Frycek, she enjoyed writing them down. The Chopins were in the eyes of many a model family, and their home a place where all the right values of goodness and decency reigned in an atmosphere of music and culture.

One of the visitors to the Chopin apartment was Elsner. Józef Xaver Elsner was born in 1769, in Grodków, Silesia, a small town south-east of Wrocław, then called Breslau, of German-speaking parents of Swedish descent. As a young man he went to Breslau to study theology, but gave it up when he found he had to learn Polish, which he was not willing to do. He tried medicine instead, and then he went to Vienna where he finally settled for music. After a brief spell in the theatre orchestra at Brno, in Moravia, he was appointed conductor at the Lvov Opera. In this beautiful city in the Austrian province of Galicia, he found again a need to learn Polish. This time he willingly conceded, and not only learnt to speak Polish but also to be Polish and to marry a Polish girl. He changed the spellings of his Christian names to Józef Ksawery and embarked on a career of indefatigably promoting – and composing – Polish music. Józef Elsner lived at today's 56 Krakowskie Przedmieście. A commemorative plaque marks the rebuilt house.

In 1799 he was appointed chief conductor at the Warsaw Opera, which was all but dead from Prussian suppression of Polish culture. It was housed at the time in the National Theatre. He revitalized it, and mounted his own short and light-hearted operas, as well as those of other composers. He scoured the European opera scene, and imported the operas of Salieri and Mozart from Vienna, and Cimarosa, Paisiello and Cherubini from Italy. In Napoleon's time Warsaw was introduced to Méhul and Grétry from France. In 1810 he enlisted the talented young Polish composer, Karol Kurpiński, as his deputy, which enabled him to expand on his progressive ideas backstage. In 1811, finding a need for greater basic training for the operatic stage, he set up a progressive series of music- and drama-teaching establishments, until, in 1821, while still holding the post of chief conductor at the Opera, he founded the Main School of Music as a department of the Faculty of Sciences and Arts at Warsaw University. The Main School of Music became familiarly known as the Warsaw Conservatory. With its strong operatic connections, Elsner appointed Italian-born Carlo Soliva, or Karol Soliwa as he chose to spell it, as teacher of singing. The Conservatory was situated in the Krakowskie Przedmieście close to the Castle.

This interested the Chopins; Frycek, at twelve, was too young to attend, but now it was possible for Nicolas to plan for the future. Elsner knew that one day Frycek would come to him for formal training, and began to sow some preliminary seeds by listening to the boy's playing, and giving him tips on composition, form and counterpoint.

Over the next two years, Frycek's only surviving composition was the Polonaise in G sharp minor, written some time between 1822 and 1824, and published posthumously. It was the work of an accomplished composer, who had outgrown the traditional simplicity of the salon polonaise as understood by Ogiński, and had now composed his first full-bodied concert piece. Although it does not feature in the established chronology of Chopin's six polonaises, this is the first of those great, passionate masterpieces of the form, for which the three childhood polonaises were as studies.

Frycek had now embraced the new, fashionable piano concertos in the Romantic style. On 24 February 1823, Julian Niemcewicz put on a charity concert at the Benevolent Society building. Frycek played one of the nine piano concertos by the German composer, Ferdinand Ries, at that time resident in London. Two days later, the *Warsaw Courier* reported the concert: the greater part was a eulogy about the incredible talent of Warsaw's very own young genius, and compared Frycek's achievement with a similar concert in Vienna, where another little genius, one Franz Liszt, enchanted his Viennese audience with a piano concerto by Hummel. There was a second such concert organized by the Benevolent Society on March 17, at which Frycek played. The report in the *Courier* this time eulogized more about the charitable aspect of making music for the benefit of the unfortunate poor than about the music.

The summer term of 1823 came to an end, to Linde's relief. In June his wife, Ludwika, had died, leaving him to care for their two little daughters, Ludwika, eight, and Anna, two. He was glad of the opportunity to be alone with his thoughts. His students, and those at the university, went home – or on holiday. The Chopins went to spend the summer with Countess Ludwika at Żelazowa Wola. The estate had changed since the Chopins' departure thirteen years previously. In 1814 the main manor had burnt down, leaving only the two wings, including Frycek's birthplace.

His godmother Anna Skarbek was no longer there; in 1821 she had married Stefan Wiesiołowski, an official at the Warsaw Treasury with an estate at Strzyżewo, beyond Kalisz in Prussia. Stefan Wiesiołowski was related to Konstanty Wolicki, at whose salon Frycek played to Angelica Catalani. Old Count Kacper Skarbek returned to Poland from Paris, and moved in with his daughter and son-in-law at Strzyżewo, where he died in February 1823. He was buried at the church in nearby Kotłów.

The Chopins had been back to Żelazowa Wola since the fire for brief visits, but this time it was for a longer stay. Despite the absence of the manor, it was an idyllic summer spent in simple circumstances, with hot days and sultry nights. The children enjoyed the full benefit of the countryside, and went for long walks along the River Utrata, and played games in the surrounding woods. Frycek spent a great deal of time playing the piano:

On beautiful starlit nights, the piano was hauled out of the house and placed under a fig tree. The pianist was bidden to sit at it and play, and with his improvisations he enchanted his listeners and brought tears to their eyes. The sounds wafted through the orchards and reached the ears of the villagers, who all came to the house, and stood outside the palings to hear the young visitor from Warsaw.

One of these villagers was Antoni Krysiak, who was exactly the same age as Frycek. He recalled the occasion clearly, despite advancing senility, and he recounted the story to Mily Balakirev in 1890, when the Russian composer came to Żelazowa Wola that year to unveil a monument to the memory of Fryderyk Chopin.

Today the one remaining Żelazowa Wola wing, the left one in which Chopin was born, although completely rebuilt, is Poland's premier Chopin site. Set in a beautifully tended park, it contains a reconstruction of the alcove in which Fryderyk Chopin was born. There is a small recital room with French windows opening onto a terrace. Every Sunday piano recitals are given here, and in summer a larger audience can sit on the terrace, to listen to the music in the open, as did Antoni Krysiak.

FOUR
Domuś Dziewanowski's Mazovia

The summer of 1823 drew to a close, and Frycek returned to Warsaw with a measure of apprehension; that autumn he was to start his formal education in Class IV of the Warsaw Lyceum. His father had been promoted to Head of the French Department and was in charge of Class IV. First he had to pass his entrance examination, but Nicolas and Justyna had already taught him basic reading, writing and numeracy at home. Among the requirements were dictation, setting out a letter, a knowledge of the conjugation of Latin, German and French verbs, the general outline of basic history and geography, arithmetic, algebra up to four variables, square roots, and in geometry a knowledge of circles and the relationships of the angles of a triangle. The examination was difficult, and the standard expected by Linde was high. Frycek passed the exam with flying colours.

On September 15 the newly teenaged Frycek travelled the distance of a flight of stairs to his new class at the Warsaw Lyceum. He was dressed in the strictly enforced uniform, after the style of the warrior Uhlans: knee-length blue frock coat with epaulettes, buttoned up to the neck and belted at the waist, long matching trousers, black shoes and a tall peaked cap. The curriculum was comprehensive, and included ancient and modern languages: Latin, Greek, French, Polish, Russian; mathematics included geometry. Science was a growing subject, and chemistry, physics, botany, natural history, topography, geography, minerology and entomology were essential subjects. History included Russian as well as Polish, and the Czartoryski Constitution was thoroughly drummed in. Drawing and design included architecture, and Nicolas himself taught the art of calligraphy. At the apex was religious education: the Roman Catholic Church of the Visitation next to the Casimir Palace was the spiritual soul of the Lyceum, and the priest, a semi-permanent fixture on the campus, was considered a most important person.

Overseeing the six hundred boys was the rector, Professor Samuel Linde. A widower since June, he lived on the first floor with his daughters, little Lulu and Anna. He had married their mother, Ludwika Burger, in 1804, the year of the institution of the Lyceum. Of their seven children five were stillborn. The professor was popular with his charges because of his discipline laced with kindness, his dry sense of humour, and the way in which he peered at the boys through his spectacles. His German accent (he hailed from Toruń, and was the butt of rhyming jibes about Copernicus, also born there, and the famous Toruń cakes, *Kopernik-piernik*) and the fact that he affectionately called the boys 'my children!' gave him an avuncular air and set a happy atmosphere in which the cream of Polish youth could grow and develop its full potential.

Among Linde's staff was the young mathematics assistant Antoni Barciński, who had lodged at the Chopins', but left shortly after Frycek's enrolment. Ten years later he married Frycek's sister, Izabela. Some of the teachers worked at the university as well as the Lyceum; among them was Deodat Vögel, who taught perspective and optics at the university and drawing at the Lyceum. His well-known drawings of Warsaw are still used as contemporary illustrations. Frycek took a particular interest in his lessons; from an early age he had shown an aptitude for meticulously detailed designs. The name-day card created for his father when he was six is a prime example. His still life and landscape drawings were delicate, accurate and beautifully executed; but his caricatures were his greatest and most popular output. Those few that have survived show a remarkable capacity for humour. Adolfa Cichowska, a relative of science teacher Józef Skrodzki, recalled how Frycek drew caricatures of the whole editorial staff of the *Polish Courier*, which her uncle edited, by observing them through a keyhole. Closer to home, Frycek's caricature of Linde found its way into the rector's hands, to Frycek's consternation. Fortunately, the rector saw the funny side, wrote 'well done' on it, and returned it to the much relieved perpetrator.

Frycek's sense of humour was not confined to pencil and paper; he was a talented mimic, and caused hilarity with his impersonations. His gift for story-telling, which he embellished with facial expressions, overacting and the liberal use of foreign accents, especially the Germanic cadences of Żywny and Linde, kept his peers amused for hours. Józefa Kościelska was the younger sister of Frycek's later love, Maria Wodzińska. In her *Memoirs* she recalled that Frycek 'was the very soul of fun; he rushed about, joked, mimicked all those he knew, drew their caricatures. . . .' He also used his acting talents in the drawing-room dramas and charades in which young people emulated the satires and farces of the salons. As an adult Fryderyk Chopin was renowned as an amusing and witty raconteur who regaled dinner party guests with his sophisticated humour.

Frycek's wit, charm and sense of fun made him many friends. Wilhelm 'Wiluś' Kolberg, who lived downstairs, was three years older. Julian Fontana, pianist and eventual editor of Chopin's posthumous opus numbers, was born the same year as Frycek. He remained Frycek's friend for life, as did another pianist, Tytus Woyciechowski, who joined the Lyceum later. Józef Jędrzejewicz, twenty at this time, later married Frycek's older sister, Ludka. Two other friends were Jan Białobłocki, also a pianist, and Jan Matuszyński.

But his closest friend that year was thirteen-year-old Dominik 'Domuś' Dziewanowski, whose father, Juliusz, had an estate at Szafarnia, near Toruń, in deepest, most rural Mazovia. Domuś, who lodged with the Chopins, had a love of music in common with Frycek – a love inherited from his mother, who played the piano. The two boys worked competitively and played hard, their sights set on the Class IV Prize at the end of the year.

But despite the fun and hard work all was not well in the Chopin house. Frycek was frail, and the first signs of consumption, as tuberculosis was known at the time, were emerging and causing concern. Also Emilka, now ten, was showing similar symptoms. Dr Gerardot was called, and prescribed a diet of fine-ground bread, only the ripest fruit, small quantities of sweet wine in preference to water, acorn coffee, pills and half a carafe of tisane – a distillation of herbs – to be taken at one draught. Despite these set-backs, Frycek and Domuś achieved their aim, and in July, they both won the Class IV Prize *ex aequo*. Nicolas admitted, putting his worries to the back of his mind, that Frycek's first year at the Lyceum had been a success.

That summer Domuś invited Frycek to stay with him at Szafarnia. The small but fine manor, with two ornamental lakes, stables and outhouses, was situated just outside the village. The family consisted of Juliusz Dziewanowski, his wife and his two sisters, Ludwika and Honorata, and his son Domuś. It was Aunt Ludwika who played merry host to Frycek, made sure that he stuck to his diet, and took the boys on outings.

On August 10 Frycek wrote home to say that he was well, was having a lovely time, did no reading or writing whatsoever, and spent his time playing, drawing, running about, enjoying the fresh air and going for coach rides. 'I eat with an enormous appetite,' he wrote, 'and I need nothing to satisfy my thin stomach, which is becoming fatter, except permission to eat country bread.' For the next page and a half he launched into a diatribe about why Dr Gerardot had forbidden him to eat country bread. He compared the wholemeal local loaves, whose delicious aroma drove him mad, with the fine-flour white bread of the city, and saw no reason why he should be forbidden to eat it. He even offered to send the doctor a loaf to taste just to prove his point.

Apart from reporting the social life – the local families took turns visiting one another – Frycek asked his father, who was expected to arrive at some time, for some music. 'I ask Papa if he would be so kind to buy at Brzezina's [the music publisher] the Variations on a theme of Moore for piano duet by Ries, and to bring it, so that Mrs Dziewanowska can play it with me.'

The composer Thomas Moore was born in 1779 in Dublin. He emigrated to England, where he made a name for himself as a latter-day troubadour. His romantic and poetic ballads were popular in the drawing-rooms of England during the first half of the nineteenth century. Moore died in Bromham, Wiltshire, in 1852. Ferdinand Ries, one of whose piano concertos Frycek played at the Radziwiłł Palace, was living in England at the time, and wrote a set of variations for piano duet on one of Moore's most popular airs – which he had actually 'borrowed' from the famous

'Carnival in Venice'. Frycek was very fond of both the tune and Ries's Variations.

Despite Domuś's fondness for music and the fact that his mother played the piano, the main thrust of Frycek's creative drive was directed elsewhere. With Domuś at his elbow, he compiled his own distinctive brand of newsletter in the form of a home-made newspaper, based on the format of the *Warsaw Courier*, yet imbued with his own zany humour. The 'Szafarnia Courier' was a double-paged broadsheet, in which all events of note were recorded in schoolboy journalese. At the head was the title, in printed letters, and the date. The left-hand side was devoted to home, that is, local news, while the right side was devoted to 'foreign' news – covering anything outside the immediate vicinity of Szafarnia. As editor, he came to call himself in later editions Mr Pichon – an anagram of Chopin – and referred to himself in the third person. The various names and misnomers are cryptic references to persons real and imaginary.

When completed, he sent the 'Szafarnia Courier' home, where it was eagerly awaited and avidly read. Four issues have survived out of six, which cover the period 10 August to 5 September 1824. The dates of the individual entries are not always chronological, suggesting some entries are afterthoughts. Much of the content of the lost issues has survived in a mixture of legend and transcription.

Issue No. 1 is dated 16 August 1824. Under 'Home News' is recorded:

On August 11 Mr Fryderyk Chopin went riding on a charger. He ran several races, but every time he failed to overtake Mrs Dziewanowska, who was on foot. But that was the horse's fault, not his. He won a victory against Miss Ludwika, who came close to her goal.

Frycek qualified his lack of prowess on horseback in a letter to Wiluś Kolberg:

You're not the only one who can ride; I can as well, but don't ask how well; but I can, enough to let the horse go slowly wherever it wants to, while I sit on it, terrified, like a monkey on a bear. So far I haven't fallen off yet, but I may do so one day.

The 'Courier' continues:

Mr Franciszek Chopin goes for a drive every day, with such honour as always to sit at the back.

Mr Jakub Chopin drinks six cups of acorn coffee every day, and little Nicolas has four rolls a day, apart from a large lunch and a three-course dinner in the evenings.

On August 13 Mr Better played upon the fortepiano with uncommon talent. The Berlin virtuoso played just like Mr Berger, the fortepiano player from Skolimów; in his skill and digital dexterity he excels even over Mrs Lagowska, and he plays with such feeling that every note seems to come not from his heart, but from his mighty stomach.

On August 15 the important fact was learned that one of the turkeys gave birth behind the granary. This event signifies not only an increase in the turkey population, but also profit to the Treasury, thus assuring its increase.

Last night a cat crept into the cupboard and broke a flask of syrup; however, although he had thus earned the shadow of the gallows, he none the less deserves praise for having chosen the smallest flask.

On August 12 a hen went lame, and a drake lost a leg during a confrontation with a goose.

A cow, suddenly taken ill, now grazes in the garden.

On August 14 a decree was issued that no piglets were to walk in the garden, under pain of death.

Under 'Foreign News':

A certain citizen wished to read 'The Monitor'. He sent his servant to the Carmelite Fathers in Obory, to get the periodical. As the servant had never heard of this periodical, he confused the words [periodical with haemorrhoidical] and asked the Fathers for a journal on haemorrhoids.

In Bocheniec a fox consumed two defenceless geese. If anyone catches him, he must inform the Bocheniec Court, who will punish the miscreant according to law, and hand the fox over as compensation for the two geese.

Issue No. 2, dated 19 August 1824, is lost, but some details survive. Under 'Home News':

> On August 15 there was a musical gathering at Szafarnia, of a score or so of miscellaneous persons. Mr Pichon figured in the programme with a piano concerto by Kalkbrenner. This did not have as much effect on the miscellaneous persons as the 'Żydek' also performed by the same Mr Pichon.

Friedrich Wilhelm Kalkbrenner was born in Germany in 1785. He was a brilliant pianist and his four piano concertos are virtuoso works. Frycek already had Gyrowetz's and Ries's concertos under his belt. To be able to play a Kalkbrenner concerto testified to an accomplished technique. Perhaps the concerto in question was too 'modern' for the miscellaneous persons at Szafarnia on that occasion. Chopin dedicated his E minor piano concerto to Kalkbrenner, and they became friendly rivals in later life in Paris, Kalkbrenner adhering to the Liszt-Thalberg school of pianistic 'thunderers', Fryderyk Chopin to his own more delicate, subtle style.

The 'Żydek', which means literally 'little Jew', was a mazurka that Frycek had been toying with at the time. He was, after all, in Mazovia, the land of the mazurka. It was in Szafarnia that Frycek became acquainted with the mazurka, a dance in three-four time which was to the peasants what the polonaise was to the upper classes. Frycek was exposed to the mazurka in all its guises, from the wild ones in which the boys threw the girls into the air in displays of machismo, to the more ethereal, wistful ones which sang of love and melancholy. These are similar in feel to the *kujawiak*, a very slow dance in three-four time which comes from the Kujawy region. Frycek's Żydek was such a one. He was experimenting with the modal qualities of this rural music, and his Żydek, although in the key of A minor, had a tonal pull towards F major. The result was an extraordinarily chromatic piece for its time, and Frycek did not get it right till much later, when it was published as the Mazurka in A minor Op. 17 No. 4.

Frycek's Mazurka in B flat, without an opus number, was written

at this time. This is another example of his experimentation with
the modal tonalities that he was hearing all around. Many mazurkas
used the Lydian mode, with the fourth note of the scale sharpened.
This bright and breezy mazurka uses this device in its main theme.

Frycek's third mazurka written at this time was dedicated to
Wiluś Kolberg. In it Frycek explored the 'bagpipe' drone found in
many mazurkas: an unchanging bass note was kept going whatever the harmonies and modulations above. Mazovia had its own
bagpipes, and some of the music reflected this. Again, this mazurka,
with its discordant passage in the middle, was perfected later and
published as the Mazurka in A flat, Op. 7 No. 4.

The 'Szafarnia Courier' Issue No. 2 recorded that the editor
had drunk seven cups of acorn coffee, and was expected soon to
drink his eighth. Also reported was the story of a group of Jewish merchants who arrived at the neighbouring village of Obrów
to buy wheat from the lord of the manor, a Mr Ramocki. Frycek
went to call on them, and played them the Majufes, a Jewish
wedding march. This caused such paroxysms of delight among
the Jews, that they frolicked, skipped and danced to the music,
and asked Mr Ramocki if he would arrange for the boy to play
at a forthcoming Jewish wedding. 'Because', they maintained, 'he
plays like a born Jew.' Poland had many folk and dance bands –
and the Jewish ones were considered the best.

Issue No. 3, dated August 24, is lost, but details of the saga of
Mr Ramocki and the Jewish wheat merchants have been preserved.
Under 'Foreign News', the editor recorded that there was an *okrężne*
in Obrów, at the Ramocki estate. This was a harvest festival event.
The peasants, having gone round all the fields and collected the
harvest, celebrated by making wreaths from the grain stalks, to
present to Mr Ramocki, as a symbol of the gathered crops – the
ones bought by the Jewish merchants in the previous issue. Mr
Ramocki responded by laying on a splendid open-air feast complete with apple and plum cordials, vodka and beer. There was
music and dancing of mazurkas, *kujawiaks*, waltzes, polkas and
obereks. The merry gathering assembled outside the manor, and
two girls were, in the editor's words, screeching in harmony a
semitone apart.

The screeching referred to another facet of Polish folk music:
open-throat singing in harmony. When the vocalists, usually girls,

are in tune, open-throat singing is very effective. The editor, whose interest in the folk traditions of Mazovia was all-consuming, was fascinated with – if not actually enamoured of – Szafarnia's offering during this *okrężne*. The lyrics of the ditty concerned a bride and a bridegroom, which suggests that a wedding had been planned to coincide with the harvest. Whatever the quality of the singing, everyone had a marvellous time.

The saga continued with a prank played by Frycek on the Jews, which backfired. He wrote a letter to Mr Ramocki, supposedly from the Jewish wheat merchant, indicating that he had changed his mind, and did not want to buy his wheat after all. Frycek's mimicry included Jews, and he was an expert in Jewish accents, mannerisms, ways of saying things and commercial jargon. Now he tried his hand at Jewish forgery. He did it very well, using the atrocious Roman handwriting for which Jews, more accustomed to the Hebrew script, were noted. Mr Ramocki was fooled, and was set to do violence to the merchant. Frycek, seeing that he had overstepped the mark, confessed and salvaged the situation.

Issue No. 4 was dated 27 August 1824. The 'Home News' reported that:

On August 25 Miss Kosteria, shouting to Mr Szymon with her alluring voice, came out of the kitchen with a bucket full of water, and, stopping abruptly, knocked the bucket over. So momentous an accident was instantly brought to the attention of the editor of the Courier, who, considering it a feat of extraordinary eptitude, deemed it worthy of international awareness.

On August 26 a monster in the guise of a chicken was found in the hen-run. This terrifying object with two legs and a wing, lacked a head. Sending it to Warsaw, or one of the other capitals, as one of nature's wonders, is being considered.

Mr Pichon is being worried by his country cousins [gnats], who are many. They bite him wherever they can, but fortunately not on his nose, else it would grow even bigger than it is already.

On August 26 Sudyna the dog caught a partridge in a wheat field. Miss Kozaczkiec, seeing this, took the dead thing away from her, and hung it in a pear tree. She shook the pear tree while jumping up and down until the partridge fell out of it, and she consumed it with a great appetite.

The descendant of the famous heroes who had defended Gaul, the melancholy gobbler, the turkey's brother, was stricken with the fever, and now lies without hope of recovery.

On the very early morning of August 25, a drake came out of the hen-run and drowned himself. Up to the present the reason for his suicide cannot be determined, as the family of the deceased choose to remain silent.

The cow is much better and her complete recovery is no longer in doubt.

Under 'Foreign News' we read:

On August 26 in Sokołowo a turkey climbed into a garden, where there was a kite that had lived there from an early age. He had never before seen a turkey and wanted to peck out its eyes. Both took to their beaks, and a duel took place. In the end the turkey won.

Frycek's school friend Jan 'Jasio' Białobłocki lived at Sokołowo, very close to Szafarnia.

'Mr Pichon was in Golub. Amongst other wonders and foreign details he saw a foreign pig, which took the attention of this intrepid traveller.'

Golub was the frontier town. The border with Prussia was the bridge over the little river Drwęca at what is today Golub Dobrzyń. In Chopin's day they were two separate towns: Golub was in Poland, while Dobrzyń was in Prussia. Under the terms of the Congress of Vienna Poles in all three partitions were allowed freedom of national expression, and the borders were treated by the ordinary people as administrative boundaries. The peasants and artisans whose lifestyle traditionally crossed these artifical frontiers took no notice of them.

Aunt Ludwika took the boys to Golub market, a seething hive of activity and trade, where swineherds rubbed shoulders with itinerant musicians, and Jewish merchants did business with counts. In one corner of the square is the Protestant Church, which was being renovated at the time. The Protestant pastor was a German whose name is not recorded; he had trouble delivering his sermons in Polish, a language that gave him grief. Frycek and Domuś went in, intent on teenage mischief. They climbed into the pulpit, where Frycek assumed the part of the pastor, and, with Domuś's encouragement, regaled his congregation of workmen who were restoring the church and the party from Szafarnia, with an exhibition of mimicry at the expense of the inarticulate – and mercifully absent – pastor.

Issue No. 4 continued:

On August 25 a cat strangled a chicken.

A Jewish milkman at Rodzoń was letting his calf feed in the manor courtyard. He got away with it several times, but on the night of August 24 a wolf came and ate it. The lord of the manor was glad that the Jew was paid in this way for his dishonest conduct, but the old Jew was more angry at the wolf. He is offering a whole calf to whomseover delivers the culprit to him.

Issue No. 5 was dated 31 August 1824. 'Home News':

On August 29 Mr Pichon was engaged in his toilet and was contemplating breakfast when with a scream, a barefooted woman rushed into the room. Mr Pichon was so startled that at first he stood with his mouth wide open, but after a while he learned the cause of her complaint. Mr Wiktor Sikorowski had quarrelled with Miss Kocaczka, and had decorated her head beautifully with his fist, so she was forced to seek satisfaction from a higher authority.

On August 29 a cart full of Jews was driving along. The whole family consisted of an old sow, three big Jews, two little Jews and six head of children. The whole lot were sitting in a heap, squashed like Dutch herrings. Then a stone in the road upset the cart, and it overturned. They all lay on the sand in the following order: first the children, each in a different position, most of them with their legs in the air. On top of them was the old sow, groaning under a load of Jews, who in their consternation, had lost their black skull-caps.

On August 30 three wenches fought in a cowshed. Two, armed with sticks, were belabouring the third, who was not.

On August 30 Mrs Zakierska, a resident of Szafarnia, having quarrelled with another was so enraged that nothing could be done with her, and she wanted to drown herself. Fortunately Mrs Szrederowa, the wife of Mr Gartner, an elderly resident, seeing what was happening, came running over. When she had already put her head in the pond, she dragged her out by the legs, thus saving her life.

Sudyna the dog, following on the heels of Miss Józefka through the village yesterday evening, caught a goose, strangled it and ate it.

On August 31 four geese were placed under house arrest, each not knowing how it would all end.

The cow is getting better, and on general consensus the doctors deem that there is no longer any danger.

'Foreign News':

On August 29 Mr Pichon, while passing through Nieszawa, heard a Catalani as she sat on a fence, singing at the top of her lungs. He became so absorbed, but although he heard the tune and the voice, he could not hear the lyrics. Twice he came past, but still he could not understand a single word. Finally, to satisfy his curiosity, he took from his pocket three *groszy* and offered them to the singer to repeat her song. For a long time she fidgeted, pulled faces and refused, but encouraged by the idea of the three *groszy* she began to sing the little mazurka, from which the editor, with permission from the authorities and the censor, quotes the following sample verse:

> Look, there beyond the hills,
> How the wolf is dancing;
> Alas he has no wife,
> That is why he is depressed.

The reason Frycek could not understand it was that the lass had a very rich Mazovian accent and used peasant diction, which would qualify as a Polish form of Unwinism. Besides, the words are nonsense. The incident shows Frycek's interest not only in local music, but also in local girls.

On August 29 at Radomin a cat went mad. Fortunately it did not bite anyone, but ran around until it jumped into a field where it was killed. Only then did it stop playing the fool.

In Dulnik a wolf ate a sheep for his supper. The desolated shepherds of the remaining lambs offered the tail and ears to whomsoever catches the wolf and brings him to a family enquiry.

The final Issue was No. 6, dated 3 September 1824. 'Home News':

On September 1 Mr Pichon was playing a *żydek* on the piano when Mr Dziewanowski called the Jewish milkman to ask him his opinion of the Yiddish virtuoso. Moshe came up to the window and poked his long tall nose into the room and listened, saying that if Mr Pichon would agree to play at a Jewish wedding he could earn himself 10 thalers. This pronouncement encouraged Mr Pichon to take up that kind of music as much as possible, and, who knows? he may devote himself completely to such profitable harmonization.

On September 2 a recently acquired cat escaped from his room. The housewife ran out and, seeing he was escaping, chased him. She had just caught up with him when the cat jumped over a fence and took a rest on the other side. The lady, desperate to catch him, climbed on to the fence with the intention of getting to the other side. However, her foot slipped . . . she lost her equilibrium . . . and . . . fell like a pancake on to the ground.

On September 3 Mr Łukasz, an official, having climbed into a pear tree, began to shake the branches to make the pears fall to the ground. Having been shaken several times, no pears were willing to fall, but, it should be noted well, by chance, instead of the pears, he shook himself on to the ground.

On September 2 Miss Brygida, a cook, who was making bread, turned round, and through her grace and agility knocked all of it to the ground.

On September 1 Negro [black dog], going out one evening into the fields, killed a partridge without a rifle or powder.

The cow is definitely recovered.

'Foreign News':

On September 1 a turkey devoured a partridge in the woods.

On September 5 in Bocheniec the marriage will take place of Mr Jan Lewandowski with Miss Katarzyna Grzewska, the daughter of the Governor of Bocheniec. The Governor's wife is preparing a great feast and the bridegroom is already inviting the guests, among them Mr Pichon, who is unspeakably happy to accept. The editor of the 'Courier' will be reporting the event in a future Issue.

Posterity will never know about Mr and Mrs Lewandowski's wedding since this was the last issue of the 'Szafarnia Courier'. As with its predecessors, the final issue ends with 'Passed by the censor – L.D.' – Aunt Ludwika Dziewanowska.

It was against the law in the kingdom to publish any journal without censorship. Despite all the promises of the Congress of Vienna, Poland had become a virtual police state. In charge of censorship and internal security was the loathed Russian Commissioner in Warsaw, Count Nicolai Novosiltsov. In the same way as many cultured Russians looked upon Poland as their civilized western province, so Novosiltsov represented to the Poles the barbaric east. He was a personal friend of the Tsar's, even though he was a drunken and debauched womanizer with a sadistic streak. Censorship enabled him to spy on everyone to whom he took a dislike by reading between the lines of their writings. He had cause to, since many of the younger generation of Poles were no longer content to go along meekly with the compromise of the Congress Kingdom, and talk in the cafés and drawing-rooms had become dangerous. Vilnius and Warsaw, both university cities, became hotbeds of dissenting talk, and Nicolas became worried by snippets of conversation that reached his ears.

Novosiltsov pounced, and many arrests were made; the most notorious, which gnawed deeply into the Polish psyche, was the Łukasiński affair.

Major Walerian Łukasiński's regiment was the Fourth Infantry. He was a dashing and popular soldier who formed a secret patriotic society. Novosiltsov got wind of this, and in 1824 Łukasiński and three ringleaders were arrested and charged with high treason. They were first publicly humiliated on the parade ground, lined up in front of the regiment and the public, in full dress uniform. Their epaulettes and their medals were torn off, and their swords were broken by an executioner dressed in black. This piece of theatre was followed by the shaving of their heads and the placing of shackles round their ankles. Then they were forced to push wheelbarrows full of stones along the lines of their men. Some of them were unable to control their feelings, and wept. Łukasiński was tried, found guilty and imprisoned. He survived in a Russian prison till 1868, blind after forty-six years spent in darkness.

In Szafarnia life was simpler. The seasons, not Novosiltsov, ruled; September was advanced, the harvest was in and the first leaves were turning to gold. The summer holidays were drawing to a close, and a new term at the Lyceum was beckoning. Frycek and Domuś returned to Warsaw, armed with some hilarious recollections of rural Mazovia.

Firmly etched on Frycek's soul were the sounds of Mazovia, which caught his attention whenever he heard them. One wintry evening he was coming home with his father, when he heard from a tavern the sounds of a fiddler 'chopping' mazurkas and *obereks* with his bow. Struck by the originality and distinctive character, he begged his father to stop and listen. Despite his father's impatience to get home, Frycek made him stay for half an hour while he listened. He loved peasant open-throat singing as much as *bel canto*, and found this rough, violent style of fiddling, though anathema to the musical academic, fascinating. He was never slow to appreciate and assimilate music at every level.

December 6 was Nicolas's name day, and he was entertained, along with the boarders and other guests, with a performance of 'The Mistake, or the Pretended Rogue'. This light-hearted farce was written for the occasion by Frycek and Emilka, whose literary talents were beginning to blossom. Now nearly eleven, Emilka was showing remarkable literary promise. She had been an avid consumer of poetry and literature from an early age, and had for some time been writing poems and stories of her own. She was fond of drama, especially the homespun, drawing-room carpet variety. Nothing is known of the plot of this play, except that Frycek played a paunchy mayor, and Emilka his ethereal daughter. With Emilka's literary talents and Frycek's penchant for over-acting, the offering was well appreciated by everyone present.

Despite her growing frailty, Emilka continued to develop her interest in writing. Frycek, who was devoted to her, encouraged her with his total involvement in her worlds of the imagination. Together they formed a 'Literary Society', whose aims were to write poetry and stories for the benefit of anyone who cared to listen, which in effect meant the boarders. Frycek was the president, and Emilka was the secretary. The society's mouthpiece was the 'Literary Amusement Journal'. The creative writing was Emilka's, while the editing was in the hands of the already experienced proprietor of the late 'Szafarnia Courier'.

FIVE
A Visit from the Tsar

In September 1824 the boys returned to the Lyceum at the start of the academic year to find that their rector had married, at fifty-two, the eighteen-year-old Ludwika Nussbaum. The question again arose about the possibility of a male heir, which had always been close to Linde's heart. So far he had been foiled by Providence, on some occasions tragically. The new Mrs Linde soon won many hearts, including Frycek's, and everyone wished the professor the fulfilment of his desire.

At the end of April 1825, the Tsar arrived in Warsaw for the reopening of the Seym, a duty that had been shelved since the establishment of the Congress Kingdom. The Czartoryski Constitution was not observed, and despite the outward air of well-being, the mushrooming of secret patriotic societies threatened the Russian administration. The Tsar had to act, and his first move, a popular one, was to announce the opening of the Seym. An air of reconciliation pervaded the Warsaw spring, yet there were still undercurrents of resentment. Novosiltsov and Grand Duke Constantine were loathed heartily, and many Varsovians were still smouldering from the Łukasiński affair of the previous year. Both the university and the Lyceum rumbled with frustrated student dissent, and the city only grudgingly settled for a politically correct stance in the face of a genuine attempt by the Tsar to mend fences. The Chopin family, living squarely in the centre of this student disaffection, had to beware. The long arm of Novosiltsov's spy network had targeted all places where students could talk mischief. But Nicolas was prudent, and the family managed to maintain a safe distance from danger. Frycek's mind was firmly on school and his music, specifically his new Rondo in C minor. He was on good terms with Grand Duke Constantine, and wanted to keep it that way. He saw the Tsar's visit as an opportunity for further recognition.

The Tsar's policy became obvious soon after his arrival. He had not visited Warsaw since a whistle-stop during his 1816–17 tour of his Empire, and this time he decided to devote time and attention to his western kingdom. He arrived exuding goodwill. He dispensed with the high-handed aloofness of his previous visits, and elected to mingle with the people, talk to them and listen to their petitions and problems. During his six-week stay he attended balls and concerts, and took an interest in all things Polish, including industry. When Fidelis Brunner, the instrument maker, sent him an invitation to listen to his choralion in action, he accepted.

The choralion was the brainchild of Jakub Fryderyk Hofman, Professor of Botany at the university and a zealous inventor of unusual gadgets and musical instruments, including the eolimelodikon, melodikordion, melodipantaleon and orchestron. Hofman's designs were realized either by the piano maker Fryderyk Buchholtz or by Brunner. They were all variants of the harmonium, or harmonium-fortepiano hybrids, but with a bigger, richer tone designed to fill a large space. These instruments had systems of pedals and levers for controlling tone and volume. They were originally built for churches as movable alternatives to organs; or they were used experimentally as a substitute, or booster, for an orchestra – a selling point being that piano concertos could be performed by two keyboard players. They were the results of the experimentation with novelties so beloved of nineteenth-century European inventors. But despite their curiosity value, they have not stood the test of time.

Brunner, a friend of the Chopins, had installed his choralion in the Evangelical Church of the Holy Trinity. It was then a question of finding someone to play it for the Tsar. Hofman suggested Frycek Chopin, who played the piano, sang in the church choir, and could put his hand to any keyboard instrument. He was also good at improvising, useful when putting an instrument with built-in special effects through its paces. Throughout history fifteen-year-old boys have embraced new technology with enthusiasm, and Frycek was no exception. Going beyond merely playing written piano and organ music on the choralion, Frycek figured out the instrument's possibilities and peculiarities through a free ramble, or a fantasia, as a prepared improvisation was called. Soon he mastered the choralion, not as an organ substitute, but as a musical instrument in its own right. The Tsar had been briefed beforehand by his brother, Grand Duke Constantine, about this young pianist with a gilded and growing reputation. He was fascinated not only by Brunner's choralion, but also by the pale, delicate fifteen-year-old, immaculate in his dark blue Lyceum uniform, as he played with what the Warsaw press described as the demure shyness of a young girl. His programme included his prepared Fantasia, which showed the choralion off to best advantage. Afterwards the Tsar, when dispensing diamond rings as gestures of imperial approbation, gave one each to Frycek and to Fidelis Brunner.

The rotunda-shaped Evangelical Church of the Holy Trinity catered for Warsaw's Protestants. At this time about half the population of Warsaw was German, many of whom were Protestant. The Germans were divided into two camps; the first, like the Kolbergs, had chosen to become Polish and to assimilate themselves into the Polish nation. This group eschewed the language and culture of their roots, and made a point of speaking only in Polish. Juliusz Kolberg discouraged the use of German in his home. Some converted to Roman Catholicism, and changed their names to a Polish spelling; for instance Schmidt became Szmit, Schultz became Szulc and Schroeder became Szreder. Frycek's own surname had been spelt Choppen, Szoppen and Szopen, though the family chose to retain the French spelling. The second camp pointedly chose to retain their Germanness, their language and their religion. Warsaw's most successful theatre was the German Theatre. The result was a distinctly multicultural city, with Jews and Russians making up the rest of the ethnic mix. All lived in mutual tolerance, if not friendship, and there were curious unwritten laws that everyone obeyed: for instance Catholics did not mix socially with Jews, and 'real' Germans, either local or foreign, never stayed at the Hotel Niemiecki (German Hotel) on principle – only true non-Germans stayed there. Racial and religious prejudice was a traditional institution, which everyone happily preserved.

The Evangelical Church was nearly destroyed in World War II, but was rebuilt in 1960, and is situated in Królewska Street. In keeping with its musical associations, regular concerts take place there.

On Friday, May 27, Frycek performed his Fantasia again at an 'Artistes' and Amateurs' Grand Vocal and Instrumental Concert' at the conservatory, this time on the eolopantaleon, designed by Długosz. These fanciful creations enjoyed great success, and the orchestra was augmented with a choralion. Frycek also played Moscheles's Piano Concerto, the latest addition to his growing repertoire of Romantic piano concertos. Other items briefly recorded by the *Warsaw Courier* were: an Overture by Józef Nowakowski (a composition student at the conservatory), a duet from the opera *Achilles* by Pacer, the Rondo Brilliant by Hummel, the Violin Concerto by Rodeg (the soloist, a student of the conservatory, received special applause for this), a choral work by Beethoven accompanied by the choralion (possibly Frycek again), an aria from Rossini's *Otello*, and, as a finale, a cantata by Józef Elsner, the rector of the conservatory.

A week after this concert, Frycek's Rondo in C minor was published as his Op. 1. 'A new rondo for the pianoforte,' wrote the *Warsaw Courier* on 2 June 1825, 'composed by Fryderyk Chopin and dedicated to Madame Linde, was published by A. Brzezina. Price, 3 *złoty*.' The Rondo is based on a folksy *krakowiak* for its main theme. This lightweight polka-type dance in two-four time from the Kraków region in southern Poland is the starting point for a series of episodes, each a different world of chromaticism and feeling, that show not only mature musicianship, but also a remarkable understanding of musical syntax and form. Difficult keys such as D sharp minor, enharmonic devices such as calling an F an E sharp, and the use of double sharps flowed from Frycek's pen with the ease of an experienced composer. The dedicatee was the new Mrs Ludwika Linde, testimony of Frycek's approbation.

On June 10, the conservatory mounted another concert, at which Frycek again played the eolopantaleon. This concert also featured a set of Variations for the flute played by P. Kresner, which were loudly applauded, and arias by the Italian soprano and friend of

Paganini, Antonia Bianchi. As the summer progressed, Frycek's end of year examinations on July 26 loomed high, and he had to settle down to some hard work. His musical activities had taken a toll on his school work, and he wrote that 'tomorrow I have to get up early and tonight to sit up, sit up, still sit up, and perhaps even sit up all night'. His perseverance partially paid off, and he and fellow pianist Julian Fontana both received commendations. But no prizes – Frycek wrily wrote that those all went to 'enemas'.

With the school year over, Frycek prepared for his stay in the country with the unbridled enthusiasm of a teenager looking forward to long, hot summer holidays away from schoolwork, stifling city streets, and parental constrictions. The Dziewanowskis had invited him again to Szafarnia. On the Monday after the exams, when Domuś's Aunt Ludwika came in her carriage to fetch him at the Casimir Palace, he was wearing a new pair of breeches and a muffler round his neck for protection against catching a chill on the road. Having once again been warned against eating country bread and unripe fruit, the carriage set off along the River Vistula towards the green fields, farms and meadows of Mazovia. By Wednesday they were at Szafarnia, and Frycek and Domuś resumed their exploration of the countryside and the pursuit of local girls. The 'Szafarnia Courier' of the previous year was just a memory, and the idea was not revived.

Besides, this year there was not the time. Aunt Ludwika had prepared for the boys an action-packed schedule of social and tourist rounds. First stop was a trip abroad to visit the Prussian city of Toruń, then called by its German name, Thorn.

Again they visited the frontier town of Golub and crossed the bridge over the River Drwęca, into the Prussian town of Dobrzyń, where they went to see the mediæval castle perched spectacularly on top of the hill. The castle, now a museum, was originally built by the Knights of the Cross, although today only one Gothic tower survives from the original. In the seventeenth century King Zygmunt III gave the castle to his sister Anna, whose alterations exist to this day.

Like the market in Golub, the courtyard of the castle was full of German and Polish traders and street entertainers – specifically, barrel organists and hurdy-gurdy men. Frycek, with his voracious interest in folk music, came across one such hurdy-gurdy man in the castle compound, who was rolling out a German waltz, or *staierek*. He was struck by the sheer horribleness of the noise, and showed his disdain for it by writing a little rhyme to fit with it:

> Miss Ludwika gave half-*złoty*
> To listen to a Prussian waltz;
> If it hadn't been for Miss Ludwika
> For such songs there'd be no calls.

In Toruń Frycek stayed at the Fenger Palace. Wealthy banker Jakub Fenger, who died in 1798, was the father of Countess Ludwika Skarbek. It was the house where Fryderyk Skarbek was born. The house is still there, at No 14 Mostowa Street, bearing a commemorative plaque.

Frycek loved the magnificent German mediæval city, and his descriptions are valid today, as little has changed of the historic centre from Chopin's day. 'I saw the entire fortifications on all sides of the town,' he wrote to his school friend Jan Matuszyński in Warsaw.

> I saw a marvellous machine for moving sand, which the Germans call a *Sandsmaschine*. I also saw Gothic churches, founded by the Knights of the Cross; a crooked tower, a beautiful town hall with as many windows as there are days in a year, as many halls as there are months, and as many rooms as there are weeks. The whole magnificent building is in the Gothic style.

The *Sandsmaschine* is long gone, but the vast dark red brick Gothic buildings – which have given rise to the Polish saying, 'as red as a Toruń brick' – have all survived the ravages of time. The great churches are St John's, with its enormous bell, the Church of the Blessed Virgin, with its mediæval wood carvings, and the Church of St Jacob, with its decorations in glazed brick. The fortifications, which include the crooked tower, line the banks of the Vistula, with arched gateways at regular intervals – one of them leading to Mostowa Street and the Fenger Palace. The gigantic town hall is one of the most glorious buildings in all Poland, set in the middle of the Market Square. Outside it stands a statue of

Toruń's most famous son, Nicholas Copernicus. The house where the astronomer was born is in nearby Kopernik (Copernicus) Street.

> I have seen the whole house, though at the present it is some-what profaned. Think of it, Jaś, in the corner of that very same room where the great astronomer first saw the light, now stands the bed of some German, who, probably on ac-count of having eaten too many potatoes, emits foul odours; and on those same bricks . . . bedbugs now crawl. Yes, brother, that German doesn't care who used to live in that house.

However, it was not the architecture that most excited Frycek about Toruń. He continued:

> But never mind Copernicus, let us come to the Toruń cakes. . . . According to the custom among the pastry bakers, the cake shops are stalls fitted with locked cupboards, in which all the different kinds of cakes are kept, assembled in dozens. . . . Now all I can say is that out of everything it is the cakes that have made the strongest impression on me. Nothing outshines the cakes!

Toruń's gingerbread cakes were famous in all Poland, and the tradition thrives to this day. They came in all shapes and sizes, from biscuits to gingerbread sculptures of castles and horse-drawn carriages. Frycek loved Toruń cakes, and sent one home for Emilka.

Back at Szafarnia, harvest was in full swing, and it was time for the harvest *okrężne* celebrations. One evening, just as supper was finishing, the family's attention was drawn to the noise of caterwauling in the courtyard. Frycek and Domuś got up and rushed to the door. There they found two local girls with gar-lands on their heads open-throat singing a ditty in execrable har-mony, accompanied by a youth on a battered violin with one string missing. They were leading a procession of peasants in festive mood. When the boys appeared, they sang – Frycek recorded that they screeched without mercy, one half of their jaw a good semi-tone out of tune to the other half – a verse about 'our skinny Varsovian', and how 'fast' he was, a quality which may well have been borne out by the girls. The peasant serenade was taken in good humour, and ended up with a good deal of horseplay involving throwing buckets of water over the girls, in which other local lads and stable boys joined in, until the hallway was flooded. A second musician turned up, armed with a tattered, one-stringed double bass, so Frycek grabbed the violin, and with only four strings between them they duetted while the others leapt about, waltzed, and *obereked* until eleven o'clock.

One Sunday Frycek visited his school friend Jasio Białobłocki at nearby Sokołowo, where he lived with his stepfather, Antoni Wybraniecki. He had visited him the previous year as well. Like Frycek, Jasio was a music lover, and, like Frycek, he had been a victim of tuberculosis for a long time; this was aggravated by a wasting disease which had attacked his legs, and he was virtually a cripple. Frycek learned that it was unlikely that Jasio would be returning to the Lyceum that autumn. Mr Wybraniecki had bought his stepson a pantaleon, and the two boys spent the day messing about in the music room and eating apples in the orchard. Frycek was very supportive of his friend, understood his problem and did everything he could to cheer him up.

The summer holidays came to an end, and Frycek and Domuś returned to the Lyceum for their third year. As expected, Jasio Białobłocki was too ill to go back with them. Frycek missed his friend but they maintained a lively correspondence together. Because Jasio was musical, Frycek's letters always contained music news, and regular inquiries into his health from Żywny.

Ludka Chopin, emulating her brother, had tried her hand at composition, and had written a mazurka. Frycek was very complimentary, and even wrote to Jasio that 'Ludwika has done a splendid mazurka, such as Warsaw has not danced for a long time. . . . It's sprightly, delightful, in a word, danceable. Without boasting, it's exceptionally good.'

Apart from the Rondo in C minor, Frycek's Mazurka in B flat, written the previous year, and another in C, were published. Both exist today, but without opus numbers. Frycek went to see a performance of Rossini's *The Barber of Seville*. He enjoyed it so much that he wrote a polonaise on themes from it. 'I have done a new polonaise on THE BARBER, which is fairly well liked,' he wrote to Jasio. 'I'm thinking of sending it off to be lithographed tomorrow.' In the event he did not do this, and the polonaise is now lost.

Frycek's prowess at the harmonium hybrids during the summer months in Warsaw may have contributed to his appointment as organist at the Lyceum, a post of which he was justly proud: 'Aha, noble sir, what a head I've got,' he wrote to Jasio, 'the most important person in the Lyceum, after his reverence the priest.'

He played the organ every Sunday for the nuns at the Church of the Visitation, next to the Casimir Palace. The December 1849 issue of the *Biblioteka Warszawska* contained an article by music critic Józef Sikorski entitled 'Wspomnienie Szopena' ('Recollections of Chopin') to mark the composer's death in Paris only a month previously:

While the University of Warsaw was still in existence, mass was celebrated on Sundays and feast days at the Church of the Visitation for the students. A choir composed of pupils and ex-pupils of the Conservatory under Elsner sang religious songs accompanied by organ, or sometimes an orchestra. Chopin was a frequent guest there, especially during his last year in Warsaw, and played the organ, either fugues of the old masters, or his own improvisations. The use of pedals, one of the more difficult aspects of organ playing, came to him easily and naturally. . . . It happened once between the parts of a mass, which were sung by the choir with orchestra, that Chopin sat at the organ and, in the manner of great organists, took the theme of the part of the mass that had just ended, and improvised on it. He did so with such brilliance of ideas, and poured them out in a great, continuous stream, that all those who had crowded round him listened spellbound, forgetting where they were and the duties for which they had congregated. They were awakened from their reverie by the angry sacristan, who ran upstairs and cried, 'What do you think you're doing, in God's name? The priest has tried twice already to sing the *Dominus Vobiscum*, the acolytes keep ringing their handbells, and still the organ continues to play.'

The Church of the Visitation was scarcely damaged in World War II, and a plaque in the entrance commemorates Chopin's playing the organ, which is still there.

During that autumn Frycek had become a regular visitor to Princess Ludwika Czetwertyńska. Larger than life, ebullient, and with a mane of luxuriant hair that was the talk of Warsaw's fashionable set, she ran one of the most lively salons in the city. She made Frycek welcome at any time, showered him with hospitality and patronage, and became almost a second mother to him. Prince Antoni Radziwiłł, the Governor of Poznań, stayed at her house whenever he visited Warsaw; it was during one of his visits that Frycek first met the Prince, a meeting that led to a deep and significant friendship.

At the beginning of December Tsar Alexander I died of malaria at Taganrog in the Crimea (or, according to some sources, went secretly into exile as a religious recluse). Warsaw and all Poland fell into shock. Since Alexander had no progeny, the succession was originally to pass to his younger brother, Grand Duke Constantine. But the latter's divorce and consequent remarriage presented constitutional problems which in effect disqualified his heirs by the Princess of Łowicz from the throne of Russia. He had renounced any claim to the throne, and was happy to remain in his position as Commander of the Polish Garrison in Warsaw, so the succession passed to Alexander's youngest brother, Nicholas. As the year came to its end a cabal of officers and aristocrats, known by history as the Decembrists, hatched a plot, which originated in Warsaw but spread to the military establishment at St Petersburg, to put Constantine on the throne. Constantine, like Alexander, was in favour of Poland's existence as a nation, but within the Russian tsarist framework. Nicholas, on the other hand, was a dark horse. The Decembrists questioned the succession, Nicholas stood his ground, and the remainder of the year saw a tense interregnum, in which everyone involved tried to keep their heads, and the whole population of Warsaw talked of nothing else.

But the New Year was at hand. In Poland this was an unwritten generic term for the festivities of the Christmas season, which lasted from December 24 until January 6: the former was often referred to as New Year's Eve, as well as *Wigilia* – the 'vigil' leading up to the moment of Christmas at midnight; and the latter, the Feast of Epiphany, was Christmas in the Russian Orthodox calendar. Since Poland was on one hand a staunchly Roman Catholic land, and on the other within the cultural orbit of St

Petersburg, a confusing duality existed. This is why Frycek, in his letter to Jasio Białobłocki dated December 24, wrote that he was about to sit down to New Year's Eve supper.

Frycek and Ludka had been invited to spend the Roman Christmas with Countess Ludwika Skarbek at Żelazowa Wola. Frycek and his father were also invited to lunch that day at the Jaworeks, musical friends of the family. 'Papa and I were invited to a "lax" (laxative?),' he wrote to Jasio. 'I at first thought he had been seized by diarrhoea, and was offering me the same; but when the "lax" was brought out . . . I found that it was a salmon (in German *lachs*) which had been sent to him from Gdańsk.' Among the guests were a Czech pianist from Vienna called Czapek and a Mr Zak from the Prague Conservatory 'who played the clarinet as I've never heard the clarinet played before; he gets two notes at once with a single breath.' Whether Frycek was being complimentary or disdainful is not clear. Playing two notes simultaneously on the clarinet testifies either to technical brilliance, or to painful ineptitude.

There is an old Polish folk tale for children which tells the story of a poor beggar tramping through the snow on Christmas Eve, cold and hungry, with nowhere to stay. He called at a manor from which came the sounds of music and merrymaking; the smell of cooked food, orange candlelight and plumes of smoke from the chimney testified to a house of plenty. Hoping for a crust of bread with a lump of cheese, and a corner in a barn where he might spend the night, the beggar knocked on the door, only to be told in no uncertain terms that the lord of the manor did not wish to be disturbed from his celebrations, and the beggar was sent on his way into the snow-filled night. He then chanced upon the hut of a poor peasant in the forest. From within came the faint light of a solitary candle and a small fire. In desperation the beggar knocked on the door, which was opened by an old peasant and his wife. One look at the inside showed extreme poverty, but when the beggar asked if he might have a crust of bread and a night's lodging in the shed, the old peasant couple invited him in warmly. They shared their meagre Christmas Eve supper of weak cabbage soup, stale bread and a lump of cheese with him, and gave him the straw mattress while they slept on the mud floor. The following day the beggar thanked the old couple and went on his way. Within a year the lord of the manor had hit upon hard times, and lost his estates, while the old peasant couple enjoyed a string of good luck, and became rich. The reason for these changes of fortune was that the beggar was Jesus Christ in disguise, come down to earth at Christmastime to test the goodness of man.

It has been a tradition to this day that a spare place is laid at table on Christmas Eve 'in case Jesus comes disguised as a beggar'. The Skarbeks observed this tradition, especially when the children were small. While Frycek was writing that 'you already know why I'm writing, so don't be surprised if it's short and dry, because I'm too hungry to write anything fat', Countess Ludwika was supervising the preparation of the *Wigilia*. Straw was placed on the table under a white tablecloth, symbolising the manger. Everyone came to the table when the first star appeared in the sky – it was the children's job to look out for it. Bread was put on the table, and before sitting down everyone broke off a piece, and shared it in turn with everyone else, to the accompaniment of hugging, kissing, and the wishing of a prosperous New Year.

Christmas Eve was a religious day of abstinence, so meat was never served. The traditional fare is largely the same today as it was in Chopin's day. It consisted of beetroot soup, with filled pastries floating in it. Mushrooms and rice wrapped in cabbage leaves, served with a mushroom sauce, constituted the second course. The rich sauce was imbued with the flavour of dried *boletus* mushrooms left over from the autumn forays into the forests – for mushroom gathering and drying was always an integral part of Polish culture. The main course was carp, which was plentiful in the then unpolluted rivers of Poland, with dill potatoes. After that compotes of dried fruit were served, along with poppy-seed cakes, honeycakes and gingerbreads. Fruit cordials, vodka and beer were drunk throughout. After supper presents were exchanged while carols were sung, and towards midnight everyone set off to the local church for Midnight Mass, at which the crib was unveiled, and everyone sang carols. Fryderyk Chopin never forgot the music of his childhood. One of his favourite Christmas carols was the gentle 'Lulajże Jezuniu' ('Lullay little Jesus'), perhaps the best loved of all Polish carols.

SIX

The Silesian Waters

The opening weeks of 1826 were bitterly cold. Some 20,000 mourners attended the funeral of Stanisław Staszyc. This statesman, academic, geologist and man of science had been a thorn in the side of Novosiltsov's secret police. He had been a political writer sailing dangerously close to the wind. He was chairman of the Society of the Friends of Learning – and as a member of an academic society automatically suspect. He had travelled round the countryside studying rock formations, mingling with the peasants and lodging in their cottages in preference to inns. He had bought the estate of Hrubiesz with the aim of liberating 4,000 peasants from serfdom, and setting them up as small farmers. He was a man of enormous stature, and all Poland mourned his death. The funeral procession set off from the Church of the Holy Cross, which was packed with the great man's colleagues, family and friends.

Frycek was there, in the crowd that included Fryderyk Skarbek, who was then a professor at the university. He followed the procession along the Krakowskie Przedmieście, past the Royal Castle and the Stare Miasto, and northwards to Bielany on the Vistula, where Staszyc had asked to be buried. His coffin was carried by his fellow academics, some of whom even argued over the privilege. Members of the public also claimed a share of this privilege, and on occasions punches were thrown. At the graveside Fryderyk Skarbek delivered an oration, and when the coffin was lowered into the grave the pall was torn to shreds as mourners clamoured for a remnant as a memento. Frycek himself managed to get a piece.

Observing the funeral with interest was Novosiltsov, who correctly read it as a statement by the population of Warsaw. Staszyc
had become a central figure in dissident circles, and Novosiltsov
noted who was mourning with the greatest enthusiasm. The
Decembrist Plot had been crushed with characteristic ruthlessness,
and Nicholas had ascended the throne at St Petersburg as undisputed Tsar of Russia and King of Poland. The plotters were dealt
with mercilessly, and its ringleaders executed. Warsaw, as one of
the hatcheries of the plot, bore the brunt of the new Tsar's suspicion. Active dissidents and innocent suspects were hunted down
and arrested in their hundreds, and hundreds more were placed
under close observation. The knock on the door in the middle of
the night became a real fear for many. The dungeons of the Carmelite
Monastery were requisitioned as detention centres, and when they
were full, the cellars of the City Hall and the Bruhl Palace served
as prisons.

The death of Alexander was observed in Warsaw with a display of loyalty that was also read as a political statement. It was
the end of an era; the late Tsar had been a benevolent ruler who
had made mistakes. But despite the Grand Duke Constantine, despite
Novosiltsov, despite reneging almost completely on the Constitution of the Vienna Congress, Poland had been better off under
Russia than under any other occupying power. Warsaw pulled
out all its musical stops for him. In St John's Cathedral Karol
Soliwa, professor of singing at the conservatory, conducted a two-
hundred-strong force of players and singers in the *Requiem* of the
prolific Józef Kozłowski. It was interspersed with commemorative music by other local composers. Mozart's *Requiem* was performed at the cathedral, with additions born perhaps of enthusiasm
rather than taste: Karol Kurpiński, who conducted the performance, added an extra wind band to the Dies Irae and the Sanctus,
a host of harps to the Hostias and Benedictus, and a full military
band to the Finale. Elsner's darker-toned *Requiem*, scored for male
voices, cellos, bassoons, horns, trumpets, trombones and drums,
took place at the Evangelical Church.

The unsteady ten-year Russian-Polish honeymoon was over, and
the next decline of Poland's fortunes had begun. The year dragged
on with fear and uncertainty hanging over Warsaw like the sword
of Damocles. The optimists carried on as before, while the pessi-

mists were speculating on a repetition of the unrest of recent decades. Insurrection had been mentioned, but dismissed; the consequences were too horrendous to contemplate.

At the Lyceum, the new Mrs Linde was pregnant, and everyone hoped for a boy for her husband's sake. Frycek was now
half way through his third year, a 'one year' student, which meant
that he spent only one year in Class VI, instead of the usual two.
During his third and final year at the Lyceum his health had
taken a knock. That he had been staying out till the early hours
may have had something to do with it. He fell prey to headaches
and his glands had swollen. The doctor had forbidden further
nocturnal socializing, and had prescribed bed rest and the wearing of a night-cap. Leeches were applied to his throat in an attempt to reduce the swelling of the glands, on the advice of a Mr
Kozicki, who was peddling the idea at the time in the name of
progressive medicine. Nor was Frycek's health the only worry for
Nicolas and Justyna; Emilka suffered similar symptoms.

Doctors came and went as the Chopins tried to find a cure for
their sick children: Dr Gerardot was replaced by Dr Romer, and
he, in turn was followed by Dr Wilhelm Malcz, the vice president
of the Benevolent Society, and a physician with a remarkable record
of success in healing disease and in operations. All three, although
agreed on Frycek's potentially serious condition, had diagnosed
Emilka's symptoms as a 'catarrh-linked affectation'.

That summer the terrible wasting disease of tuberculosis was
on everyone's mind. Frycek shared news of his illnesses with Jasio
Białobłocki, and the two boys found a certain strength from each
other's plight. Jasio was now permanently at home in Sokołowo,
and the two friends kept in touch by letter. Frycek tried to keep
Jasio's chin up with some witty writing, such as reminding him
that 'when people have a tie of eleven years of friendship, when
they have counted the months together 132 times, have begun
468 weeks, 3,960 days, 95,040 hours, 5,702,400 minutes,
342,144,000 seconds, they don't need reminders or complimentary letters.' Jasio's illness was far in advance of Frycek's, and he
was wasting away at an alarming rate, and Frycek was aware
deep down that a similar incapacity might befall him one day.
The previous year Jasio's parents had sent him to take the waters
at the East Prussian spa town of Bischoffswerter – today Biskupiec

in the Lake District of Mazury – but the visit effected no change. Jasio still found strength from his music, and Frycek kept him supplied with updates on the Warsaw music scene. He wrote with great enthusiasm about the impending première of Weber's *Der Freischütz*, on July 3, but doubted whether Warsaw, accustomed to the lightweight melodies of Italian opera, both Rossini and of the homegrown variety of Elsner and Kurpiński, would react favourably to the growing trend of German Romanticism. Frycek always sent Jasio things to play. Aleksander Rembieliński, the nephew of the President of the Education Commission, was a talented young pianist and composer. 'You would not believe how beautifully he plays,' wrote Frycek. He sent Jasio a set of Rembieliński's Waltzes to play, 'which I think you will like'. Rembieliński died young, and his Waltzes are lost. Frycek obtained for Jasio a volume of Rossini arias in arrangements for the piano, and a polonaise by Józef Kaczkowski, which he recommended. He usually included some of his own 'scribblings'. One of these was a Waltz in C, written that year and now lost. Inspired by Ries's Variations on a theme of Thomas Moore for piano duet, he wrote a set of his own, which were published posthumously without an opus number. He wrote a set of Three Ecossaises, a misleading title if one is looking for a Scottish sound. As in his later Tarantella and Bolero, Frycek was interested in form and time signature, rather than ethnic feel. These short, polka-like dances in two-four time, in D, G and D flat, were published together posthumously, as Op. 72 No. 3.

In the absence of Jasio, Frycek's closest friends at the Casimir Palace that year included Julian Fontana, Jan Matuszyński, Wiluś Kolberg, and now, Tytus Woyciechowski, recently arrived to lodge with the Chopins. His father had an estate beyond Zamość. Frycek, Jan and Tytus were all in Class VI. Tytus was a good pianist, and often played duets with Frycek, who wrote a set of Variations in F for piano duet, now lost, which he dedicated to Tytus.

Meanwhile, from the floor below came the sounds of a baby crying. Mrs Linde had presented her husband with Bogumiła.

The Długosz-Hofman-Brunner instrument enterprise was thriving, and news of Frycek's prowess at their products was spreading. He was invited to Teresa Kicka's house to play her eolimelodikon to an assembled company. After two or three pieces by other composers Frycek became carried away by the eolimelodikon, and went off at a tangent from the piece he was playing into an improvisation, after which there was no stopping him. 'There was general admiration,' wrote poet Antoni Odyniec, 'his hearers no longer criticized, only listened. He played on and on, ever more expressively and plaintively, and there was no knowing how long he might have continued.' Another time he visited the Zamoyskis to try out a newly acquired eolopantaleon. The whole evening was spent gathered round the instrument as Frycek wove yet another instant and extended tone picture.

Jasio's stepfather, Antoni Wybraniecki, came to Warsaw to order a second choralion from Brunner, for his local church in Sokołowo. He called on the Chopins, and the subject of consumption and its treatment dominated the conversation. Wybraniecki saw that Emilka was becoming increasingly frail. The Literary Society that she ran with her brother was thriving and was very popular with the lodgers, but Nicolas and Justyna were worried. The idea of spas had been discussed, and Wybraniecki told the Chopins about the waters at Bischoffswerter.

Elsner recommended Duszniki, which was then called by its German name, Reinertz, in Prussian Silesia. A Silesian himself, born not far from there, he knew it well. He painted an attractive picture of a pretty spa town in the valley between the Table Mountains and the Bystrzycki Range almost on the borders of Bohemia. After deliberation the Chopins decided to try Duszniki.

The idea of taking the waters caught on. Sixty-year-old Countess Ludwika Skarbek, who was suffering from tuberculosis, decided to go too, as did her son Fryderyk, who opted for Duszniki's twin spa town of Kudowa-Zdrój, a few kilometres beyond Duszniki, right on the Bohemian border. While Izabela and her father stayed at home, the Chopin-Skarbek contingent divided into three, and left in a staggered convoy.

On Tuesday June 27 Fryderyk Skarbek, his wife Prakseda and their seven-year-old son Józef, or 'Józio', set off in their own carriage. Ludka, who had spent the early summer with Countess Ludwika at Żelazowa Wola, went with them. On their way they called at Strzyżewo, near Ostrów, to see Fryderyk's sister and Frycek's godmother, Anna, and her husband, Stefan Wiesiołowski. Fryderyk also wanted to visit nearby Kotłów to see the grave of his father, Count Kacper, who had died at Strzyżewo three years previously. After five days at Strzyżewo they went on to Kudowa-Zdrój, which they reached on July 9.

On July 15 Countess Ludwika left with Emilka by diligence, and arrived at Duszniki on July 23.

Frycek had to wait for his final examinations. His school year drew to a close, and with it his elementary education. His parents were pleased when the Class VI Prize went to Frycek, Tytus and Jan Matuszyński. On July 27 Frycek and Wiluś Kolberg celebrated the end of term by going to see Rossini's *The Thieving Magpie* which opened that night at the opera. It was a memorable occasion for the two boys, not only because of the music and the drama, but it was also the end of an era. For a popular sixteen-year-old boy, leaving for ever a school where he had been happy is often an emotional experience, when classrooms are looked at for the last time, books are returned, goodbyes are said and thanks expressed to favourite teachers. Frycek said goodbye to Wiluś in his characteristic way, with a composition. The goodbye was a little exaggerated, as Frycek was only going to spend summer in Duszniki, and Wiluś would still be living downstairs after his return. Perhaps it was just an expression of thanks to the older boy for his friendship and guidance, and an excuse to compose something. He wrote a Polonaise in B flat minor, which he subtitled 'À Guillaume Kolberg, Adieu'. For the theme of the trio section he used one of Giannetto's arias from *The Thieving Magpie* – thus cementing for ever the association with their evening at the opera. The Polonaise was published posthumously without an opus number in 1878 in Leipzig.

The following day, July 28, Frycek and his mother set off for Duszniki by diligence, and arrived on August 3.

On August 18, two weeks after his arrival, Frycek wrote to Wiluś that he had passed 'through Błonie, Sochaczew . . .' At Sochaczew, on the River Bzura, is the turn-off to Żelazowa Wola. Once a ducal seat, it suffered greatly from the ravages of endless wars. The ruins of the castle, destroyed by the Prussians during the final partition, are still there. In Chopin's day it was a garrison town.

'. . . Łowicz . . .' The post house, in Wjazdowa Street – today May 3 Street – is still there as it was in Chopin's day. The well-maintained building is now the Post Office. The beautiful Col-

legiate Church, where the body of Prince Józef Poniatowski lay
after it had been brought back from Leipzig, still dominates the
Market Square.

'... Kutno, Kłodawa, Koło...' At Koło the road crosses the
River Warta. Just beyond the town the old post road turns off
the modern main road, through undulating countryside and pine
forests towards '... Turka...' Turek, as it is called today, is an
industrial and mining complex.

'... Kalisz...' The Chopins' friend, Dr Adam Helbich, lived in
Kalisz. Frycek always stayed with him whenever he passed through.
Once on the main Baltic-Adriatic amber route and Poland's oldest
city, Kalisz is today industrialized. It was the last Polish town
before the Prussian border at Biskupice Ołoboczne, today just off
the Kalisz-Ostrów road.

'... Ostrów...' Ostrów Wielkopolski is close to Strzyżewo,
the home of Stefan and Anna Wiesiołowski, and their children
Ludwika and Roman.

'... Międzyborz...' Międzyborz is a crossroads village set among
birch and pine forests.

'... Oleśnica...' Oels, as it was called in German, is, as it was
when Chopin passed through, dominated by its fourteenth-century
castle.

'... Wrocław...' The historic capital of Silesia (Śląsk) was
known in Chopin's day by its German name, Breslau. In 1109
Bolesław Krzywousty (Wrymouth) defeated Emperor Henry V and
the Duke of Bohemia at the bloody Battle of Psiepole. In German,
the name 'Hundsfeld' means, literally, 'Dog's Field'. According to
legend, after the Germans' headlong flight the battlefield was strewn
with so many uncollected corpses that it attracted packs of dogs
to feed off them. The victory forced the Germans to renounce all
claims to Polish territory. The Chopins passed the site just before
entering the city. Today Psiepole is a built-up suburb.

The Skarbeks and the Chopin girls stayed at the Golden Tree
in the Market Square, opposite the Town Hall, with its astronomical clock, in the centre. Today it is situated at Nos 31/32,
on the corner of Olawska Street. The square itself was a hive of
narrow alleys between the stalls and the tents of merchants, many
come in from the country and further afield, selling anything from
vegetables to foreign trinkets.

Frycek and his mother stayed at the Golden Goose, a prestigious hostelry situated in Olawska Street, on the corner of Ofiar Oświęcimowski Street opposite the Evangelical Church.

Wrocław was a city of gardens and waterways, and well-dressed people strolling along the banks of the River Oder (Odra) testified to a thriving city. The ancient fortifications by the river had been landscaped into gardens and parks, and the dykes beside the moats had been gravelled and turned into walkways. There were canals everywhere, with attractive bridges from which young couples would gaze at the swans before entering one of the waterside beer gardens. In Warsaw such establishments were the exclusive preserve of men, but in Wrocław they were patronized by both men and women, young and old, drinking beer and enjoying live music.

Elsner had given Frycek three letters of introduction to musicians of his acquaintance in Wrocław, but it was a brief stop, and he only had time to call on one of them, a Herr Latzel, a visit 'with which,' Frycek wrote to Elsner, 'he was much pleased'.

Wrocław suffered heavily in World War II, although the present city, as in Chopin's day, still has many parks and gardens; the Town Hall is still there and there are eighty bridges over the waterways and canals connected to the River Odra and its tributary, the Ślęża.

'. . . Nimsch, Frankenstein, Warta and Glatz . . .' Today the Polish names are respectively Niemcza, Ząbkowice Śląskie, Bardo and Kłodzko. The later boasts a bridge over the River Nysa Kłodzka, which is a miniature replica of the Charles Bridge in Prague.

'. . . we reached Duszniki, where we are now staying.'

Ludka's record of the journey was far more creative than Frycek's stark list. She kept a detailed diary on the route, and later wrote a novella for children about the journey, of the moral kind that were in vogue at the time. Ludka, now twenty-one, was becoming increasingly interested in children, child psychology and early education, and she saw this journey as a mind-broadening experience packed with history, geography and morality. She entitled her book 'Józio's Journey from Warsaw to the Silesian Waters, as told by himself'. It is written in the first person, and the hero is Józio, a fictionalized version of Fryderyk Skarbek's seven-year-old son, with whom she had established a strong rapport. The story is based on their journey, and describes each place they passed through. It is written to suggest that Józio – and thus the reader – learns from the journey. Every new piece of knowledge and every experience helps Józio to become a better person. The story abounds with moral values as well as historical and geographical background. There is no more vivid a picture of Frycek's journey to Duszniki than his sister's novella.

Józio Skarbek eventually married Fryderyk Chopin's one-time fiancée, Maria Wodzińska.

Because different circumstances prevailed when travelling by diligence and a private carriage, the itineraries taken by the three contingents were not identical.

Between Kalisz and Wrocław, Frycek and his mother, travelling by diligence along the post road, passed through Ostrów, Antonin, Międzyborz and Oleśnica. After Kalisz the Skarbek carriage went cross-country to Strzyżewo, to call on Stefan and Anna Wiesiołowski. Ludka Chopin fictionalized this visit in 'Józio's Journey', but did not mention the Wiesiołowskis by name, or the village of Strzyżewo. Instead she describes a visit to 'Auntie and Uncle', and their two children, Ludwisia and baby Romanek. These children are actually based on the two Wiesiołowski children, Ludwika, then four, and baby Roman.

After the family visit, the Skarbek carriage continued through Mikstat, Ostrzeszow (Schildberg) and Syców, where they picked up the main road again to Oleśnica and Wrocław.

The Skarbeks with Ludka arrived in Kudowa on July 9, and stayed there until about July 23, when Countess Ludwika and Emilka arrived in Duszniki. This consisted of the village, and the spa, two kilometres away. Fryderyk Skarbek then went on to Prague, while Prakseda Skarbek, little Józio and Ludka all moved into Burgemeister August Heine's house, which was situated at the end of the spa closest to the village. Frycek and his mother, when they arrived a week later, lodged at Burgel's Hof, in the centre of the spa.

Frycek's day began when he and his mother left their lodging by the River Bystrzyca to be at the Lau-Brunn, the well house, by six in the morning. The whole spa was criss-crossed by paths and walkways lined with lawns, trees, shrubs and flower beds. Frycek was very taken with all these 'beautiful avenues'. One such avenue connected Burgel's Hof with the Lau-Brunn. It was already full by that time with everyone bound for the well houses, for the programme was the same for everyone.

The wells were built on podiums, and were surrounded by safety railings, and guests were not allowed to help themselves; the water was scooped up in jugs at the ends of rods, and served to the guests by attendant girls, who dispensed gingerbread biscuits afterwards to disperse the unpleasant taste of the water. Contemporary medical knowledge held that the waters contained properties which, if taken in moderation, were beneficial, but could, if taken without care, be dangerous and even fatal. The measures were not only safeguards against anyone falling in, but also against inhaling the vapours when leaning into the well, and tales were told of people who had died from so doing. In fact the waters exuded quantities of carbon dioxide, which caused dizziness at close quarters.

In the 20 August 1892 issue of the Polish periodical *Musical Echo*, an article appeared under the title of 'Chopin's Youthful Love', which documents the story of one particular well attendant. Libusza was the daughter of a Czech worker at the Mendelssohn iron foundry in the Strążyska Valley. The owner was an uncle of the composer, Felix Mendelssohn, who was a frequent visitor to Duszniki. Every day she served Frycek with his two cups of water and a biscuit. Libusza's mother had died several years previously, and as well as being housewife and mother at home, she worked at the Lau-Brunn to help support her four brothers and sisters. Despite the hardships, she managed to keep up a bright and optimistic temperament with which she charmed everyone – especially Frycek. She in turn found the pale, delicately featured sixteen-year-old attractive, and was flattered by his attention.

The morning water intake lasted till eight, when everyone returned to their lodgings for breakfast, at which whey was one of the dietary mainstays. After breakfast the walkways were full, with many guests joining in the festive atmosphere created by the local wind band, an atrocious outfit which welcomed new arrivals and played in the park for the arguable delectation of guests. Józio liked the band, but Frycek, whose aural sensibilities were finer, described it as 'a dozen caricatures of miscellaneous types gathered together; the leader, a thin bassoonist with a snuff-stained, bespectacled nose, frightens the ladies who are scared of horses by freely playing at the strolling guests'. The guests, either more tolerant or tone deaf, joined in the carnival spirit by wearing masks and dressing up.

At noon the walkways emptied as the guests went back to their lodgings for dinner, after which everyone changed again for the second visit to the wells, and for the afternoon walk. Frycek wrote that 'there's usually an even bigger masquerade than earlier, as everyone dresses up in something different from the morning. Again there is vile music'. The day was rounded off with supper, after which the Germans opted for an early night, while the Poles tended to spend the evenings socializing.

The guests at Burgel's Hof were of mixed nationalities, Germans, Poles and Czechs; but as the season progressed the Poles returned home, leaving mostly Germans, and evening visits ground to a halt. Frycek, as always gregarious and enquiring with foreigners, befriended a lady from Wrocław and her children, who spoke a little French, so some conversation was possible. He managed to teach the boy 'Good day' and 'Good evening' in Polish, but the lad became confused, and ended up greeting Frycek with 'Day evening'. 'I don't know how he got it to that,' wrote Frycek, 'and we had quite a job explaining it to him.'

One of the most delightful features of Duszniki were the walks in the hills. Green and clad in forests, they were perfect for excursions for the more energetic, even though none of the hills could really be classified as mountains. Medical opinion of the time had words to say about air quality as well. 'There is a mountain here called the "Heu-Scheuer", with a beautiful view,' wrote Frycek. 'But the air on it is not good for everyone, and unfortunately I am among those not allowed to go there.'

But he did climb the one hundred and fifty steps to the Hermitage, which was occupied by an officiating hermit – a solitary Catholic cleric with his parish of a patch of hillside, supported by the people and guests of Duszniki. Consisting of one room and a chapel, it was built in 1698 on the site where, according to legend, the children of Duszniki knelt to pray for salvation from a plague that was raging in the region. Their prayers were answered, the plague subsided, and Duszniki was spared. In commemoration, the local people established the Hermitage on the hill known as Einsiedelei. Another favourite walk was to the paper mill beside the river, where the manager took guests on guided tours.

One day Frycek learned that Libusza's father had had an accident at work. An iron roller had become dislodged, fell on top of him and crushed him to death. Libusza and her brothers and sisters were orphaned. Libusza, as new head of the family, was devastated. Frycek tried to console Libusza and the children, and wanted to do something for them. His mother suggested that he give a concert for their benefit. Frycek liked the idea despite the fact that 'there is not one good piano, and all I have seen are instruments that cause me more distress than pleasure'.

With the cooperation of the council, a concert was arranged at the small manor hall for the benefit of the orphans, for around August 11 – the exact date is not known. Chopin's first public performance abroad was a resounding success, and the applause was so great that a repeat performance was arranged for August 16. Fryderyk Skarbek, who had been travelling around in Bohemia, was back in Duszniki at the time, and attended the concert. The episode drew the council's attention to the children's plight, and they were placed in care, while Libusza went to Prague to stay with an aunt.

The event evinced favourable reactions at home. Żywny wrote to Frycek, congratulating him on his charity, and commenting on 'a nobility of character uncommon in one so young'.

The *Warsaw Courier* may have got it wrong when, on August 22, it reported that 'the young Polish artist, Fryderyk Chopin, gave two concerts for several children who, through the death of their father who had been taking the waters at Duszniki, became orphans. All proceeds were given for their benefit'.

Countess Ludwika, Frycek and Emilka continued to follow their regimes. Frycek's health improved a little, and he gained weight. Countess Ludwika and Emilka went further, and took baths in the waters. 'My dear Lulu,' Emilka wrote to her best friend, Ludwika Linde, the Professor's eldest daughter, on August 18, 'I drink the whey, the water, and I bathe every day, and Mama seems to think I'm looking better, and that I've put on a little weight.' Justyna, who was suffering from rheumatism, also took advantage of the baths.

The Chopin cult at Duszniki is based partly on legend and partly on documentation. The Libusza story, though the stuff of romantic novels, is based on fact. Burgel's Hof has been rebuilt on the same site, and in the same style, and is now the nursing home 'Nokturn'. A plaque on the wall testifies that 'Fryderyk Chopin stayed in this house in August 1826 with his mother and sisters'. Documentation showing that Ludka and Emilka did not stay there surfaced after the plaque had been installed. The hall where Frycek gave the concerts has been the venue of an annual Chopin Music Festival since 1946. The Hermitage on the hill no longer houses a hermit, but is the Museum of the Music Festival. The old paper mill is now one of Poland's most important industrial museums, and produces paper using the same methods as in Chopin's day. The Lau-Brunn still yields its waters and is renamed 'Pieniawa Chopina' – Chopin's spray. The iron foundry is no longer there, but the rebuilt Mendelssohn house is, and the winding path leading up to it is called Libusza Way.

From the Józio story, the village of Kohlaw is now called Podgórze. In Chopin's day its coal mine serviced the foundry. The inn 'U Niedźwiedzia' (The Bear) in the market square was a famous hostelry situated at the eastern end of the lower side. A plaque commemorating the stay of King Kazimierz marks the site of what was in fact 'Pod Czarnym Niedźwiedziem' (The Black Bear). The waterfall mentioned by Józio is the source of the Biały Potok, one of the streams that feeds the River Bystrzyca, on the hill of Złota Sztolnia (Hohe Menze). Zimmermann's Rest, on the western slopes above the spa, is now overgrown, and August Heine's house is no longer there.

By the end of the first week of September, Frycek was bored. Libusza, the Skarbeks, Emilka and Ludka had all gone. He was not actually an invalid, and the lack of friends, a decent piano, and city life strained his patience. The harvest was in, and the greens had begun to turn to gold, the sun was not as warm as it had been, and Frycek was more than ready to leave. The waters and the fresh air had done him some good, and he was looking forward to life at the conservatory.

On September 11 Frycek and his mother set off for home. Their first stop was Wrocław, where Frycek called on two musicians, Schnabel and Breuer, with Elsner's other two letters of introduction. Josef Schnabel, the kapellmeister at the Cathedral of St John the Baptist, was particularly friendly. After that Frycek and his mother went on to Strzyżewo, to call on Stefan and Anna Wiesiołowski,

and their children, Ludwisia and Romanek. Anna was pleased to
see her godson, and they stayed for a few days. During their stay
Frycek was invited for the day to Antonin, the Hunting Lodge of
Prince Antoni Radziwiłł, fifteen kilometres away.

The Radziwiłłs were one of the wealthiest magnate families in
the Commonwealth era, whose roots were in Lithuania. Prince
Antoni was born in 1775 in Prussia. He showed an early talent
for music, and was trained in singing and cello in Berlin. In 1796,
when the Kingdom of Poland belonged to Prussia, he married
Princess Ludwika of Prussia, and thus into the royal family. At
the Congress of Vienna in 1815 the Poznań region was given to
King Friedrich Wilhelm III, who created from it the Duchy of
Posen (now called Poznań), and appointed Prince Antoni Radziwiłł
as Governor. The Prince consequently moved his court from Berlin
to Poznań. He was a fine singer and an able cellist. At his Poznań
residence he maintained a permanent string quartet, in which he
himself played the cello. Haydn, Mozart and Beethoven were the
mainstays of the repertoire at the weekly performances at his salon, Poznań's premier rendezvous for leading artists, writers and
musicians. His residence was the former Jesuit college, close to
the Market Square. He was a highly rated composer, and his
setting of the first part of Goethe's *Faust* evinced great admiration from contemporary commentators, including the King and,
later, Franz Liszt. The King honoured his achievement by ensuring
that his *Faust* was performed annually at the Berlin Academy of
Singing. Prince Radziwiłł was a patron of the arts, specifically of
music. After hearing Frycek playing at Princess Czetwertyńska's
salon in Warsaw the previous year he was very aware of a rare
talent in the making. Now, with the boy only fifteen kilometres
away, the Prince took the opportunity to invite him to visit Antonin.

Prince Radziwiłł's remarkable hunting lodge was only just completed that year. He built it to accommodate his large hunting
parties, for the surrounding forests were full of wild boar, roe
and red deer and wolves. Designed by Karl Schinkel, the lodge
was a tall, octagonal timber building of three storeys, with four
wings. The central hall was as high as the building, and had a
central column – the chimney. The floors were balustraded galleries
with rooms coming off them. The lodge was described in *The
People's Friend* of 2 July 1836:

In the forest, among the treeless terrain and lakes between Szerpka and Kociemba, on a site completely surrounded by pine and fir woods stood, as if conjured up by magic, a stately building. . . . Its exterior, form and construction blended with the silent wildness of the forest. It was made entirely of timber, itself the colour of the forest.

Frycek was introduced to the Prince's two beautiful daughters, twenty-two-year-old Eliza, and eighteen-year-old Wanda. Both played some piano, especially Wanda. Frycek and Eliza immediately found a further common interest in drawing, in which the young princess excelled. The pencil sketch that she made of Frycek playing the piano on the day of his visit has survived to this day.

The Radziwiłłs' hunting lodge is still there, unchanged, beautifully set among woods, meadows and lakes. Today it is an hotel, restaurant, Chopin museum and recital hall, where concerts are held.

When Frycek returned to Warsaw after an absence of two months he was ready to take his place at the Warsaw Music Conservatory.

SEVEN
Emilka

Warsaw was depressing. At Duszniki Frycek could not wait to be home again, but now that he had returned to the care of Dr Wilhelm Malcz and his regime, he lapsed into a state of indolence. Bedtime, he told Jasio, had been ordered for 9 p.m., thus precluding 'all teas, evenings and balls'. He was forced to drink 'emetic water', a type of cough mixture, and to eat oatmeal '*quasi* a horse'. A return trip to Duszniki next year was threatened. 'Since Sokołowo,' he wrote, 'I got so fat and lazy that I don't want to do anything at all.' Frycek informed Jasio that the choralion that his stepfather had ordered from Brunner was finished and awaiting collection, but by November Brunner had heard nothing from Wybraniecki so he dismantled it.

Frycek's enrolment at the conservatory was also depressing. For a start, he was late. Then Dr Malcz had decided that sitting all day at a desk, studying, was detrimental to his health, and had prescribed walking as much as possible, despite that 'the air here is not as good for me as in Duszniki'. So Frycek settled for part-time attendance. He was more advanced than the other students, and time that might have been spent sitting at a desk was better spent at the piano. He had hoped to see some familiar faces among the intake, but as he looked about the hall on his first day, he found only Julian Fontana.

Julian was born in Warsaw in the same year as Frycek, was a pianist and composer, and they were lifelong friends. They corresponded regularly, and Julian was largely responsible for collating and editing Frycek's unpublished manuscripts for publication after his friend's death.

There was no sign of Tytus Woyciechowski: he had opted for law at the university. They remained close friends, and Frycek developed a particularly strong affection for him.

Jan Matuszyński's aptitude for music was limited to a little flute, and he had chosen medicine at the university, so Frycek remained in touch with him, as well as with Domuś Dziewanowski, Wiluś Kolberg and the Wodziński brothers. Evenings were spent either in one another's houses or in Warsaw's many cafés.

The most famous was Mrs Brzezińska's, sited at today's 626 Kozia Street, which branches off the Krakowskie Przedmieście near the castle. It was Warsaw's premier meeting place of artists, writers and musicians – and others who might attract the attention of Novosiltsov's henchmen. Mrs Brzezińska's had a rich and varied reputation. In Chopin's day it was separated from its rival, the 'Baroka', by Warsaw's main Post Office, with its enormous archway always busy with diligences pulling in and out. The closest café to the Casimir Palace was Mrs Stypułkowska's, next to the Riding School in Królewska Street. There were two cafés in Miodowa Street, which would have been convenient from the conservatory – the 'Dziurka', colourfully meaning 'little hole' and situated in the Tepper Palace, and the 'Honoratka'. This café, in the Chodkiewiczowski Palace, was a cosy, smoky room with an arched ceiling, its panelled walls covered with paintings. Seated at the tables men would be seen, talking, drinking coffee or playing chess. Frycek patronized all the cafés, and saw in the early hours with his friends, while putting the world to rights – when he could get away with defying Dr Malcz.

Frycek's course consisted of seven hours per week of harmony, counterpoint and composition with Elsner, six hours of practical exercises, and one hour of theory, which was held at the university. The course aimed to train the complete artist, and Frycek, in addition to music, studied poetry and literature with Kazimierz Brodziński, who introduced him to the work of Poland's greatest poet, Adam Mickiewicz. Frycek set some of his verses to music.

The core of Frycek's training consisted of his intensive sessions with Elsner. He taught harmony and counterpoint strictly by the book, but had the vision to realize that his young charge should not be slavishly sticking by the rules regulating the use of consecutive fifths and doubled thirds. Frycek knew these rules by instinct. Elsner none the less formally imparted them, working on the theory that if rules are to be broken, they should be broken on purpose, not through ignorance. Creativity had to be confined within a structured framework; and Elsner encouraged Frycek to establish his own, and then to work within it. Like everyone else he was required to do exercises in fugue and classical sonata form.

One of the disciplines that Frycek had to learn from Elsner was the art of orchestration, in which he was by no means a shining star. He liked the sound of the orchestra, but found orchestration boring – preferring to devote all his creative energy to the piano.

Frycek admired Elsner tremendously, both as a musician and as a man. History has seen Józef Elsner more as the guru of Polish Romanticism than as a composer in his own right. His numerous compositions, attractive and of their day, have not stood the test of time. He came from a generation to whom consecutive fifths and doubled thirds were forbidden, and even Beethoven initially used them at his peril. Under Elsner's influence – rather than tuition – Frycek learned to balance the rule book against his creative flow.

The flow became a flood in which this balance was evident. Frycek's main interest was in composition, and he quickly learned the techniques of other composers, notably Bach, Mozart, Haydn and Beethoven, and could not wait to put these techniques to the test. During his first year at the conservatory he wrote formally and prolifically, dedicating his compositions to his friends.

He dedicated his *Rondo à la mazur* in F to his childhood friend, Countess Alexandrine 'Moriolka' de Moriolles. It was published by Brzezina as Op. 5. The *Rondo* was closely followed by two mazurkas, both published posthumously, the first one, in G, without an opus number; the second, in A minor, published as Op. 68 No. 2. A third mazurka, in A, is now lost. He sent the G major to Jasio Białobłocki at the beginning of 1827, along with the vague promise of another one to come later because 'two together would be too much of a good thing', and 'two arias from Freischütz, with which you ought to be pleased. They are for female voice . . . but as I know how squeakily you sing . . . when your leg hurts you they are just the thing for you.'

The Elsners were also beneficiaries of Frycek's dedications. He was a frequent visitor at their house next to the Church of the Visitation, as were his fellow students. They were welcomed and entertained by Elsner's second wife, singer Karolina, one of the principals of her husband's Warsaw opera. Their fifteen-year-old daughter, Emilia, had a lovely voice and played the piano, and was in her element when surrounded by male students. The Elsner piano was constantly open to students wishing to work at it, and the approval of the Elsner ladies was just as important as a good mark by the master. Frycek, when not taking advantage of the piano himself, often listened with the others as Emilia played duets with Ludwik Nidecki, who was the same age as she was. Gradually it became obvious that these duets were expressions of more than just musical appreciation. Young love was definitely in the air in the Elsner house.

Emilia maintained an album, for which she requested musical contributions from students and other visitors to the house. She was often the first to hear any new composition, usually by dint of having been present at its conception and birth. To be asked by Emilia to write in her album was a sign of approval. Frycek's contributions, no less than seventeen items, included settings of poems by Mickiewicz and Witwicki, some mazurkas and waltzes. Two of the latter, in E flat and A flat, were formally dedicated to Emilia Elsner, and published posthumously without opus numbers.

The romance between Emilia Elsner and Ludwik Nidecki eventually blossomed into marriage, and Emilia's album survived until its destruction in World War II. The rebuilt Elsner house in the Krakowskie Przedmieście bears a commemorative plaque.

Apart from the two-part Fugue in A minor, submitted, rather than dedicated to his counterpoint teacher, Frycek honoured Elsner with the initial dedication of his first piano sonata, in C minor. This work evolved from one of Elsner's set tasks on classical sonata form. Frycek sent it to Haslingers, in Vienna, for publication, but dithered about the dedication, feeling that it was not good enough to bear his teacher's name. Haslingers also dithered in its publication, and only after his death was it published as Op. 4. This uncertainty showed the first signs of a capacity for self-criticism. Accustomed to adulation since he was eight, Frycek was now beginning to fear that he was not that good. Not once did Elsner let him know that he was his star pupil, which, academically speaking, Frycek was not. From a scholastic viewpoint both the Nidecki brothers, by watching their consecutive fifths, attained higher marks for their assignments.

Frycek became friendly with Ludwik Nidecki's older brother, Tomasz, who was in his third year at the conservatory. He was born in 1800, and was one of Elsner's most successful students, as a composer very much in the Elsner mould of technical competence.

As was second-year student Ignacy Feliks Dobrzyński (1807–67). The younger students looked up to him and admired his capacity for hard work, with which he overcame a certain lack of natural talent. He was an aspiring symphonist, but his art did not come to him easily, and he came to Elsner to learn orchestral techniques. In this he far surpassed Frycek, who was plainly not interested. Dobrzyński's output, popular in his lifetime, is currently enjoying a revival in Poland.

Józef Stefani (1802–76) was one of Emilia Elsner's favourites, and her album contained more Stefani than anyone else. On graduation he made a name for himself as a composer of polonaises and an opera, *Krakovians and Górals*, which played to full houses in the 1840s. He became teacher of singing at the Lyceum, and eventually took charge of the ballet at the opera.

There were two other schools where Frycek learnt as much as in any study session with Elsner. Firstly there was Brzezina's Music Shop, where he had several of his works published, including, that year, the *Rondo à la mazur*. He spent hours going through Brzezina's wares, trying out imports from Paris, Vienna, Berlin and St Petersburg. In this way he got to know the latest trends, and learned from the example of the fashionable virtuosi of Europe's salons and concert platforms. As well as for himself, Frycek was always on the lookout for something for Jasio.

The other 'school' was Buchholtz's piano factory. The Chopin apartment had a Bucholtz piano, but Warsaw, as all Europe, was in the throes of a boom in musical instrument manufacture. It was keeping up with the New Romanticism and its demands for instruments of high quality to accommodate the increasing army of virtuoso performers. It was a self-perpetuating upward spiral of technical achievement, where piano manufacturers acceded to the requirements of the artists, who, in turn, saw greater possibilities in finer instruments. This trend was not lost on Frycek, who saw the technology of piano manufacture as one of the great essentials of his art. Both Brzezina and Buchholtz saw the advantages of having this brilliant youth trying out their wares, and Frycek was always welcome to browse, try out – or just be – in their shops. What was good enough for 'Chopinek' was good enough for anyone.

At Brzezina's Frycek discovered the music of Irish pianist and composer, John Field. He was born in Dublin in 1782, but emigrated to Russia in 1803, and settled in St Petersburg where he found patronage and fame. Especially popular were his Nocturnes, a form of his own devising. These were sensuous tone poems, usually featuring a singing melody line weaving lyrically over an accompaniment of arpeggios or moving chords. Frycek was utterly seduced by them. He had been captivated by the soaring melodies of Italian opera from an early age, and now here was a composer who had captured the very qualities of the human voice on the piano. For the first time, the world *cantabile* was used as a dynamic. Frycek saw endless possibilities in this for phrasing that 'breathed', and even bent the rhythm by barely perceptible speeding up and slowing down, as the human voice does to fit the words, over a steady, undulating accompaniment. He wrote two nocturnes that year, in C minor and in E minor, which were published posthumously: the C minor without an opus number, and the E minor as Op. 72 No 1.

Fryderyk Chopin met his role model in Paris in 1832, and was disappointed in both the man and his playing. Field died in Moscow in 1837 after a life of touring and music making alternating with drunken dissipation and extensive fornication.

Frycek's Contredanse in G flat, written in 1827, lay dormant for over a century, until it was published in 1934. In 1939 it was banned by the Nazis, and for that reason was secretly reissued in Warsaw and played as an act of defiance to the occupying power.

The year 1827 dawned very cold, and snow lay thick on the streets of Warsaw. All the sleighs were out, and there were numerous accidents. Justyna's rheumatism became worse. Frycek had started lessons in Italian. The Carnival period was in full swing when he heard the news that Jasio Białobłocki had died. He was devastated. Their friendship was something very special, with music and poor health having been the primary bonding factors. Jasio had always been in Frycek's thoughts, especially during his forays into Brzezina's. He had always been popular at the Chopin apartment. 'What a young gentleman that was,' said 'Józef's missus', the cook, 'more handsome than any of the other young gentlemen that come here. Neither Mr Woyciechowski not Mr Jędrzejewicz is as handsome, none of them, none. Lor', I remember the time he ate a whole cabbage straight out of my pot just for a lark.'

The Mr Jędrzejewicz mentioned by the cook was Józef, Ludka Chopin's future husband. He had even written an appreciation of Jasio for the *Warsaw Courier*, when the news suddenly came that it had been a false alarm, and Jasio was alive.

Frycek was a turmoil of emotions. 'Are you alive? Or not ...?' he wrote to Jasio in the middle of March. 'They say that you're dead. We all cried our eyes out – all for nothing ... I take up my pen to ask you if you're alive, or have you died? If you are dead, please let me know, and I'll tell the cook, because she's been saying prayers for you.'

All was as well as could be expected in Sokołowo, and there was even a chance that Wybraniecki would eventually get his choralion. It had been reassembled and was being prepared for transportation to Mazovia by river. But at the Casimir Palace ominous clouds had been gathering since the middle of February. Emilka became so weak that she was confined to bed. She had been coughing and spitting blood. She had stopped eating, and had grown thin and emaciated, a shadow of her former, lively self. Dr Malcz was very concerned, and twice ordered her to be bled, with a knife. Leeches were applied, as were hot plasters, which blistered the skin. She suffered sinapisms – hot mustard plaster dressings; wolfsbane – a herb that contains the poison aconite – was administered.

It was, as one would expect, to no avail. On 10 April 1827 Emilka Chopin died at her home of tuberculosis of the lungs and, it must be added, benevolent but ultimately unenlightened medicine. She was fourteen. The Chopins were inconsolable at the loss, at such a young age, of their extremely talented daughter.

Eugeniusz Skrodzki, the son of Józef Skrodzki, lecturer in science at the university, was a little boy at the time, and was at Emilka's funeral. Nearly sixty years later, writing under the pen

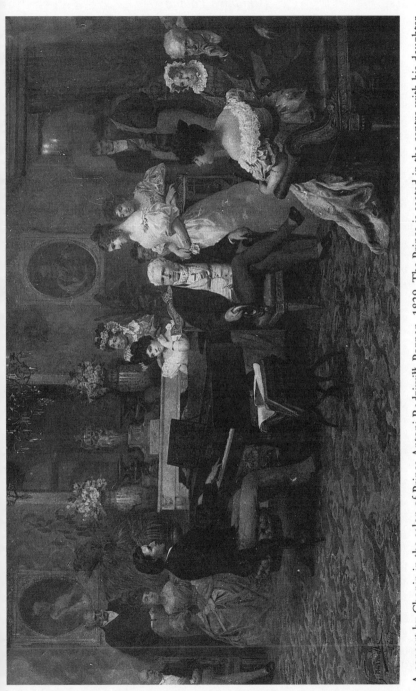

A concert by Chopin in the salon of Prince Antoni Radziwiłł, Poznan, 1829. The Prince is seated in the centre with his daughter Eliza beside him. Alexander von Humboldt is on the extreme right.

name 'Wielisław', he recalled that it was a day in early spring.

A white coffin, resting on a bier bedecked with garlands of spring flowers, was placed outside the front door of the apartment. Emilcia looked radiant and appeared to be only sleeping. Her still bonny cheeks, a sweet smile and a gentle air seemed to radiate through her emaciated and pallid face. We children could not comprehend what had happened to her. Then the hearse arrived for the coffin, and the priest, Father Rzymski, dressed in a black cape, put on his biretta, and intoned the hymn for the dead. When the procession moved off, the wailing and crying of her family drove it home to us that we would never see our Emilcia again.

Their 'Emilcia' used to assemble all the Casimir Palace children in the park to tell or read them stories under the linden trees. And her mother used to come out at intervals to refresh her with cups of hot, sweet milk.

Emilka Chopin was laid to rest at the Powązki Cemetery in Warsaw. The exact site of her grave is not known as her headstone has been moved next to Ludka, who is also buried there. The inscription says 'Emilia Chopin, passed away in the fourteenth spring of her life like a flower blossoming with the hope of a beautiful fruit 10 April 1827.'

Fryderyk Skarbek's obituary of Emilia Chopin was published in the May 1 issue of the periodical *Children's Recreations*, to which Klementyna Tańska added an additional contribution. As well as being the editor of *Children's Recreations*, Klementyna Tańska was a popular writer of children's stories and moral tales. She had been a great favourite with the Chopin girls during their formative years, and her writing inspired all three to write. For Emilka she was a literary role model, as was the German author Salzmann, whose children's tales she translated, with Izabela, into Polish. Emilka, with plays in verse such as 'The Mistake, or the Pretended Rogue' (in which Frycek also had a hand) had been the most creative and imaginative, and her poetry was of an exceptionally high quality.

The two older girls were more practical in their aspirations. They had embraced the Napoleonic ideal of the education and improvement of the working classes, and as adults wrote articles on the subject. Ludka had shown a particular interest in the education of young children and, although the term had virtually no meaning at the time, child psychology. The closest that literature came to guidance on the subliminal education of young children was the trend for moral tales. These were stories in which every event was served with a moral judgment, either good or bad. Love of family, respect for elders and ancestors, patriotism, love of God, gratitude, good manners, compassion for the unfortunate and an enquiring mind were virtues to be pursued at every opportunity. Historical, geographical and scientific facts were liberally included, usually with some moral involved, such as thanking God for the beauties of a mountain range, or that plagues could be punishments for wrongdoing.

Tańska's books were the inspiration for Ludka's 'Józio's Journey', which, in its entirety, is full of such moral judgements.

It is no coincidence that Frycek wrote two tragic compositions at the time, of which only one survives. An 'Andante Dolente' in B flat minor is now lost. The other, the Funeral March in C minor, is one of a pair, both in the same key, that were published posthumously as Op. 72 No 2.

Kazimierz Wójcicki, writing in 1856, described Emilka Chopin:

This young girl has astonished all who knew her with her intelligent ideas, mature thought and a thirst for knowledge. At thirteen she had surpassed in achievement many young ladies who have completed their education. She was bright and witty, and all her observations on daily life were invariably apt. She banished sorrow with jest, to make everyone happy. She was adored by her family, and what her brother and sisters could not get from their parents by asking, she managed through jokes and wiles. In learning she was mature beyond her years, and eagerly devoted herself to hard work. At eleven she transcribed the whole of Ignacy Humnicki's tragedy *Oedipus*. The writings of Klementyna Tańska inspired her to set her literary aims to the highest possible levels. Gifted with an easy facility for verse, she achieved a considerable poetic skill by perseverance and hard work. Her character and talents were akin to those of her brother Fryderyk.

If that were true, the world lost a literary genius that spring.

The Lindes saw another addition to the family that year; the baby was baptized Emilia.

The summer term was a bleak one for Frycek and the family as they tried to come to terms with the death of Emilka. On July 17 Frycek sat his first-year examination in composition and counterpoint. Elsner's comment on Frycek's result was 'special ability', exactly the same comment as had been bestowed on Tomasz Nidecki. Now graduated, Tomasz received a grant for further study in Vienna, approved by the authorities. Ignacy Dobrzyński perhaps did a little better with 'uncommon ability'.

The Chopins' apartment was to be given over to the expanding university during the summer holidays, and the teachers of the Lyceum had been relocated to the left-wing annexe of the Krasiński Palace opposite the university. The Chopins' new apartment on the second floor was even more spacious. Despite many memories of happy times gone by, of young lodgers come, gone and grown up, visitors, name-day performances, the sound of music and conversation, and, above all, the love that held the family together, the Chopins knew that the cloud that now hung over the Casimir Palace would never disperse. They were happy to move: free of the ghosts of Emilka, they were in a better position to try to rebuild their lives. But Justyna never got over the tragedy, and wore black for the rest of her life.

The Krasiński Palace, with the Chopin apartment, survived until the 1944 destruction of Warsaw. After World War II the palace was rebuilt. On the second floor one room, the salon, has been reconstructed from a drawing by Antoni Kolberg. The room, now at No 5 Krakowskie Przedmieście, is a memorial to Chopin.

In the summer of 1827 Frycek needed to get away, and his chance came after his exams.

Among the Chopins' circle were the wealthy Mazovian landowners, the extensive Zboiński family, who were related to the Dziewanowskis. Count Ksawery Zboiński, latterly Superintendent of Płock Castle, was a senator, with an estate at Kowalewo, twenty-five kilometres north-east of Płock; Count Karol Zboiński had an estate at Kozłowo, near Świecie on the Prussian stretch of the Vistula; and Count Józef Zboiński was the owner of the magnificent Kikół Palace, near Płock. Through the Zboińskis the Chopins met Count Antoni Sierakowski, who was married to Karol Zboiński's sister Antonina. Count Antoni was a wealthy landowner with an estate at Waplewo, to the south east of Malbork, in eastern Prussia. He was a published composer, virtuoso violinist and a patron of music. He was now planning to invite summer guests to Waplewo, with a trip to Gdańsk. Among those invited were Count Karol Zboiński and his family, and Count Ignacy Dembowski, who was also married to a Zboińska. As Count Dembowski lived in Warsaw. To complete the party Frycek was also invited. Frycek jumped at the opportunity, and accepted Count Antoni Sierakowski's invitation.

Count Ksawery Zboiński was also Emilka Chopin's godfather. Because of the tragic death of his god-daughter, he wanted to do something for the Chopins, and involved himself in Count Antoni's invitation to Waplewo, making all the arrangements for Frycek's journey. So Frycek's first port of call was to Count Ksawery's Kowalewo estate, the expedition's starting point. During his short stay at Kowalewo Frycek managed to compose a waltz, which he intended to send to Ludka and Izabela. But, he wrote, he 'did not have the time to write it out'. The waltz is now lost.

Count Ksawery had three daughters, of whom the youngest, Kamilka, was not yet two. She took a fancy to Frycek, and used to lisp, much to his amusement, 'Kagila pana kotech' ('Kamilka Pana kocha – Kamilka loves sir'). His 'chaperon', Count Ignacy Dembowski arrived, and on the morning of the departure, a Friday in late July, Frycek found time to write to his parents:

I have no time to write, as we're just starting; it's eight o'clock in the morning, and we never get up before seven. The air is fine, the sun is shining beautifully, the birds are twittering. If there were a brook, it would be babbling, but there is a pond, and the frogs are in excellent voice. But the best of all is a virtuoso blackbird performing under our windows.... Today, then, to Płock....

The historic city of Płock is situated on high ground on the River Vistula. It is the oldest urban settlement in Mazovia, and had grown rich from the cloth trade, until it was ravaged during the Swedish invasions of the seventeenth century, after which it went into decline. Today, despite pollution from the huge petrochemical works and an oil refinery, the Old Town, known as 'Little Kraków', is still very beautiful, and unchanged since Chopin's day. The Romanesque cathedral dates from 1075, but was rebuilt in the middle of the eighteenth century, in which form it exists today. The two towers, the Zegarowa (Clock) and the Szlachecka (Noble) bear witness to ancient fortifications long since destroyed.

'. . . tomorrow to Rościszewo . . .' After Płock, the party turned north, away from the Vistula, through forests of birch and pine, to the town of Sierpc. Here they left the main post road and turned to Rościszewski, a few kilometres away, to stay with the Rościszewski family, whose single-storey manor in the village is there to this day, housing an agricultural office and a nursery school. The following day was Sunday, so, in keeping with tradition, everybody attended mass at the village church, which is still there.

'. . . the day after to Kikół . . .' After mass, the party retraced its wheelmarks back to Sierpc to rejoin the post road, lined with linden trees in full flower, through Lipno, and on to Kikół. There they stayed at Count Józef's sumptuous palace, which was situated on a hill, whence there was a beautiful view of the lake. To Frycek's delight, Count Józef had a fortepiano in the Knights' Hall. The Zboiński Palace is still there, its view now obscured by the village that has grown round it.

'. . . two or three days in Turzno . . .' The party continued along the Toruń road till it reached Lubicz on the River Drwęca, the Prussian border. There they turned north, bypassing Toruń, to Turzno, where they stayed with more relatives, the Gajewskis. The Gajewski manor is still there today, and houses administrative offices and a school.

'. . . a couple of days in Kozłowo . . .' Leaving Turzno, the party rejoined the northern post road to Świecie (then called Schwetz) on the Vistula. Count Karol's estate at Kozłowo was situated on the River Wda, nine kilometres before its confluence with the Vistula near Świecie. No trace is left of the Zboiński estate on the banks of the river, but a plaque embedded in a boulder at the entry into the village commemorates the Chopin visit. Count Karol Zboiński joined the party, and they continued on their journey.

'. . . and the next moment, Gdańsk . . .' On August 9 journey's end came as the carriage drove through the Golden Gate into the main town, and on to the Holzgasse and the 'Hotel Drei Mohren'

(Three Moors), the finest in the city. Count Karol and Count Ignacy, with Frycek, registered, as was the norm for underage guests, merely as '*nebst Familie*' in the care of Count Ignacy, booked in for five nights. They were joined by Count Antoni, come to meet them from Waplewo to show them round. The purpose of the visit was purely recreational, so sightseeing was the primary objective.

There were certainly sights to see in Danzig, as Gdańsk was called in German: the Długi Targ (Long Market), an extension of Długa Street, Neptune's Fountain and the Artus Court are among the sights that Frycek saw, as well as the nearby stark and severe St Mary's Church, the world's largest brick church, which boasted an astronomical clock dating back to 1470. Frycek saw the cathedral at Oliwa, which today is a northern suburb of Gdańsk, as it boasted the world's largest organ at the time, built in 1755. It took seven men to operate the bellows.

Pastor Johann Wilhelm Linde would have been offended if Frycek had not called on him. The older brother of the rector of the Warsaw Lyceum lived in Tobiasz Street.

No traveller visited Gdańsk without seeking out the Baltic Sea. To the north of Gdańsk, the pretty little town of Sopot was just beginning to attract attention as a fashionable seaside resort. In 1797 Count Kajetan Sierakowski, Count Antoni's father, had built a small manor on a hill overlooking the vast expanses of sandy beach as a summer residence. Although it was no longer in Sierakowski hands at the time, Count Antoni might have taken Frycek to see it, or at any rate to see the Baltic Sea from its viewpoint. As the then owner was a close friend of the Sierakowskis, speculation exists that Frycek may have played there. The Sierakowski manor is still there, situated at 12 Czyżewski Street, and on the strength of this speculation, chamber concerts are held in the room in which Chopin was reputed to have played. The house is a cultural centre in Chopin's name, and is run by the Society of the Friends of Sopot.

Gdańsk suffered heavily at the start of World War II, but has largely been rebuilt as it was prior to 1939. The site of the 'Drei Mohren' is now in Kładki Street, close to the Church of the Holy Trinity, but no trace remains of the site of Pastor Linde's house.

After five days, the tourists left Gdańsk, and turned south-east-

wards to Count Antoni's estate at Waplewo, some twenty kilometres to the south-east of Malbork. For Frycek, who enjoyed
travel and the foreign experience, this was a splendid opportunity
to make music with Count Antoni, in the sure knowledge that his
host was appreciative of his art. It was a musical week at Waplewo,
after which the touring party paid a second five-day visit to Gdańsk,
for further sightseeing.

'. . . and home.'

Frycek was also invited to spend the late summer with his godmother Anna Wiesiołowska at Strzyżewo. Since his stay there on
his way back from Duszniki the previous year, his relationship
with his godmother had turned to a closer, more mature friendship.
Frycek gladly accepted, and by the end of August he was again in
the Duchy of Poznań. Prince Antoni Radziwiłł was at his hunting
lodge at Antonin, and Frycek was invited, with the Wiesiołowskis,
who were friends of the Radziwiłłs, to spend a few days there.
Now seventeen, Frycek was beginning to hold his own at the
dinner table as a sophisticated and witty young man and an ex-
ceptional, published musician, rather than an interesting curiosity
to be patronized and studied. And he was able to enjoy the company of Eliza and Wanda Radziwiłł, who, although older than he
was, held feminine charms which did not go unappreciated.

At holiday time, Frycek's mind turned to romance, relaxation
and the enjoyment of countryside and fresh air, but he also had
the need to compose, and it was at Strzyżewo – and Antonin –
that Frycek embarked on his first attempt at writing a concerto
work, the Variations in B flat on 'Là ci darem la mano' from
Mozart's *Don Giovanni*, for piano and orchestra. The composition showed his preoccupation with opera, and was dedicated to
Tytus Woyciechowski, along with the Polonaise in D minor, published after Frycek's death as Op. 71 No. 1. Despite the Variations' very basic orchestration, after their publication in Vienna
in 1830 as his Op. 2, they became Frycek's first composition to
earn a place in the international concert repertoire. When he had
finished them, he sent the package off to his friend at Poturzyn.

Autumn came, and Frycek returned to Warsaw. The new apartment at the Krasiński Palace was ready – this time there would
be no more boarders. Frycek embarked on his second year at the
conservatory with enthusiasm.

EIGHT
Drama at Sanniki

Frycek, like most seventeen-year-olds, adored all girls, but purely, romantically and idealistically, partly because of shyness, and partly because he put feminine beauty on a pedestal. He loved the company of young women who were beautiful, intelligent and witty. Eugeniusz 'Wielisław' Skrodzki recollects in his *Memoirs* that Frycek's first love was Countess Alexandrine 'Moriolka' de Moriolles. Since their first meeting as children at the Belvedere Palace they had become close, but in those days games and pranks were the order of the day, interspersed with some music. As they grew into their teenage years, the friendship assumed touches of innocent, totally unpossessive romance. If not actually inseparable, Frycek and Moriolka were often seen in each other's company.

Eugeniusz claimed Moriolka had assignations in the Botanical Gardens behind the university with Frycek, and that it was he, Eugeniusz, who, on seeing Mr Chopin going there in search of his son, waylaid him and assured him that Frycek was nowhere to be seen, thus causing Mr Chopin to go away. He was rewarded later with a bag of sweets for his part in the conspiracy to salvage the young pair's honour. If Nicolas had come across Frycek and Moriolka in the Botanical Gardens they would have been innocently walking, talking or just sitting on the grass, the only suspicious circumstance being that Moriolka was unchaperoned. If a kiss were stolen, it would have been instigated by her; Frycek would not have called her a 'little devil' for nothing. It was a close, semi-platonic, semi-romantic teenaged friendship, based on mutual attraction and confidence. Whatever Frycek's feelings might have been he did not show them, and only a keen observer like Eugeniusz would have noticed the occasional far-away gaze or a twinkle in the eye. Frycek and Moriolka remained good friends until Frycek's departure from Poland.

On 2 January 1828 Countess Ludwika Skarbek died in Warsaw of tuberculosis of the throat, and in April came the news of the death, from tuberculosis of the bone, of Jasio Białobłocki on March 31. For Frycek these two deaths were a terrible blow. Over the last two years Frycek was in no doubt that Jasio would die, and did everything he could to support him. But what was perhaps most disturbing was his increasing awareness of his own mortality. He knew he had the beginnings of tuberculosis, and he had first-hand knowledge of the toll this disease could take. Exactly a year previously he watched Emilka dying, and now it had claimed Countess Ludwika and Jasio as well. Frycek sublimated his fears and staved off depression by composing. He composed furiously that year, never letting up, accepting any challenges that Elsner gave him. He beavered away at the unfamiliar techniques of writing for the violin and the cello, and wrote two more major works for piano and orchestra, the *Fantasy on Polish Airs* and the *Rondo à la krakowiak*.

On the pianistic front, he wrote a Rondo in C, with which he was not entirely happy and, having sought Tytus's opinion, as he often did, decided to rewrite it.

That spring Hummel came to Warsaw to give a series of concerts. Johann Nepomuk Hummel was one of the guiding lights of the virtuoso piano during the first part of the nineteenth century, and one of Frycek's major influences at this time. Żywny was an admirer of Hummel, and had introduced his music to Frycek at an early age. Hummel was born in Pressburg, now Bratislava, in 1778. As a little boy he lodged with Mozart in Vienna for two years, taking lessons from him, then toured Europe as a child prodigy. He lived for a while in London, where he was further trained by Clementi, before returning to Vienna to study composition with Salieri, Albrechtsberger and Haydn, from whom he took over the musical soul of the Esterházy estate in Hungary. Among his own piano pupils were Czerny, Henselt and Thalberg. The previous year he had been at Beethoven's death bed, remaking their friendship after an old quarrel. Hummel was a pallbearer at Beethoven's funeral.

The fifty-year-old virtuoso and artist, with a string of names to drop that would read like an almanac of the greatest musicians of the age, held a fascination for Frycek. He attended every one of Hummel's concerts, and found a performer with a singular skill for off-the-cuff improvisations, whose control of his art was total. Here was a musician who could do anything, at any time, at the drop of a hat, and always come up with a superb performance. This was a far cry from the established procedure of contrived formality which allowed no room for bending with the atmosphere. In a word, this was the artist against whom he had to measure his own art. He analysed and digested every note and every nuance at every concert of Hummel's.

Frycek needed to meet this phenomenon, and they became friends. Hummel told Frycek stories about people who had only been names at the head of sheets of music: of how Mozart was a superb improviser while Salieri was not; of how Mozart was not very taken with a sullen youth by the name of Beethoven when he arrived for a course of lessons while he, Hummel, was staying there – until Beethoven started to improvise. 'Watch that one,' Mozart said at the departing Beethoven, who only stayed with Mozart for a few days before having to return home. 'One day he will have something to say.' And of how he played a Haydn piano sonata at London's Hanover Rooms, after which he was tipped a guinea – by old Papa Haydn himself, who happened to be in the audience.

Hummel acknowledged Frycek as the true inheritor of the art of improvisation after Mozart and Beethoven.

Frycek had been singing in choirs for several years, and towards the end of May he was in the middle of a choral rehearsal in preparation for the feast of Corpus Christi, when one of his student friends from the university by the name of Oborski burst in excitedly, and informed Frycek that Tytus Woyciechowski had left in the middle of the night, and that he had asked him, Oborski, to say goodbye to Frycek on his behalf. Tytus's mother was seriously ill, and he had to abort his course at the university and return home to Poturzyn to manage the estate. Frycek was shocked and concerned that he might never see his friend again. He had written and dedicated four works to Tytus between 1827 and

1829: as well as his 'Là ci darem la mano' variations, there were the three Polonaises, in D minor, B flat, and F minor, all published posthumously as Op. 71.

Shortly after Tytus's departure Frycek began work on his Piano Trio in G minor, intending to dedicate it to Prince Antoni Radziwiłł. Elsner had been encouraging him to try forms other than piano music. Frycek, who would try anything once, conceded, and embarked on a period of experimentation that would never again be repeated. This was his first foray into chamber music; and it cost him some blood, sweat and tears. By July he had managed to complete the Allegro first movement, and tried it out with the help of a couple of string players.

That year saw the first of many published works of the literary collaboration of Ludka and Izabela Chopin. It was a moral tale for children, entitled *Ludwik and Emilka*. All three surviving Chopin children were now published artists. The second-year examinations at the conservatory took place on July 22. Frycek had been exempted from attending, but Elsner in his habitually terse end-of-year report wrote: 'Chopin Fryderyk (a particular ability, second year, gone away for the improvement of his health).' This compared with Ignacy Dobrzyński and the other students, who were assessed (many abilities).

Frycek had left early because of his health, and gone to stay in the country with his friend Konstanty 'Kostuś' Pruszak at his parents' manor at Sanniki, a small village about eighty kilometres to the west of Warsaw. The Pruszaks, a gregarious family, were friends of the Chopins, and Kostuś had been Frycek's school friend. 'Old' Pruszak was a friendly and genial character who was constantly 'taking the waters' wherever there were fashionable waters to be taken. His wife Marianna was a hospitable hostess who liked nothing better than to have a house full of young people, friends of Kostuś or his sister Aleksandra, known as Olesia. Frycek had been trying to pair Tytus, who had been to Sanniki himself, with Olesia, much to Tytus's irritation. Now that Tytus was a farmer with other things on his mind in distant Poturzyn, Frycek's matchmaking machinations had come to naught. Kostuś invited Frycek to spend the summer holidays at Sanniki.

The whole region has traditionally been imbued with folk lore, and the local lads and lasses would don their regional costumes and have a party at the slightest instigation. Musicians specialized in the *kujawiak*, the dance originating in the Kujawy region further to the west. This dance comes in two parts. The first part is in a slow, seductive three-four time with a strong accent on the third beat. When this comes to an end, the tempo changes abruptly into the *oberek*. This is in very fast three-four time, again with the accent on the third beat, and usually features the band's virtuoso, as the melody line invariably consists of fast quaver runs in *perpetuum mobile*. The dance develops into a frenzy, with the boys swinging the girls round and round until everyone becomes dizzy, to the accompaniment of much clapping, whooping and cheering. With such dances on offer, it is hardly surprising that Sanniki in the summer of 1828 was one mad round of parties, dances, romance – and amateur dramatics. Marianna Pruszak was a drama enthusiast given to mounting amateur productions at their Warsaw house. At Sanniki she liked to arrange comedies and charades, and Frycek took wholeheartedly to the drawing-room carpet with his peculiar brand of zany showmanship. There was a suggestion that Frycek's frequent walks in the gardens with Olesia's governess held hints of romance.

Halfway through the stay Tytus wrote to Kostuś asking him to call at his former lodgings in Warsaw to arrange for his things to be sent on, and to check his piano. So Frycek and Kostuś returned to Warsaw for a few days. Together they went to Tytus's lodgings and Kostuś sent his effects on to Poturzyn.

While they were in Warsaw they went to the opera to see Rossini's *The Barber of Seville*, which was playing in Italian. Frycek wrote to Tytus about the leading man that

I could have murdered Colli. He played the part as a low buffoon and sang so out of tune it was dreadful. In one exit he went head over heels. Imagine Colli, dressed in breeches, with a guitar and a round white hat, sprawled on the floor. Shame! The Barber was dreadful!

Back at Sanniki Frycek set about reworking his Rondo in C, which he had discussed with Tytus. He rearranged it for two pianos, and it was published posthumously as Op. 73.

On September 4 Frycek left Sanniki and returned to Warsaw.

Today the old walls still surround the estate, and the trees are old enough to have witnessed those open-air dramas of that heady summer of 1828. The original timber manor was destroyed by fire, and the one now standing on the site was built in 1910. The building houses administrative offices, including the Register Office – sometimes used by Chopin-loving couples looking for an extra touch of romance to their wedding day. Part of the manor is a Chopin and Regional Folk Centre. There is a recital hall and a music library, and accommodation for those wishing to take advantage of the concerts and local folk festivals; for the folk art tradition is still strong and maintained throughout the region, with Sanniki Manor as its epicentre. There is a commemorative plaque on the wall of the manor.

Back in Warsaw Frycek got together with pianist Maurycy Ernemann, and they went to Buchholtz's piano factory to try out the Rondo in C. 'It went fairly well,' Frycek informed Tytus, 'We're thinking about playing it at the Resursa (Merchants' Hall).' He paid another visit to the opera to see one of his favourites, Weber's *Der Freischütz*, which was 'most appallingly performed. The chorus were a quarter of a beat out with each other.'

King Friedrich Wilhelm III of Prussia, inspired by the spate of academic congresses in Switzerland, decided to place Berlin on the scientific map of Europe, and set up his own Congress of Naturalists, under the aegis of the University of Berlin, in the autumn of 1828. The eminent Professor Alexander von Humboldt was appointed President. Born in Berlin in 1769, the son of the King's Chamberlain, he was a traveller, explorer and author of a thirty-volume set of books describing his discoveries in Central and South America, where he spent five years in the jungles in the cause of natural science.

Representatives from all of Europe's centres of scientific learning were invited to take part, with all expenses paid by the Prussian government. Professor Feliks Jarocki, a friend of the Chopins, received an invitation. The Professor was a former student of the Berlin Academy, a doctor of philosophy, professor of zoology at Warsaw University and a member of many learned societies. When the Professor asked Frycek if he would like to accompany him to Berlin, Frycek was beside himself with excitement. 'I'm writing like a half-demented lunatic,' he wrote to Tytus, 'because I really don't know what's going on. Today I'm off to Berlin to see an opera by Spontini. . . .'

It was Tuesday, September 9, the day of departure of the diligence to Berlin. Frycek's interest in natural history was limited, but it was a rare chance to visit one of Europe's greatest cities, and to sample a professional performance of Spontini's *Fernand Cortez* or *Olimpie*, especially after the recent *Barber* and *Freischütz* fiascos. Frycek blamed the fact that Karol Kurpiński, Elsner's assistant and inheritor of the mantle of Polish opera, had gone to Kraków, and his place had been taken by one Żyliński, who, in Frycek's opinion, was making a mess of things. So it was no wonder that Frycek was acting like a 'half-demented lunatic' at the prospect of some good opera well mounted.

Gasparo Spontini was born near Ancona in Italy in 1774. As a composer of operas he had only limited success until 1807, when his *La Vestale* was enjoyed by Napoleon. This ensured his musical future, and he was appointed chief director of music in Berlin at an enormous salary. From this exalted position he could do no wrong, and he enjoyed continuing success until the German Romanticism of Weber's *Der Freischütz* nudged Italian opera into second place. He was still enormously popular, and Frycek entertained hopes of meeting him at the far end of a veritable Establishment maze: 'Jarocki's friend Lichtenstein,' he explained to Tytus, 'the secretary at the Congress, used to be a friend of Weber and is a member of the Academy of Singing and thus on good terms with Zelter its president, so by making the acquaintance of Lichtenstein I shall get to know the best musicians in Berlin except Spontini, whom he can't stand. . . .'

With hopes of rubbing shoulders with the famous, dreams of fortune in his heart and teeth gritted against the gruelling, five-day, six-hundred-kilometre drive to Berlin, Frycek and Professor Jarocki climbed into the coach in the courtyard of the Post Office. The other travellers were a heavy-humoured German lawyer from Poznań and a fat, greasy Prussian farmer who spent most of his life travelling. The coach was Prussian, and badly sprung, and soon Frycek began to feel uncomfortable. The post road left Warsaw through the toll at Wola, and passed through Sochaczew, Łowicz, Kutno and Kłodawa. After that the post road continued to the north-west to Sompolno, Ślesin and Kleczew, rejoining the E30 just before Słupca, the last Polish town before the frontier at Staw. After Poznań the route went through Grodzisk, Wolsztyn, Sulechów, then cross coun-

try through Kije, Sycowice and Radnica to Krosno Odrzańskie,
Cybinka and on to the bridge at Frankfurt-am-Oder, today's frontier with Germany. Just before Frankfurt the party was joined by
'a Teutonic Corinna, full of *achs*, *jas* and *neins*, a veritable romantic doll who amused us all by continually nagging the lawyer'.

The diligence arrived in Berlin at 3 o'clock on the afternoon of
Sunday, September 14. Rooms had been prepared for 'Professor
Jarocki's party' at the comfortable Kronprinz Inn, with many of
the eminent naturalists. Frycek commented, 'we are comfortable
and content here'.

That evening Frycek went with Professor Jarocki to meet the
President, Professor Humboldt and his secretary, Professor Martin
Lichtenstein, also an eminent natural scientist. He was director of
the Berlin Museum and Professor of Zoology at the university
and the founder of the Berlin Zoological Gardens. The fact that
Professor Lichtenstein had promised to introduce him to Berlin's
top musicians was the only saving grace of the evening for Frycek,
who rued the fact that he was missing a performance of Munich-
based Peter Winter's *Das Unterbrochene Opferfest*.

The following day, Monday, Frycek wandered round the wide
streets of Berlin, marvelling at the fine buildings and bridges over
the River Spree. Although he did not consider Berlin particularly
beautiful, he noted the order, cleanliness and tidiness, and recognized
that a lot of forethought had gone into its planning. He was
struck by the absence of crowds, and reckoned that the city could
easily hold twice its population. After some research, Frycek found
Berlin girls wanting. 'They all have the same empty jaws, or toothless
mouths,' he wrote home, '... it's true that they dress well, but
what a waste of good muslin cut up for those kidskin dollies.'

That evening his indifference to eminent natural historians turned
to annoyance when he was forced, screaming within, to sit through
a banquet, listening politely to endless plant and animal talk. He
was missing a concert by a brilliant nine-year-old violinist called
Birnach, whom he wanted to hear. He took out his irritation by
sketching caricatures of some of the delegates, whom he considered
a bunch of old fogeys. 'Figures of fun' and 'monkeys' were among
his written descriptions.

On Tuesday morning Frycek did the required tour of the thirteen rooms of the Zoological Exhibition, which, he conceded, was

very good; but he would have preferred to visit Schlesinger's Music Shop. He did get to visit two piano factories, but, unlike at Buchholtz's, here there were no pianos ready for him to try. Fortunately there was a piano back at the inn, which Frycek played, to the pleasure of the innkeeper. That evening, 'to avoid the possibility of ending up again with the "caricatures" he chose to dine early and alone, because Spontini's *Fernand Cortez* was on, and this time he was determined to see it.

After that Frycek managed largely to keep clear of natural science functions, and got to see a good deal of opera: apart from Spontini's *Fernand Cortez*, Frycek took in Cimarosa's *Il matrimonio segreto*, *Colporteur* by the Anglo-French composer, George Onslow, and a decent performance of *Der Freischütz*; he also caught a repeat of Winter's *Das Unterbrochene Opferfest*. Best of all was Handel's *Ode to St Cecilia* at the Academy of Singing, which came closest to Frycek's idea of great music. The fact that a pretty and talented seventeen-year-old soprano by the name of Schatzel was one of the leading singers may have affected his judgement. Frycek went to see her on several occasions.

On Thursday the Congress was formally opened in the presence of Crown Prince Friedrich Wilhelm. Lichtenstein reserved a ticket for Frycek, as there would be many celebrities present. For that Frycek was grateful, but when Jarocki offered to get him an invitation to Humboldt's private reception for the natural historians later that evening, Frycek frantically begged him not to go to the trouble as 'it would be no advantage to me, and anyway, the gentlemen might look upon me as an outsider in their midst'. This was Frycek's polite way of saying that he could not stand another boring evening of natural history, and he would much rather go to an opera.

At the reception there was, as Lichtenstein had predicted, a considerable array of well-known personages. From the world of music there was composer Karl Zelter, the president of the Academy of Singing and friend of Goethe; Spontini was there, as well as the brilliant nineteen-year-old Berlin pianist, Felix Mendelssohn. Frycek wanted to approach him and introduce himself, but the grandeur of the occasion inhibited him, and the two giants of early Romanticism missed each other by a whisker of shyness. Frycek looked about for a familiar face, specifically that of Prince Antoni Radziwiłł, who was supposed to come. He was a small fish floundering in a big academic pond, surrounded by the rich, the famous and the eminent, and had not the maturity and self-confidence to realize his own place in this assemblage of eminence. He had hoped to be introduced to the best of Berlin, but everyone was preoccupied with their own spheres of interest. Frycek hardly knew anyone, and hoped that Prince Radziwiłł would rescue him and introduce him to Berlin's musical inner circle. But the Prince was nowhere to be seen.

That same day Jarocki and Frycek visited the Berlin Library – one of the biggest and finest in the world. Seated at a table, poring over a manuscript of a letter written by Kościuszko, was the secretary of the Dresden Library, twenty-seven-year-old Karl Falkenstein. The previous year he had published a highly acclaimed biography of Kościuszko in German, which had just been translated into Polish. When he realized that Jarocki and Frycek were Polish, he asked for a translation of the letter. Jarocki, a fluent German speaker, complied, and dictated the translation to a grateful Falkenstein.

On Tuesday, September 23, the eve of the end of the Congress, there was a celebratory banquet. Frycek was there. 'The banquet was accompanied by songs,' he wrote.

All those present joined in, and those seated at the tables drank liberally and beat time to the music, while Zelter conducted. Beside him a huge gilt cup had been placed on a crimson pedestal as a symbol of his exalted musical rank. Everyone ate more than usual because the scientists, especially the zoologists, had concerned themselves foremost with the improvement of meats, sauces and soups, and they had made considerable progress in the science of eating during the last few days of the Congress.

It was a rip-roaring finale to the Congress.

On Wednesday the Congress was wound up and pronounced a great success. Jarocki and Frycek stayed on until Sunday, September 28, when they climbed once more into the coach. Their destination was Poznań, where they had been invited to a banquet by Archbishop Wolicki. They came to Züllichau, a small town situated at an important intersection. The diligence passed through the western Krosno Gate straight into the Market Square to the post stage, where it stopped to change horses. As there were none available, the driver announced a delay of an hour, so Frycek and Jarocki decided to go for a walk. Neither the site of an historic battle nor the streets of the little town were of any interest, so they returned to the post house and found that there were still no horses.

The friendly postmaster, sensing the irritation of the travellers, invited them all to his house in nearby Tuchmacher Street for refreshments. As this was preferable to wandering the streets, Frycek and the others gratefully accepted. Seated in the postmaster's lounge, he noticed an old piano in the next room. Bored, he strolled over casually, sat down at the piano, and tried out a few arpeggios. It was actually in tune, so he did what he did best on such occasions – he started to improvise. Züllichau was small, with a village atmosphere, and the postmaster's door was always open to locals, who came in and out at will.

Frycek noticed an elderly gentleman had entered the room, and was listening, transfixed. He thought he would give this German a taste of Polish music, so his improvisation took on an ethnic feel as he wrapped his fingers round some Polish tunes that came to his head, strung them together into a medley and the result was an instant fantasia on Polish themes. The other travellers and more locals filtered in, as did the innkeeper, his wife and two very pretty daughters. Everyone was amazed, especially the innkeeper, who had never heard his piano sound so good. After a while the postilion barged into the room with a cry of 'The horses are ready!' Frycek stopped, pleased at the prospect of being on his way again, but his audience waved the astonished postilion away, and made Frycek continue. So he struck up again and the impromptu session continued, with everyone in raptures over the music. When he finally stopped all language barriers were brought down with the arrival of wine, cakes and sweets, on the house. And admiring looks from the girls for Frycek.

Toasts were drunk, congratulations were expressed, and it turned out that the elderly gentleman was Cantor Kahler, who taught music at the Züllichau Pedagogium. 'Young man,' he cried, 'I'd have given ten years of my life to be able to play like you. If Mozart had heard you, he'd have shaken your hand and cried "Bravo!" It would not be right for me to do so.' In later years Kahler published works and commentaries about Chopin.

Frycek was utterly exhausted, and wanted to be on his way, but still they would not let him go. The innkeeper got all the passengers to admit that they were in no hurry, so Frycek had no option but to play just one more piece. After that he finally stopped. The passengers, seeing that this was truly the end, filed out of the inn and got back into the coach, the pockets of which had been crammed with extra cakes and sweets by the innkeeper's daughters. The postilion climbed on to his horse, the driver got into his seat, cracked the whip, and the coach pulled off towards Poznań, with a grateful group waving them off. Frycek tried to relax in his seat. He had given a great deal of pleasure to these people, but his exhaustion was total, and he felt ill. He could not wait to get to Poznań.

The story was recounted years later by Frycek's sister Izabela Barcińska to Chopin's biographer, Maurycy Karasowski. The inn at Sulechów, as the Polish town is now called, has been pulled down. On the site at No. 9 Rynek (Market Place), a plaque dating back to when Sulechów was in Germany, was removed in 1945, along with all signs in German. It has not been replaced.

The postmaster's house was pulled down in 1945. The site is a children's playground beside a block of flats in today's Handlowa Street. On the wall of the Town Hall a plaque commemorates Chopin's visit to Sulechów. In 1949, the centenary of Chopin's death, the town honoured the legend with the establishment of a Chopin Festival, which is now held every May.

It was already October when the diligence reached Poznań, where Frycek and Jarocki broke their journey at the invitation of the Archbishop of Poznań and Gniezno, Teofil Wolicki.

The Archbishop's family had known the Chopins for many years, and it was in the salon of Konstanty Wolicki in Warsaw that Frycek met Angelica Catalani. The Wolickis were also related to the Skarbeks through the Wiesiołowskis of Strzyżewo: Stefan Wiesiołowski's mother was born Wolicka. The Wolickis were further related to the Wodzińskis, whose estate was at Służewo, in Mazovia. Two of the three Wodziński boys, Antoni and Feliks, lodged with Nicolas on the Wolickis' recommendation, and became Frycek's close friends; of their two sisters, Maria, at this time only nine, later became, for a while, Frycek's fiancée, and little Józefa, then seven, writing years later under her married name of Kościelska, mentioned some Chopin anecdotes in her Memoirs.

The brief stopover as guests of the Archbishop at his residence beside the cathedral on the 'Holy Island' of Ostrów Tumski, on the River Warta, was a good opportunity for Frycek to call on Prince Radziwiłł to pay his respects. The Prince and his family were in residence in the Governor's Palace, which is today the former Jesuit College. The Prince welcomed Frycek warmly, and a musical evening was promptly arranged. Henryk Siemiradzki interpreted the scene in his painting of 1887, 'Chopin playing in the salon of Prince Radziwiłł'. Among those present in the painting are the Prince, his daughter Eliza and Professor Humboldt.

Neither the Prince nor his string quartet were involved in performing, although Frycek told Prince Radziwiłł about his Piano Trio. The soirée was Frycek's, and only the Prince's Kapellmeister Klingohr joined him in some duets. At the back of his mind Frycek compared the two impromptu sessions that had taken place within a couple of days of each other: the first, at Züllichau, was in a postmaster's house, where he played on an old piano, and now he was in the salon of the Governor of Poznań, seated at the best fortepiano that money could buy. His first audience had consisted of a select group of locals and travellers, and now he was performing for an equally select group of the highest Prussian society. At the first he had played folk tunes, and enjoyed the adulation of the innkeeper's daughters. Now he gave a programme of sonatas by Beethoven, Hummel and Mozart, and his delicate features were again contemplated by a Princess called Eliza, who had already sketched him the previous year, and would sketch him again. In both cases he improvised, and in both cases he enchanted his audience, who always wanted to hear more. The two sessions took place at opposing ends of the social scale. Frycek's music belonged to both.

The piano that Frycek played at Prince Radziwiłł's is now in the Museum of Musical Instruments in the Market Square in Poznań. The room in which he played has been restored, and is now the sumptuously decorated White Room, where recitals are arranged by the Poznań Philharmonic Society.

Frycek also called on his mother's relatives, who lived in Poznań. Frycek and Jarocki only stayed in Poznań for a couple of days, and on Monday, October 6, arrived back in Warsaw.

NINE
Konstancja Gładkowska

Back in Warsaw Frycek walked straight into the affair of Olesia
Pruszak's governess. After the family's return from Sanniki to their
house in Marszałkowska Street, it was discovered that the governess was pregnant, and that conception must have occurred at Sanniki
during the summer. The obvious culprit had to be Frycek, who was
often seen with her in the gardens. Marianna Pruszak confronted
Nicolas and Justyna, but the accusation was found to be false. Marianna
apologized, and the matter was cleared up. Frycek, having got over
the shock, found the whole matter funny. 'You will be amused by
the story. . . . I was at Sanniki for over a month,' he wrote to Tytus,
'and always walked in the garden with the governess. But I only
walked, that's all. She was not attractive, and I had no appetite for
such good fortune anyway.' The hapless governess was dismissed,
and Frycek was appointed to give Olesia lessons for a fee, an advantage to an eighteen-year-old student. He also gave music lessons to
nine-year-old Maria Wodzińska, his future fiancée.

Marianna Pruszak's predilection for amateur dramatics continued, and she put on a play by Duval entitled *Les Projets de
Mariage*, in which Frycek, played the part of 'Pedro'.

Nicolas and Justyna had made alterations at their new apartment.
On the floor above there was an attic room with no access, and
they made plans to convert it into a study for Frycek. At the
beginning of 1829 a staircase was built from the dressing-room
to the attic, and Frycek had a den of his own, complete with an
old piano and a bureau.

Frycek completed his next two compositions for piano and orchestra before the builder had finished the staircase. They came in quick succession that autumn, but were not published until 1834. The first was the *Grand Fantasy on Polish Airs*, Op. 13. This work was a direct result of his Sulechów improvisations. On his return from Poznań he consolidated those ideas into a free-form work in three sections, each a set of free variations on a different folk song. His greatest efforts went into the piano writing, the orchestral scoring only fleshing out the background with chords and the occasional imitative phrase. The first section is based on 'Already the Moon Has Set', the second is the folk song, 'Laura and Filon', and the third is an *oberek*, bringing the *Fantasy* to a sparkling finale.

If the orchestral scoring of the *Fantasy* was basic, the same could not be said of the *Rondo à la krakowiak*, Op. 14. This work, based on the dance in two-four time from the Kraków region, is widely regarded as Frycek's greatest concerto achievement from the viewpoint of orchestral writing. Perhaps Elsner had words with him about the lackadaisical scoring in the *Fantasy*, because the attention to orchestral detail is superior in the *Krakowiak*.

On his return from Berlin Frycek had turned up at the conservatory late. Elsner did not mind, as he knew that Frycek was working and studying at his own speed. 'It is a bad master', Elsner said, 'who is not surpassed by his pupil.' Frycek had done that, even if the scoring was not up to diploma standard. He realized that in the *Fantasy* Frycek aimed at a virtuoso concert romp through Polish folklore, whereas the *Krakowiak* was a miniature concerto in which both piano and orchestra explored rondo form around a folk motif.

Frycek's visits to Elsner were not so much lessons as critical sessions and analysis, despite the gradual opening up of a generation gap. Frycek's was a new music belonging to a new generation, and Elsner, now sixty, did not always understand it. Frycek still sought Elsner's advice as an impartial judge who never flattered for flattery's sake. He continued to visit the Elsners and added a Mazurka in D into Emily Elsner's album, which was published posthumously without an opus number. According to Ludka he also wrote a Waltz in D minor, which is now lost. Controversy about the authenticity of a Polonaise in G flat has now been resolved, and it was published posthumously without an opus number. And all the while Frycek was still working on the Piano Trio, which was giving him problems.

Julian Fontana took a liking to the rewritten Rondo in C for two pianos, and spent a month learning it. He and Frycek went to Buchholtz's to try it out on two pantaleons, to hear how it might sound. 'Might,' qualified Frycek in a letter to Tytus, 'because as the pantaleons were out of tune with each other, the effect did not really come off.'

Frycek spent the Christmas and New Year period in a social round of parties and dinners, including several evenings at Marszałkowska Street with the Pruszaks. As always, he was asked to play, and charades were a feature after dinner. Also there were opera and theatre performances to see, including *Pan Geldhab*, a comedy by Polish playwright Aleksander Fredro.

In the new year the talk turned to the impending coronation of Tsar Nicholas as King of Poland. The equilibrium of Warsaw life was disturbed as dissident whispers began to be heard in Mrs Brzezińska's and on the university campus. Novosiltsov's men appeared and began to maintain a high profile, to ensure that all street level expressions would be favourable to the new King. Despite the restlessness, the Establishment played things straight, and Elsner composed his *Coronation Mass* for the occasion.

Spring arrived, and with it Frycek's nineteenth birthday. A series of concerts had been arranged by Karol Soliwa at the university to air some of his pupils' talents. On April 21 Frycek attended one of these, at which one of the performers was a student at the conservatory, Konstancja Gładkowska, the daughter of the superintendent at the Royal Castle. Three months younger than Frycek, she was one of Soliwa's star pupils. Her ambition lay on the opera stage, and Frycek often played the piano for her. She was young and slim, with blonde hair and blue eyes. Frycek thought her beautiful, but at the concert he fell head over heels in love with her, and even forgave her for singing off-key in places. Over the next weeks Frycek's mind was on little else, and whatever he did, and whatever music he wrote, he did so with her image in mind. His love for her was silent, secret and total.

On May 17 Tsar Nicholas arrived in Warsaw, with the whole Imperial Family. In his wake came dignitaries from all over Europe representing their governments, including Prince Radziwiłł. Grand Duke Constantine put on his best military parades and the Princess of Łowicz arranged the banquets. Novosiltsov's men policed the city ruthlessly, and there was no trouble. The Establishment mounted balls and entertainments, but the enthusiasm for them was muted. There was not the spirit of reconciliation that there had been for Tsar Alexander. Lip service was the only debt paid by Warsaw. There were many concerts, the most popular being those of Paganini.

Niccolò Paganini arrived in Warsaw from Poznań – where he was drawn in action by Princess Eliza Radziwiłł – a couple of days after the Tsar, as part of his gruelling, two-and-a-half year European tour. On May 23 he gave the first of his fourteen scheduled concerts. The following day Tsar Nicholas I was crowned King of Poland at the Cathedral of St John, to the accompaniment of Elsner's *Coronation Mass*. The newly crowned King of Poland left shortly afterwards for St Petersburg.

Paganini, the first virtuoso showman of the violin, was born in Genoa in 1782. His skill at improvisation on the violin inspired awed disbelief, and his performances often caused a hysteria never before seen in a concert hall. The power that he wielded over his listeners earned him the nickname, the Devil's Fiddler, and the more superstitious believed that, Faust-like, he had sold his soul to the devil in exchange for his magical gift. He found it a good marketing ploy not to refute this. His attitude brought him post-humous trouble with the Church, and after his death in Nice in 1840, he was refused burial in consecrated land for five years.

Frycek was fascinated by Paganini's virtuoso technique of improvisation, which he took to the absolute limits of music – and beyond. He achieved sounds from the violin that were not in any text books, and Frycek found in him an artist who was at one with his instrument. Of all Paganini's works Frycek most liked the famous tune, 'Carnival in Venice', a simple enough melody which Paganini skilfully put through every musical configuration. Musicians of every school from Thomas Moore, through jazz to virtuoso tuba have been doing variations on 'Carnival in Venice' ever since. Frycek was among the first, with his *Souvenir de Paganini*, written that summer, and published posthumously without an opus number. Unlike Paganini's version, Frycek's is not a virtuoso work, but a celebration of a pretty tune prettily decorated over an ostinato bass that anticipated the chromatic Berceuse.

Niccolò Paganini gave his last Warsaw concert on July 19, after which the Warsaw Establishment presented him with a gold snuff-box with the inscription: 'Al Cav Niccolò Paganini. Gli ammiratori del suo talento. Varsovia 19 Luglio 1829.' He continued on his way to Wrocław. After his departure Frycek, inspired by the notion of technical excellence, embarked on a set of what he initially called Exercises, each dealing with a separate technical skill. Gradually he built up the set over the next three years.

As the summer progressed Frycek began to take stock of his life, and his thoughts turned to his future. In ten short years he had grown from the composer of the innocent Polonaise in G minor to the composer of the immortal nineteenth-century pianistic classics, the 'Là ci darem la mano' Variations and the *Krakowiak*. He had now outgrown Elsner and Warsaw. The Polish capital had a very lively and thriving music scene, thanks to Elsner and Kurpiński, but it was still a provincial city by pan-European standards. Frycek had experienced Berlin, and now he heard the call of distant Paris, the Elysium of Milan and, above all, the city of Mozart and Beethoven – Vienna. The obvious course was to follow the example of Tomasz Nidecki, and apply to Count Stanisław Grabowski, the Minister for Public Instruction, for a grant to continue his studies in Vienna. Nicolas applied on Frycek's behalf. The reply came on June 20: the application had been turned down.

The Chopins were thunderstruck. Grabowski had pressed for an acceptance, but his recommendations had been blocked by the Minister of the Interior, Count Tadeusz Mostowski. Despite the diamond ring given to Frycek by Tsar Alexander, despite his dedication of a set of dances to the Tsarina Mother Maria Feodorovna, despite the visits to Grand Duke Constantine, and despite his reputation in Warsaw and at the conservatory, Count Mostowski on May 19 wrote an internal memorandum 're the application... that public funds should not be wasted [crossed out] assigned [substituted] for the encouragement of this type of artist'.

It was decided that Frycek should go to Vienna anyway. The previous year he went to Berlin for the ride, but this time he would go with one aim in mind: to establish himself as an international artist.

Elsner's final report was more committed than the previous two: 'Szopen Friderik (special ability, musical genius etc).' Whether Elsner's final comment was true could only be tested on the concert platforms of Europe.

On Wednesday, July 22, Frycek and four travelling companions presented themselves at the Post Office where the Kraków diligence was waiting to take them on the first leg of the journey: Romuald Hube, professor of Polish history at the university, at twenty-six the oldest and Nicolas presumed the most responsible, was asked to keep an eye on the party. The others were old school friends Ignacy Maciejowski, now classics master at the Lyceum, Marceli Celiński and Alfons Brandt.

Diligences travelled throughout the day and night, and the passengers slept as best they could 'on the hoof'. The length and timing of a journey was often a lottery subject to any one of a number of factors: a broken wheel meant a long delay. The stages were stops for rests and meals and, above all, to change horses, on average, every forty kilometres. Staging posts had stables, rooms for hire, food and refreshments. The facilities ranged from comfortable to squalid. Some halts were longer than others, depending on the availability of fresh horses. At longer stops, regardless of the time of day or night, travellers took a room for a few hours to catch up with some sleep. Often strangers asked travellers where they were going. The wise traveller would lie, knowing that the stranger could be a robber planning the best spot for an ambush. Armed robbery by highwaymen was a constant worry on the post roads. The previous year Frycek's friend, Gąsiorowski, was robbed. 'Gąsie has been in Kraków,' wrote Frycek, 'and had a lot to say about it. He told me most pathetically of how he was robbed on the journey.'

The possibility of the postilion being struck by lightning was not to be dismissed. In the middle of a flat plain their exposed position, riding on one of the near horses, was as attractive to lightning as a solitary figure on a golf course today. Many drivers and their postilions, who worked in pairs, only covered certain sections of the route, and their availability could be as scarce as that of horses.

Frycek and his friends arrived in Kraków two days later. The post road only partially followed today's trunk roads. The first stage out of Warsaw was today's E77 to Raszyn and Grójec. The next section bore south-west across country to Nowe Miasto, Drzewica, crossed Route 44 at Opoczno to Końskie, across Route 74 to Radoszyce and Małogoszcz until it rejoined today's Route 7 at Jędrzejów. After that it corresponded to today's Route 7 through Włodzisław, Miechów and finally through the Floriańska Gate into the city of Kraków.

The party spent a few short days sightseeing in and around Poland's ancient capital on the north bank of the River Vistula. After the third partition in 1795 Kraków was annexed by Austria. Napoleon restored it to the Duchy of Warsaw in 1809. After the defeat of Napoleon in 1812 it was occupied by Russia, and at the Congress of Vienna in 1815 the city and its surrounds were established as the Republic of Kraków.

The historic city that Frycek visited was largely the same as it is today: there was the Wavel, the ancient complex on the hill overlooking the river, incorporating the Royal Castle and the cathedral; during Frycek's visit it housed the military barracks of the Austrian army of 'protection'; there were the tombs of Prince Józef Poniatowski, and Tadeusz Kościuszko, to whom a three-hundred-foot-high mound, made from the soil of his battle sites, had just been completed. A French commentator said of this memorial: 'What eloquence, a nation that cannot express itself through words and books, only through mountains.'

Frycek saw the spacious Market Square with the Sukiennice (Cloth Hall) in the centre, the whole dominated by the unidentical twin spires of the Church of St Mary. From the taller of these a bugler has been sounding the hour, on the hour, every hour, day and night, once each to the four points of the compass, for the past six hundred years in commemoration of a bugler boy who had warned the inhabitants of the city during the night of an attack from Tartar hordes. The boy was killed by an arrow in mid-call. The call, known as the *hejnał*, has been aborted at that place ever since. The *hejnał* continues to this day, the only break through the centuries having been during the Nazi occupation.

To the south of Kraków is the world's oldest and biggest salt mine at Wieliczka, which goes back to the eleventh century. Today, as it was in Chopin's time, it is an underground wonderland with nine levels of rooms, passages and pit faces reaching a depth of three hundred and twenty-seven metres and incorporating three hundred kilometres of tunnels stretched over an area some ten kilometres wide. Among the almost mythological architectural features is a sanatorium – the salty atmosphere has health-giving properties, and Blessed Kinga's Chapel. Everywhere there are figures and statues, mostly of religious themes, all carved out of salt. Frycek and his group hired a coach, crossed the River Vistula into the Austrian Empire, and continued for fifteen kilometres along the road to Wieliczka.

The mine's capacity is now limited due to flooding and subsidence, and there is danger of parts of it collapsing. It can still be visited, and concerts take place in Blessed Kinga's Chapel because of the acoustics of the solid salt; the museum still has Chopin's signature.

To the north-west of Kraków is the valley of the little River Prądnik, a tributary of the Vistula. For centuries this beautiful valley has been the retreat of artists and kings. The valley is narrow, flat and green, and is enclosed by low but very craggy hills covered in forest. At the eastern end, perched on one of these crags, lie the ruins of one of Poland's most imposing castles dating from the fourteenth century: Ojców. From its spectacular perch it was visible to travellers from afar, its heavy stone structure and squat, pointed tower at one with the rough crags into which it was built. By 1829 it had lost the magnificence it once enjoyed when King Stanisław August visited it just before he was deposed. Although it had already begun its descent into ruin, the castle and its environs, including the Łokietka Grotto and the other castle at Pieskowa Skała ('Doggy Crag') never ceased to be an attraction, and Frycek and his friends decided to pay it a visit.

On Sunday, 26 July, the group hired a peasant and his cart to take them to Ojców, intending to stay the night at Mr Indyk's house in the village of Pieskowa Skała. Children's writer Klementyna Tańska had stayed there, and had written Ojców into one of her books. They visited the castle, but to get to Mr Indyk's they had to cross the rocky and swiftly flowing River Prądnik, so the peasant drove along the bank, looking for a crossing place. He got lost and the riverside became a steep rocky bank. For a while the cart lurched about without making any progress; the sun had set behind the crags, and it was getting dark. The unscheduled tour came to an ignominious end when the driver lost control and the cart ended up in the middle of the river.

By this time it was already nine o'clock, and dark. The five friends blundered back through the babbling waters on to the bank, their feet soaking, feeling tired, wet, cold and miserable. Fortunately, they met two locals who undertook to guide them to Mr Indyk's house, about two and a half miles away, crossing the river by stepping across a series of logs.

It was very late when the party reached Mr Indyk's, but he still welcomed them warmly and gave them a little guest room in an adjoining hut under the cliff. 'Izabela,' wrote Frycek, explaining the incident, 'this is where Miss Tańska slept.' The five undressed and dried their clothes over the roaring fire that Mrs Indykowa made up, with five beds on the floor. Frycek noticed a cupboard full of Kraków-style woolly hats, and bought one for a *złoty*. He then cut it in two, took off his boots, dried his feet and wrapped them in the two halves of the woolly hat, and tied them up with string for warmth. Soon everyone was happy, and the funny side of the affair was appreciated over a jug of wine.

The following morning the party returned to Kraków.

The Ojców region now is the Ojcowski National Park, and a popular tourist centre. The castle is a ruin, with beautiful views. Mr Indyk's house has burnt down and been rebuilt several times. Today the 'Chopin' villa is a small café and shop on the hillside at Pieskowa Skała.

Kraków was halfway from Warsaw to Vienna, and the time came to continue the journey. The post road followed today's trunk roads, with post stages at Lanckorona, Wadowice, Kęty, Bielsko-Biała, Skoczów and today's border with the Czech Republic at Cieszyn/Český Těšin. The route through Moravia passed Frýdek-Místek, Příbor, Nový Jičin, Lipník, Olomouc, Prostějov, Vyškov, Rousínov, Brno, Pohořelice and Mikulov. Today's Czech-Austrian frontier is between Mikulov and Drasenhofen. The final stages were at Poysdorf and Wolkersdorf.

In the approaches to Vienna the travellers had their first taste of Austrian bureaucracy. Starting with a vigorous customs and passport inspection at the gates of the city, there were further barriers all along the way, where questions had to be answered and endless forms filled in, stating age, religion, marital status and object of journey. Written proof of financial solvency had to be produced under pain of refusal of entry. Lengthy applications for a permit to stay in Vienna were filled in with orders to present them to various government officials in the city within twenty-four hours. Prospective visitors to Vienna showed dissent, impatience or sarcastic humour at their peril. The passengers from Kraków on July 31 survived these tribulations, and Frycek was high with excitement to be in the musical capital of the world.

The music traveller Edward Holmes was there the previous year. 'Vienna is a small city, thickly inhabited,' he wrote.

Its walls enclose more men and buildings than can be found in the same space as any other capital I have visited. The streets are so narrow that the eye of the passenger cannot take in the structure of the houses, and the only places where a view of the elegance of the buildings may be enjoyed are in the squares. The Graben, a broad street in the heart of Vienna, is the pleasantest part of it for a lounge, on account of the splendours of the shops, particularly those of jewellery and ladies shawls, dresses, &c, in which it is extremely brilliant. Most of the passages leading to the ramparts (which latter form the evening promenade) are not very agreeable, especially those leading from the narrower streets, as their detestable stench is continually reminding an Englishman of the peculiarity of his conformation, a nose that discriminates. There is a want of trees about Vienna.

Frycek's first visit was to Tobias Haslinger, Vienna's leading music publisher. His publishing house was called 'Odeon', and the shop, in the Graben, was a meeting place of musicians and academics, who came to browse and gossip among the neatly set out shelves of books and music beneath busts of Beethoven, Haydn, Mozart and Gluck. A chandelier hung from the arched ceiling, and the floor was of patterned marble.

Frycek had a letter of introduction from Elsner. He had sent Haslinger his Piano Sonata and the 'Là ci darem la mano' Variations. Haslinger welcomed Frycek to his shop, and expressed a particular admiration for the Variations. He suggested that Frycek should give a concert to coincide with their publication the following week. Frycek agreed, but did not want to rush things; he did not have the availability of a piano, nor had he played for a fortnight. Two of Vienna's leading piano manufacturers offered to send an instrument to Frycek's lodgings, and to provide one for his concert.

Andreas Stein, the son of Johann Stein of Augsburg, Mozart's friend and favourite clavier maker, had inherited his father's business, and moved to Vienna. The other was Konrad Graff. As in Warsaw, piano manufacturers were looking to lend their instruments to performers. Frycek was recommended by newspaper editor and music writer J.D. Blahetka, whom Frycek met at Haslinger's shop. He met Blahetka's eighteen-year-old daughter, Leopoldine, and wrote that she was 'young, pretty and played the piano'. She was a good pianist who had been taught by Czerny, Moscheles and Kalkbrenner. Blahetka introduced Frycek to the Austrian Chamberlain, Adolf Hussarzewski, a Pole and a music lover who kept an open house for musicians. Frycek, seeing that his 'Là ci darem la mano' Variations would be his passport to success, played them at Hussarzewski's to great acclaim. 'They are extremely pleased with my Variations,' he wrote.

Frycek met sixty-six-year-old Adalbert Gyrowetz, whose Piano Concerto in E minor he had played when he was eight, and Wilhelm Würfel, who used to be professor of harmony and piano at the Warsaw University, and had been for some time a director of the Kärntnertor Theatre. He had known Frycek well as a boy, had taught him organ, and now took him under his wing. His colleague and co-director at the theatre was Count Wenzel Gallenberg, a composer of ballet music, and famously tight with money. On Saturday, August 8, he offered Frycek the chance to make a name for himself by giving a concert at the Kärntnertor Theater – a euphemism for not having to pay him. Seeing his opportunity he accepted Count Gallenberg's proposal, telling himself that fees would come once he was established. Würfel took charge of arrangements, and the concert, a typical mix of orchestral, piano and vocal music, was scheduled for Tuesday, August 11 – three days later. Frycek was to perform the *Krakowiak* and the 'Là ci darem la mano' Variations. There was just the question of the piano. Given the choice of a Stein or a Graff, Frycek opted for the latter, 'but,' he wrote, 'I'm afraid Stein might be offended, but I'll thank him warmly for his kindness'.

At the rehearsal Frycek brought out his orchestral parts for the Variations, which were distributed to the musicians; and that is when the problems began. Many of the parts were either illegible, or wrong. Frycek, who was nervous enough anyway, had to run the gauntlet of an impatient orchestra while he corrected, adjusted or crossed out and rewrote. Fortunately Frycek's former colleague at the conservatory, Tomasz Nidecki, was at hand. He was living and working in Vienna as a result, ironically, of a grant from Count Mostowski's fund. His basic skill at orchestration, the fruits of paying close attention to Elsner, came into play, and eventually the Variations were sorted out.

As for the *Krakowiak*, with its more sophisticated scoring, Tomasz and Frycek became so bogged down that they decided to scrap it. Frycek's first rehearsal for his first concert in the city of Mozart and Beethoven was an embarrassing experience, and he was all for crying off. It was only the encouragement of Tomasz, Gallenberg and Würfel, that kept him going. In place of the *Krakowiak*, it was suggested he should do what he did best – improvise. Frycek chose two themes, the first from Boieldieu's opera *La Dame blanche*, which he had seen the previous day, and whose charming melodies were spinning round in his head. The second, a drinking song entitled 'Chmiel', was something ethnically Polish for the Viennese. Tomasz took the *Krakowiak* to do some badly needed editing.

At seven o'clock on the evening of Tuesday, August 11, the Music Academy's Concert at the Kärntnertor Theatre opened with the Overture to Beethoven's *Prometheus*. The orchestra was conducted by Franz Lachner. The hall was not very full, but among the audience were Frycek's friends, with instructions to gather audience feedback. Romuald Hube, Marceli Celiński, Ignacy Maciejowski and Alfons Brandt were there, as was virtuoso pianist and composer Josef Mayseder, whom Frycek had heard in concert shortly after his arrival in Vienna, and Tomasz. Waiting in the wings, shaking with fear, Frycek was taken in hand by the stage manager, Count Demar. 'He encouraged and reassured me so much before I went on stage,' he wrote, 'and kept my thoughts off it so much that I was not as nervous.'

The Overture was followed by a change in the advertised programme: the second item was the *Variations brillantes* on a theme of Mozart, composed and played by Herr Friedrich Chopin. Frycek, to his amazement, was wildly applauded as soon as he appeared. He continued to be applauded after every variation 'so loudly that I couldn't hear the orchestra's tutti'. When he had finished, to his surprise he was called back again to take another bow; the modern concept of a curtain call was beyond Frycek's experience. The next item consisted of operatic arias from Rossini's *Bianca e Faliero*, sung by Charlotte Veltheim of the Dresden Opera.

Then came Frycek's Free Fantasy on *La Dame blanche* and 'Chmiel'. 'This didn't go quite as well,' he wrote. Improvisation is a lottery. An artist on form can come up with a brilliant instant – and ephemeral – masterpiece of music when there is no one present; when the muse is absent, the improvisation can be unimaginative and pedestrian, even in the heady atmosphere of an admiring audience. Inspiration does not always come into it, and the muses will not be summoned at will. Although Frycek may not have felt that his improvisation was all that good, the audience would have been impressed anyway because of the nature, rather than quality, of the music. He received more rapturous applause, and again, was called back for a second bow. But by that time, he was getting used to it. 'That was easier to do, because the Germans appreciate that sort of thing.' The concert ended with a Rondo and Variations with Chorus from Baccaj's *Pietro il Grande*, sung again by Charlotte Veltheim.

The feedback from the hall was complimentary, and only Romuald Hube reported overhearing two ladies saying that 'it is a pity the young man has so little dress sense'. After the concert he was congratulated by Count Dietrichstein, according to Frycek 'a personage in touch with the Emperor'. They talked for a long time, the Count urging Frycek to stay in Vienna. His interest may have been lateral; his seventeen-year-old illegitimate son was also a budding virtuoso pianist, and the Count may have been sizing up the competition. The boy's name was Sigismund Thalberg.

The reviews were complimentary, although there was a general feeling that he played too quietly. Frycek dismissed this criticism: 'I expected to find this comment in the paper, especially as the editor's [Blahetka's] daughter [Leopoldine] thumps frightfully.'

Frycek had taken on the Viennese music scene. He had met and impressed some very influential people, been criticized by the orchestra, humiliated for his lack of expertise in scoring, and become very depressed about it; he was accused of not hitting the piano hard enough, and wildly applauded by a public which, according to Holmes, 'with good ears, tolerated the worst of music'. Fryderyk Chopin's debut in the city of Mozart and Beethoven had been an excellent career move. 'Today,' he wrote the day after the concert, 'I am wiser and more experienced by about four years.'

Würfel thought the concert worth repeating, so a second date was set for the following Tuesday, August 18. Again Frycek agreed to play for free on account of 'the Count's [Gallenberg's] emaciated purse'. Again he saw self-promotion as more important than financial remuneration. Tomasz had taken the *Krakowiak* in hand, and had corrected Frycek's orchestration, so his original programme was reinstated. Over the next week Frycek rubbed shoulders with Vienna's big names in music: composer and conductor Konradin Kreuzer, violinist and string quartet leader Ignaz Schuppanzingh, and Beethoven's editor Ignaz von Seyfried. He was recognized in the street and congratulated. He played duets with both Czerny and the heavy-handed but attractive Leopoldine Blahetka, whom he even persuaded to lighten her touch. Frycek took tea with the wife and daughter of Count Lichnowski, patron of music and once friend of both Mozart and Beethoven. Lichnowski offered Frycek the use of his piano – which Beethoven used to play and work at – in place of the Graff, which he said would increase the volume. Frycek politely declined, saying that the Graff suited his delicate style.

The evening of the second concert came. Again the orchestra was conducted by Franz Lachner. Frycek's reputation had preceded him, and the Kärntnertor Theatre was full. The opening Overture was to Peter Lindpaintner's opera, *Bergkönig*. Then came the *Krakowiak*. Frycek's entrance was greeted by three cheers 'going crescendo'. At the end the applause was even greater than before, and caused no less a personage than the elderly Adalbert Gyrowetz to stagger to his feet and cry 'Bravo'. Then came the Polonaise for violin by Josef Mayseder, played by Josef Khayl, which was followed by Frycek's 'Là ci darem la mano' Variations, at which the applause was as enthusiastic as before. The concert finished with a ballet.

Afterwards the congratulations poured forth like a tidal wave, not least from stage manager Count Demar and the orchestra, who gave Frycek a standing ovation. Haslinger, whose promise to publish the Variations within a week had actually been so much hot air, now made up his mind to publish them soon, but they only came out a year later, as Frycek's Op. 2. Editor Blahetka's enthusiasm overcame his tact when he gushed to Frycek, 'How did you manage to learn all that in Warsaw?' 'Under Żywny and Elsner,' replied Frycek through clenched teeth, 'any ass could learn.'

The following evening at nine, Frycek left Vienna for Prague. The newspapers were very slow in writing up the concerts. On 18 November the *German Musical Journal* wrote of 'a master of the first rank, with his exquisite delicacy of touch, indescribable finger dexterity, and the deep feeling shown by his command of shading. His interpretations and his compositions both bear the stamp of genius, and reveal a virtuoso liberally endowed by nature, who appears on the horizon like a most brilliant meteor.'

The *Vienna Theatre News* wrote that 'his touch, although neat and sure, had little brilliance comparable with the virtuosos who wish to conquer with their first few bars, but his playing was like conversing amongst clever people'.

Despite his Viennese success, Frycek realized that now, with his delicate touch and subtle nuances, he would be competing with a very different school of piano playing.

TEN

Chopin's Bohemia and Saxony

The post road to Prague evolved into today's E49, with stages at Korneuburg, Maissau, Horn, Gmünd, Veselí, in today's Czech Republic, historic Tábor, overlooking a gorge over the River Lužnice, Miličín, Votice, Benešov, Jesenice (by the northern route) and Prague. Frycek, with six letters of introduction and a signed copy of Leopoldine Blahetka's compositions tucked in his luggage, went by *eilwagen*, a smaller and faster post-chaise than the diligence. With him were three of his four companions, Ignacy, Marceli and Alfons. Romuald Hube had left them to go to Italy. On the trip they were joined by a young German merchant from Gdańsk who knew the Pruszaks and the Sierakowskis of Waplewo.

The *eilwagen* reached Prague at midday on Friday, August 21. Frycek wondered what he would find in Mozart's favourite city, where *Don Giovanni* was first performed forty years before. Edward Holmes was in Prague the previous summer. 'The situation which this city maintained fifty years since in the superiority of its taste over the rest of Germany,' he wrote, 'is now usurped by Berlin; not that the Bohemians love the art less than formerly, or that they have imbibed the flippant, commonplace notions of musical beauty which prevail in Vienna, but that their city is gone out of fashion.'

Bohemia was a kingdom within the Austrian Empire as Poland was in the Russian Empire. The language of the Establishment was German. Holmes referred to Bohemia as Germany, that being the generic term for German-speaking Europe at the time. Emperor Franz, who was King of Bohemia, paid some lip service to the agreements at the Congress of Vienna, and pursued a limited policy of ethnic emancipation, notably of Jews. The slavonic Czech language, spoken by the peasants, had started to gain ground among the intelligentsia.

The party put up at 'U Modré Hvězdy' (The Blue Star) in Celetná Street, off the Staroměstké Námesti (Old Town Square), today at No. 24. On arrival the companions sat down to a table d'hôte lunch, washed down with what Holmes described as 'a sort of beer, which to drink iced in the summertime might make the gods themselves turn pale with envy'. Having lunched well, the group went out on the town, intending to call on Václav Hanka, for whom Ignacy had a letter of introduction from Hube. Hanka was an eminent Czech scholar, philosopher, and custodian of the Prague National Museum, who knew Fryderyk Skarbek. He was an ardent slavophile and anyone from Poland involved in arts or sciences was welcome at his museum. Coming out of the hotel the companions turned left and made their way past the astronomical clock in the Staroměstké Námesti, through the narrow streets of the Old Town to the Klementinum, across the Charles Bridge over the River Vltava, then up the steep streets and stone steps of the Hradčany, or Castle Hill. They came to the Cathedral of St Vitus where, thirty-eight years previously, the people of Prague, who had come to pay their final homage to Mozart, spilled out on to the square before it and listened as Rosetti's *Requiem* wafted from the packed cathedral.

'On the whole the city, as seen from Castle Hill, is beautiful,' wrote Frycek, 'It is extensive, ancient, and was once rich.' Holmes elaborated further:

Prague has the appearance of decayed magnificence; the narrow streets of the old town look somewhat gloomy in the superb architecture of mansions, once the residence of proud Bohemian nobles. . . . Visitors of the cathedral, after toiling up the weary and steep ascent to it stand for a few minutes to take breath, and gaze round them at the beautiful panorama of the city and its environs.

'We spent so much time in the cathedral that we missed Hanka,' wrote Frycek.

Having spent Friday afternoon sightseeing, Saturday was spent delivering the letters of introduction, starting with Ignacy's visit to Hanka. The curator received them with arms characteristically outstretched, especially to Frycek as the godson of Fryderyk Skarbek. After much talk about how things were in Poland – Hanka was insatiable for such news – he brought out his album, in which various personages, including Fryderyk Skarbek, had signed their names alongside some words of wit or wisdom. Ignacy wrote a four-line stanza in the rhythm of a mazurka, to which Frycek composed a few suitable bars, in G, and they entered their contribution as a joint effort. Hanka then took them on a tour of Prague, including another visit to the cathedral to see the silver statue of St John Nepomuk, and the amethyst-studded St Wenceslas chapel.

Frycek went to the National Theatre to present his letters of introduction to Director Stiepanek and to his kapellmeister, violinist Friedrich Wilhelm Pixis, brother to the better-known pianist and composer Johann Peter Pixis. They were both interested in what the letters had to say, as Würfel had pointed out that opportunity was more important than a fee to the talented young pianist; they suggested that Frycek should give a concert in Prague. Frycek declined: he was leaving Prague the next day, and he had heard about the gauntlet of hostile critics that Paganini had been forced to run during his visit to Prague the previous autumn, and had no desire to risk having his Vienna successes reduced to nothing.

August Klengel, the Dresden-based pianist and composer, was in Prague at that time, *en route* for Italy. Würfel had given Frycek a letter of introduction to him in Dresden, but now, having met him by chance on the stairs of the National Theatre with Pixis and Stiepanek, the opportunity arose for them to get together in Prague instead. So they all went to Pixis's house for a musical soirée. Frycek was not asked to play, but was forced, with a polite smile on his face, to sit through two hours of Klengel playing all his canons and fugues, like Bach's before him, two in every key, forty-eight in all. 'He plays well,' wrote Frycek, 'but I'd have preferred him to play better (hush! hush!).'

Holmes heard Klengel playing his 'Forty-eight' in Dresden the previous year. 'I was fortunate enough to hear Mr Klengel play a great part of his collection and was delighted with the skill he exhibited in their execution, for where great contrivance is shown in the writing, the difficulty of performance is infinitely enhanced. . . . Genius reigns here.'

Klengel took Frycek aside and they chatted for two further hours, mostly about music and travel – especially Italy, where Klengel was going. As Frycek was going on to Dresden, Klengel gave him a run down on the city, and advised him where to go and whom to see, told him about its tradition of Italian opera, and the challenge to it from the new German Romanticism, specifically Weber's, whose *Der Freischütz* Frycek knew well and loved. Klengel wrote Frycek a letter of introduction to Francesco Morlacchi, composer and director of Dresden's National Orchestra, in which he mentioned his pupil, Antonina Pechwell, who, according to Klengel, was the best pianist in Dresden. By the end of their chat, Klengel rose in Frycek's estimation. 'He was very amiable,' he wrote. 'It is an excellent contact, and of more use than poor old Czerny (hush!).'

It was a hectic two days for Frycek, but without anything concrete to show for it, apart from the chance to do a whirlwind tour of Bohemia's capital. He blamed this frenetic activity for the fact that, back at the hotel, he blundered half-clothed into the wrong bedroom, to be confronted by a grinning German who bade him a surprised but cheery 'Guten morgen'. A very embarrassed Frycek burbled out an apology and fled, eventually finding his own room. 'They all look the same to me,' he complained afterwards.

At noon on Sunday, August 23, the party left Prague for the spa resort of Teplitz (Teplice), and reached their destination that same evening. The next morning, Frycek looked up the spa's guest list, on the off-chance of finding some interesting names. He found several fellow Poles, including Old Pruszak. So he called on him, and learned that the rest of the family were soon due in Dresden. Frycek promised to call on them when he got there. Also on the list was Ludwik Lempicki, whom he knew from Warsaw, a judge, senator and a landowner with estates near Płock. Frycek called on him, and Lempicki arranged to take him to dinner that evening at Prince Clary's castle.

Prince Clary, who had married the sister of Karel Chotek, the Viceroy of Bohemia, virtually owned Teplitz. The Clarys were a friendly and hospitable family, and Lempicki had no qualms about asking to bring a visiting young Polish pianist to dinner, and the Prince and Princess gladly extended the invitation.

Lempicki spent the day showing Frycek round Teplitz, and took him on an excursion to nearby Dux (Duchcov) to see Wallenstein's castle. Albrecht von Wallenstein had been a legendary soldier and veteran of the Thirty Years War, and was murdered in 1634. 'There is a fragment of the great soldier's skull,' wrote Frycek, 'and the halberd with which he was killed, and many other relics.' It was at this castle that, in 1787, Casanova took time off from cataloguing Count Waldstein's library to write his *Memoirs* and to give Mozart the benefit of his advice in matters of love while the latter was writing *Don Giovanni* in Prague.

That evening Frycek dressed for dinner, donned his white gloves, and together with Lempicki, drove to the Clarys' castle. It was a small but select gathering. Frycek noted an Austrian prince, a general, an English sea-captain, some fashionable-looking young men whom he took to be princes too, some princesses and a Saxon general by the name of Leiser, who was covered in medals and sported a scar on his face. After dinner Frycek was asked if he would improvise. Seeing that the castle boasted an excellent Graff, he agreed, sat down and asked the company to give him a theme. 'Immediately among the female company that was sitting round a big table, lace-making, knitting and embroidering,' wrote Frycek, 'came cries of "*un thème, un thème!*"' By general consent a theme from Rossini's *Moses in Egypt* was proposed, and Frycek, who had never seen the opera but knew arias from it, improvised. His fantasia went off so well that after he had finished General Leiser had a long talk with him, and, learning that he was bound for Dresden, wrote a glowing letter of introduction to Baron von Friesen, the Master of Ceremonies to King Anton of Saxony, asking him to be helpful to one of the finest pianists he had ever heard, and to introduce him to the Saxon capital's most prominent musicians.

Frycek was called upon to play four times, while the 'princesses' gathered round and tried to persuade him to stay in Teplitz, and come to dinner the next day. Lempicki was in favour of the idea, and even offered to take Frycek back to Warsaw with him at a later date. But Frycek, although flattered and tempted, was loath to abandon his travelling companions, and declined.

The following morning, Tuesday, August 25, at 5 o'clock, having hired a hackney coach from some peasants for two thalers, the party set off for Dresden. The morning was still young when they reached the border at Zinnwald, at the same place where it is today. As Frycek and his companions crossed the Erzgebirge Range into the beautiful, mountainous land, they reflected on Saxony's close ties with Poland. For three hundred years Saxony had been an Electorate, and during the eighteenth century two of Saxony's Electors were also elected Kings of Poland: Friedrich Augustus I (II of Poland) and Friedrich Augustus II (III of Poland). The latter's grandson, Friedrich Augustus III was offered Poland's throne in 1791, but declined. In 1806 he assumed the title of King of Saxony, joined Napoleon's Confederation of the Rhine, and the following year was rewarded with the Grand Duchy of Warsaw. At the Battle of Leipzig his troops deserted Napoleon in droves, and Friedrich Augustus was taken prisoner. After the Congress of Vienna he was restored to a depleted Saxony, which he ruled until his death two years before Frycek's arrival in his capital after sixty-six years at Saxony's helm. He was succeeded by his brother Anton. A legacy of the Polish connection was a sizeable Polish community in Dresden.

The hackney coach reached the Saxon capital at four o'clock that afternoon.

In Dresden, with its 'wide streets, elegant buildings and a good store of pretty girls', Holmes found 'a more polished society, a greater attention to the established formalities and etiquette of genteel intercourse, than in other cities of Germany'. Dresden competed with Prague to be Europe's most beautiful Baroque city. Frycek decided not to waste time, and the next morning, armed with his letters of introduction, he set off first thing to track down Baron von Friesen and Francesco Morlacchi. The latter was unavailable, but the Baron received Frycek courteously and promised to do what he could for him despite his short stay; but that was the sum total of the visit. 'Plenty of bows and ceremonies,' wrote Frycek. Then he went out on the town. 'I have seen the art gallery, an exhibition of local produce,' he wrote, 'and the Great Garden.' He also visited the Grüne Gewolbe in Dresden Castle, where the Crown Jewels were kept.

Holmes enjoyed driving to the Great Garden

through pleasant avenues of trees and country houses; and the agreeableness of the drive was not lessened by seeing groups of handsome girls seated in the green trellised bowers of their gardens, bareheaded, reading or working together. . . . This park . . . is a most charming place. The trees, instead of being younger than one's self, as they appear in Vienna, look ancestral and venerable. Great cheerfulness results from this open-air existence in Germany; life runs good to the last here.

His delight was to take coffee seated under the fine old arm of a tree, looking upon the evening sun or the golden clouds about it, surrounded by a throng of happy faces, listening to the music emanating from a pavilion, and thinking about Weber, who used to go the Great Garden to meet his friends, had written *Der Freischütz* in Dresden, and who had died in London three years previously.

While in Dresden a visit to 'Saxon Switzerland', to the southeast of the city, was essential, and Frycek went with his companions to this beautiful region of Saxony.

On Friday, August 28, there was a special performance of Goethe's *Faust* to commemorate the author's eightieth birthday. It seemed as if the whole of Dresden intended to be there, and Frycek started queueing at half-past four; the play lasted from six till eleven, with extracts from Spohr's opera of the same name played between the acts. Frycek recognized the famous actor Karl Devrient from Berlin, in the title role. 'It's a terrible fantasy,' wrote Frycek, 'but a great one.'

Dresden's Italian opera was housed at the 'Linkesches Bad'. Holmes enjoyed a performance of Rossini's *Italian Girl in Algiers*, and found it good. 'The company is not the worse for the admission of some German singers to make up a deficiency in number; among these is a soprano, Mademoiselle Veltheim. . . .' Charlotte Veltheim had shared the bill in both Frycek's Vienna concerts.

Klengel had advised Frycek to go and see Meyerbeer's *Crociato in Egitto* as an example of Dresden's Italian opera on the evening of Saturday, August 29, but his intended visit was thwarted because the diligence for Wrocław, the companions' next port of call, was due to leave that day. He was disappointed, even though he had already seen the opera in Vienna. That morning Frycek was collected ('He comes to me, not I to him. Ha! ha! ha!') by Francesco Morlacchi, and together they went to see and hear Klengel's pupil, Antonina Pechwell. Frycek enjoyed her performance: 'She plays well.'

Having said his goodbyes to Francesco Morlacchi and Antonina Pechwell, Frycek joined his companions at the post stage. There he came across Marianna Pruszak, with Kostuś and Olesia, who had just arrived from Antonin, where they had been spending a few days. Also present at the Radziwiłłs' hunting lodge, Frycek was happy to learn, were his parents with Ludka and Izabela, as well as Fryderyk Skarbek. Frycek, in turn, was able to report on Old Pruszak in Teplitz. The meeting was so warm and friendly, and there was so much to talk about, that Frycek was tempted to stay longer, as the Pruszaks intended to stay in Dresden until Christmas. But he had his companions to think of, so he said a fond goodbye, and the diligence set off out of Dresden and headed eastwards towards the Prussian border.

Modern through roads do not correspond to the post road along with Frycek and his companions travelled. The post road from Dresden passed through Bautzen and Weissenberg, the last stage in Saxony, with the frontier just beyond. The Prussian stages were at Gorlitz (today's frontier with Poland – Zgorzelec) Lubań, Lwówek Śląśki, Złotoryja, Legnica, Kawice, Środa Śląska, and Wrocław.

The quartet spent a couple of days in Wrocław. At Kalisz Ignacy, Marceli and Alfons went on to Warsaw, while Frycek stopped over, as usual, with Dr Adam Helbich, who had been invited to the wedding of Melania Bronikowska to Wiktor Kurnatowski. 'Melasia' was, according to Frycek, 'a beautiful child', who lived at the Bronikowski Palace at Żychlin, just to the south of Konin, about sixty kilometres to the north of Kalisz. Konin was on Frycek's homeward route, so he accompanied Dr Helbich to the wedding at Żychlin. They stayed overnight, along with other guests, and joined in the fun with party games. Then Dr Helbich returned to Kalisz, and Frycek continued on his journey home.

The Bronikowski Palace is still there today.

From Wrocław to Warsaw was a familiar route for Frycek, who had travelled that way three years previously. He arrived back in Warsaw – without his hold-all, which he had lost on the way – during the second week of September.

That year the next addition to the Linde household, Wanda, was born.

As summer waned and the trees in the Saxon Gardens turned to gold, Frycek became despondent. He had so many things on his mind, and the one person to whom he could confide his innermost thoughts, Tytus, was three hundred kilometres away at Poturzyn. 'You wouldn't believe how dull I find Warsaw now,' he wrote; 'were it not for the family making things more cheerful, I wouldn't stay. How depressing to have no one to go to in the mornings with whom to share one's griefs and joys; how awful when something weighs on you and there's nowhere to put it down.'

Over the past two years he had been spreading his wings and seeing a little of the world beyond. He had tasted Berlin, Vienna, Prague, Dresden, and now he found Warsaw wanting. Whenever he reflected on his successes in Vienna his heart beat faster, and he dreamed of returning there one day soon. At the end of September Romuald Hube returned from his travels. He and Frycek exchanged tales of their respective adventures since they parted company in Vienna. Hube had been to Trieste, and, passing through Vienna on his way home, had picked up some reviews of Frycek's performances. They were all highly complimentary, which made Frycek hanker after the Austrian capital even more. He wondered about Warsaw's cooling off towards him. Why had he not been invited to take part in the Tsar's Coronation? Why had he been refused a grant to go to Vienna? Why were the Warsaw reports about his Viennese concerts so bland and non-committal? Had the Establishment gone against him for some reason? Lovesick, he thought fondly about Leopoldine Blahetka, but, in a letter to Tytus, he added, 'Unfortunately I have already found my ideal, which I have served faithfully, if silently, for half a year; of which I dream, and to which I tender the adagio of my concerto.'

The ideal was Konstancja Gładkowska, who was now firmly back in Frycek's thoughts and dreams – and only in his thoughts and dreams. The Adagio was the first shoot of his Piano Concerto in F minor. After the success of the 'Là ci darem la mano' Variations and the *Krakowiak*, Frycek felt he was ready to tackle a full-length concerto. He began with the slow movement – ultimately a Larghetto – an extended and lyrical romance, the perfect love music inspired by a young man's silent passion for a beautiful girl. Frycek showed it to Elsner, who liked it and said it was 'new'.

Frycek's Warsaw autumn of 1829 was spent in a deep, Polish melancholy, and he needed to get out. 'If you want to know what I intend to do with myself this winter,' he wrote to Tytus, 'I'm telling you I shall not remain in Warsaw; but where circumstances will take me, I don't know.'

Circumstances first proposed Berlin. The Radziwiłłs invited Frycek to stay with them in the Prussian capital, offering him an apartment in their palace. Frycek considered this but declined on the grounds that to make a name for himself abroad, he preferred Vienna, or Paris. He wanted to maintain friendly relations with the Prince, so he finished the Piano Trio, and inscribed the dedication to him. He continued work on his concerto, and tackled the third movement. When he had finished, he was not satisfied with the first draft, and decided it needed revision before seeking an opinion. In between he managed to work on some more of his technical studies, his 'Exercises en forme'.

He called at Brzezina's music shop every day – in the hope that Haslinger might have published the 'Là ci darem la mano' Variations – and every Friday he went to pianist and teacher Jan Kessler's, where soloists and chamber players gave regular informal concerts. These varied in content, and ranged from Spohr's Octet to a special composition by one Filip, featuring two musicians, Zimmermann and Nowakowski, with chorus. 'Zimmermann', explained Frycek in a letter to Tytus,

plays the flute, but makes a peculiarly funny voice with the help of his cheeks and a hand. It sounds like a cross between a cat and a calf. Nowakowski can make a sound like an out-of-tune whistle, which he does by squeezing his lips flat. It's sheer absurdity, but well done, and very funny. It came after the Beethoven Trio. . . .

Frycek started taking English lessons with an Irishman with a predilection for the bottle by the name of MacCartney. They were a waste of time and money, as Frycek learned no English whatsoever.

Prince Radziwiłł invited Frycek to Antonin. Frycek jumped at the idea, because, having declined Berlin, he still wanted to be on good terms with the Radziwiłłs. It was a chance to get out of Warsaw, which was really getting him down, and he would also visit his godmother at Strzyżewo. The fact that Eliza and Wanda would be there might also have influenced his decision: because he was completely in love with an 'ideal' did not mean that he eschewed all other feminine charms. On October 20 at seven in the evening, with a light heart and his melancholy dissipated, Frycek caught the diligence for Antonin.

Prince Radziwiłł was no longer Governor of Poznań, having been dismissed from his post. The official reason was that he no longer enjoyed the trust of the people of the Duchy, but as he was a Polish titular head of a predominantly German-speaking population, the move was a political expedient to germanicize the region.

Frycek had tremendous respect for Prince Antoni, both as a man and a musician. His *Faust* was regularly performed in Berlin and Poznań, and he brought out his score for Frycek's benefit, and they both sat at the piano and went through it, with some vocal help from the rest of the family – who knew it off by heart. Frycek loved it, and his description in a letter to Tytus shows a capacity for critical appraisal.

I found in it so much ingenuity, even genius, that I would never have expected from a viceroy. In one scene, Mephistopheles tempts Gretschen, singing with his guitar in front of her house, while at the same time choral singing is heard from a church. On stage this contrast would be very effective; on paper you can see the skilfully constructed song, or rather, diabolical counterpoint, against a solemn chorale. He is a whole-hearted Gluckist. Theatre music, for him, paints situations and emotions; therefore his Overture has no finale, it is only an introduction.

Like everyone else who visited Antonin, Frycek signed the visitors' book, and then presented Prince Antoni with the completed Piano Trio in G minor, formally dedicated to him.

As Prince Antoni was a cellist, Frycek wrote a glitzy Polonaise for cello and piano, for him to play with Princess Wanda at the piano. This was because Frycek was asked to give her piano lessons, which he did with enthusiasm. 'I have been giving Princess Wanda lessons,' he wrote. 'She is young, seventeen [actually twenty-one] and pretty; it was really such a joy to guide her little fingers. But joking apart, she has a lot of musical feeling.'

The Polonaise is a fun-filled, macho romp, and contains a number of whimsical cello devices, such as double-stopping and 'turned' runs that Prince Antoni taught to Frycek – as well as some pianistic tricks with which to guide Wanda's little fingers. It was eventually published by Pietro Mechetti of Vienna as the *Introduction and Polonaise Brillante* in C, Op. 3, in 1833.

While Frycek, the Prince and Wanda were making music, twenty-six-year-old Princess Eliza sat apart with pencil and pad, sketching. She had already drawn Frycek two years previously, and now she did so again, while Frycek played. She was particularly fond of the Trio section of his Polonaise in F minor (Op. 71 No. 3), which he had dedicated and sent to Tytus. Eliza was so desperate for this Polonaise, that Frycek had to write to Tytus begging him to send it to Antonin by return post. Both girls were beautiful, and glittering stars often seen at the Royal Court of Berlin, where Princess Eliza had caught the eye of Crown Prince Wilhelm (from 1861 King Wilhelm I of Prussia), and the youngsters became lovers for a while. This Polish-German liaison was considered unsuitable, and the affair was quickly broken up.

A number of Eliza's drawings have survived, including the ones of Frycek.

The Princess Mother, Ludwika, was a warm, comfortable soul, who contributed greatly to the friendly and informal ethos at Antonin. 'She knows that it is not birth that makes a person,' wrote Frycek, 'and her manner is so attractive that it is impossible not to love her.'

Frycek stayed at Antonin, with visits to Strzyżewo, for a week. It had been an idyllic stay, and he was loath to leave, but he was anxious to work on the Piano Concerto. Although he enjoyed the company of the two beautiful girls, deep in his heart he knew they would never replace his 'ideal'. On the way home he stopped at a lively party in Kalisz, and he was back in Warsaw by the end of the month. A few days later came a formal acknowledgement and acceptance by Prince Antoni Radziwiłł of the dedication of the Piano Trio.

Prince Radziwiłł died in 1833, followed the next year by Princess Eliza, aged 31. Princess Wanda married Prince Adam Konstanty Czartoryski, and died in 1845. The family tombs are in the vaults at the Radziwiłł chapel at Antonin.

Frycek continued composing as winter approached. On December 22 he gave a concert at the Resursa (Merchants' Hall) – now the Belgian Embassy, opposite the Zamoyski Palace in Senatorska Street. The programme included Józef Bielawski in an unnamed violin concerto, vocal music from a Mr Copello, accompanied by Frycek, further vocal music by the visiting M. Dorville of the French Theatre, a further solo violin item by Józef Bielawski, and, to conclude, a Fantasy on well-known airs by Frycek. This was not his *Fantasy on Polish Airs*, but an improvisation on other well-known Polish tunes, including 'Miotły' (Brooms), a very popular song at the time, from a now-forgotten opera called 'The Millionth Boy'. The next day the *Warsaw Courier* asked some pertinent questions: 'Is Mr Chopin's talent not the property of his fatherland? Is Poland incapable of assessing his true worth? Mr Chopin's works bear the undisputed mark of genius.'

ELEVEN

The Piano Concertos

At the turning of the year Frycek was engrossed in completing his concerto. The Romantic musical language evolved from Hummel, Moscheles and Weber, but the form was Classical Mozart and Beethoven. The opening orchestral tutti of the first movement introduced a double exposition that built up tension before the piano's entry with a sparkling descending figure that was Frycek's only concession to the fashion of a spectacular opening designed to stun an audience into adulation. The slow movement was an expression of love, a poem to Konstancja, the untouchable girl of Frycek's dreams. For the final movement Frycek combined rondo form and the rhythm of a mazurka. Within these parameters Frycek's piano writing wove a web of virtually continuous flow, delicate even in its forte passages, seemingly improvisatory, in which the seams of classical form were barely noticeable. Frycek toiled hours to make his written music sound like an improvisation. Out of keeping with fashion, he dispensed with a cadenza as irrelevant.

His orchestral writing was essentially a background texture, a plain velvet cushion on which to display his pianistic diamonds. Some counter-melodies occasionally emerged, and there were two highly original string devices: an extended passage of tremolando in the slow movement, and a rhythmic *col legno* pattern, in imitation of the 'chopping' device of folk fiddlers, which gave the third movement mazurka a similar feel.

The effects were Frycek's own idea. They certainly did not come from Elsner. He envisaged musical possibilities that were not in any of the text books, and he was not afraid to experiment with them, even though he was not always confident that they would work. 'Perhaps that's bad,' he explained to Tytus about special effects, 'but why should one be ashamed of bad writing despite knowing better? You learn through your mistakes. Here you can see my tendency to do wrong against my better judgment. If some idea creeps into my head through my eyes, I want to indulge it, even though it may be all wrong.'

Having completed the Concerto he embarked on a campaign to perform it. He knew he would have to be careful; he had the support of family and friends, but the Establishment, to whom 'this newfangled stuff' was anathema, would not be so amenable. The Concerto was definitely 'newfangled', and some of his ideas, such as tremolando strings and *col legno* playing, were ahead of their time. So the water of Establishment opinion would have to be tested. The first performance of the Concerto was planned for Wednesday, March 3; the venue was his own apartment. Karol Kurpiński had agreed to conduct a chamber orchestra in the spacious drawing-room. The performance was a soirée rather than a formal concert.

The rehearsal was arranged for February 7, and friendly commentators were invited. This resulted in an advance report in the *Warsaw Gazette* dated February 12: 'Our virtuoso has written a new Piano Concerto in F minor for which there was a rehearsal last Sunday. Connoisseurs are already praising this new composition, which is full of fresh ideas and will surely be counted among our most beautiful works.'

On the evening of the soirée a small and select audience included the press and Elsner. In the crowded drawing-room Frycek gave the first performance of the Concerto, and followed it with the *Fantasia on Polish Airs*.

The press came up trumps. 'I am no lover of piano concertos,' wrote the *Universal National Daily* the following day:

and it must have been some classicist who first introduced into the concert hall this instrument whose strident tones and feeling depend more on the manufacturer than the player. But here I forgot this enmity, as the creative soul of this young composer took the path of genius. Gradually he aroused our curiosity, then our admiration, then our emotions. I thought

I heard the depth of Beethoven, and the sparkle of Hummel in this music. The Adagio pleased everybody, especially where the whole orchestra played tremolando while he spoke to us in a recitative through different tones.

The day after that came the *Warsaw Courier*'s report: 'Young Chopin surpasses all the pianists who have played here. He is the Paganini of the piano; his compositions are lofty and full of new ideas.'

Reassured with these reports and exhortations Frycek arranged to give his first formal concert at the National Theatre on Tuesday, March 16. Having conquered Vienna, it was only right that he should do the same to his home city. On March 8 the *Warsaw Courier* announced that 'Mr Chopin, so deservedly praised everywhere, whose talent connoisseurs compare to virtuosos of the first rank, will shortly be giving a concert on the piano of his own works at the National Theatre'.

On March 15, the day before the concert, the *Universal National Daily* wrote: 'Mr Chopin, whose incredible talent as a pianist has been well known for several years, and whose abilities as a composer have awakened the admiration of experts, will give a concert tomorrow at the National Theatre, after which he will be going abroad.'

The week leading up to the concert was for Frycek extremely stressful. 'You will not believe the torture I suffer the days before a concert,' he wrote to Tytus. He was well aware of the politics that permeated the music business, especially as he was no longer the beautiful child, or the gilded youth of yester-year. He was an adult international concert pianist, and fair game for every factional-minded critic. He could almost hear the knives being gleefully sharpened, as the pianistic thunderers of the *donner-und-Blitzen* faction prepared for bloody sacrifice. A fiasco would certainly make good copy.

Two days before the concert all tickets were sold out, to the expressed chagrin of Mrs Teresa Wodzińska, who was unable to attend. Frycek's nervous agony lasted right up to the moment he walked out on to the platform after the orchestra had played the opening item, the Overture to Elsner's opera, *Leszek Biały*. He sat at the familiar piano – it was his own – and went through purgatory while Karol Kurpiński conducted the orchestra in the opening tutti. The first movement was greeted with nothing more than polite and uncomprehending applause and Frycek's worst fears surged to the fore. 'The Allegro is accessible only to the few; there were some bravos, but I think only because they were puzzled,' he wrote to Tytus. It was customary at the time for concertos to be split by secondary items between movements, and he was visited by the prospect of a large-scale humiliation as he waited, shaking with fear, in the wings for Goerner, the horn player, to finish his Divertissement.

After that Frycek returned to complete his Concerto. This time the reaction was different. 'The Adagio and Rondo had more effect,' he wrote to Tytus, 'and there were some spontaneous shouts.'

The second half opened with Kurpiński conducting the Overture to his opera *Cecylia Piaseczyńska*, followed by Variations by Ferdinando Paër, sung by Warsaw diva Barbara Majerowa. Frycek closed the concert with his *Fantasia on Polish Airs*. Again, the applause was only polite, and Frycek admitted that 'in my opinion it did not come off'.

The aftermath of the concert was a mixed bag of impressions. Frycek had been pessimistic, but the write-ups, which were numerous and lengthy, were eulogistic, with the one proviso that was to become Frycek's constant bugbear, but ultimately his greatest strength – his soft touch. Kurpiński, who edited *The Musical Weekly*, a small-scale theatrical and operatic subscription magazine, was first off the mark the next day – having optimistically written up his piece before the concert: 'A large audience greeted the compositions and playing of the young artist with loud applause. But the instrument was not suitable for such a large venue.' Elsner commented that his instrument was 'deaf', and that he could not hear the bass properly. Frycek's most enthusiastic critic, Maurycy Mochnacki, who had praised him to the skies, at the end advised 'a little more energy in his playing'.

Everyone agreed that Frycek's music was original and sensitive. 'Harmony is the soul of Mr. Chopin's concertos,' wrote the *Fine Arts Record*, 'and this is his chief occupation; it is to this that he devotes his sensitivities of perception; it is for this that he chooses his own path far from blind imitation; it is for this that he clothes his sensitive and delicate playing in a hue of plaintive melancholy.'

The *Universal National Daily* waxed particularly eloquent: 'Mr Chopin, although still young, has with masculine strength blazed his own trail to the shrine of Euterpe, who bestows the wreath of immortality only on those who dare to approach not in the footsteps of others, but by a path discovered by themselves.'

With Warsaw's press at his feet, Frycek agreed to a second concert, also at the National Theatre, on the following Monday, March 22, with the advice that a beefier piano would stand him in even better stead. Frycek, who stubbornly continued to resist all exhortations to hit the piano harder, agreed to use a richer-toned Viennese piano belonging to the Russian General Diakov, who had offered it to him.

This time tickets sold even quicker, and authoress Klementyna Tańska asked Ludka and Izabela to reserve her a box. The programme of the second concert opened with a symphony by Józef Nowakowski, Frycek's former colleague at the conservatory. This upset Ignacy Dobrzyński, who had been hoping that his new symphony would be chosen. 'I feel, more than ever before,' wrote Frycek, 'that the man has not yet been born who can please everyone.' Next came Frycek's Piano Concerto, with violinist Józef Bielawski, first violin at the Theatre and professor at the conservatory, playing Charles Bériot's Variations between the first and second movements. This time the audience, nine hundred strong, was with him all the way. 'The audience,' he wrote to Tytus, 'even larger than before, was pleased. Clapping, and exclamations, calling me back, yelling for a third concert.'

The second half opened with Frycek's *Krakowiak*. 'The *Krakowiak* Rondo produced a tremendous effect,' he continued, 'the applause bursting out four times.' This was followed by Barbara Majerowa singing an aria from Karol Soliwa's opera *Helena and Malwina*. The concert closed with some free improvisations on songs, including 'Świat srogi' (Cruel world) and 'W mieście dziwne obyczaje' (Strange town customs). Frycek did not think this improvisation came off.

General Diakov's piano was held to have been partially responsible for the success of the second concert. Frycek saw everybody's point, but still confided to Tytus that he would much rather have played his own piano. The accolades flooded in, an adoring Moriolka sent him a laurel wreath, and he received 'some verses from somebody', actually a sonnet by Leon Ulrich, which was published in the *Fine Arts Record* and the *Warsaw Courier*. Frycek's former colleague at the conservatory, composer, conductor and violinist Antoni Orłowski, inspired by what he had heard, wrote the *Mazurka and Waltz on themes from the Concerto, the Fantasia and the Krakowiak* by Fryderyk Chopin. It was published that year by Brzezyna, despite protestations from Frycek. Brzezina also wanted to commission a publicity portrait of him, but Frycek could not be bothered, saying he did not want his face used to wrap butter in.

Every paper ran a lengthy analysis of the concert, and every critic owned that Frycek played better, had a better piano, and, most importantly, was now seen as one of Europe's greatest and most original pianists. On a more sour note, some critical analysis resulted in journalistic backbiting which got out of hand, much to Frycek's irritation. At the centre of it was the question: Was Frycek an imitator of Rossini, or not? The whole thing blew up into factionalism between German music represented by Elsner, and the Rossinists, led by Kurpiński. The offending article, in the *Warsaw Gazette*, was in reply to another article which described Frycek's originality. The *Warsaw Gazette*, although praising Frycek's achievement, advised him to study Rossini, but not to copy him, which was supposed to be a sideways swipe at Kurpiński. This article, along with a comment in the *Official Bulletin* saying that Poland should be as proud of Chopin as Germany [sic] is of Mozart, awakened in Frycek a seething rage, which led to a deep bout of depression that lasted throughout the spring. The euphoria of the concerts was followed by the inevitable come-down. He missed Tytus, the only person in whom he felt he could confide. His expressions of love and affection for his truest friend at this time were as tender as they would have been to a girl. Tytus was for him a kind of spiritual and musical guardian angel, a sexless kindred spirit who, unfortunately, was not there when he was needed most.

The Concerto in F minor was published in Leipzig by Breitkopf & Hartel in 1836 as No. 2 Op. 21. By then it had lost its Konstancja Gładkowska connection, and was formally dedicated to Countess Delfina Potocka.

Even before he had finished his Concerto, a second one was already beginning to germinate in Frycek's mind, and he began to give it serious consideration. 'I shall finish the opening Allegro of my second concerto before the holidays,' he wrote to Tytus even before the echoes of the applause at the National Theatre had died away. He added that he would have no opinion of his own about the new concerto until Tytus had heard it.

Old Pruszak was back in Warsaw after months at Teplice, and there was a party to celebrate Marianna's name day at Marszałkowska Street. On the Friday after the concert he dined with Moriolka's parents. Karol Soliwa was also there. After the dinner Frycek and Soliwa went on to a party at General Diakov's. Also present was cellist Józef Kaczyński, with whom Frycek entertained, playing Hummel's *La Rubinelle*. He attended a play at Aleksandra Potocka's salon, where the ethos of the Polish 'Old Style' was kept alive, and a soirée at the house of authoress and translator Anna Nakwaska.

Monday, April 5, was the start of the Roman Easter, one week ahead of the Russian Orthodox Easter. That evening Filipaeus, the Intendant at the Court of the Grand Duke, gave a musical soirée, at which operatic arias were the main feature. Frycek contributed as accompanist. Later that week, he and cellist Kaczyński were invited to play as a duo, as well as other musicians, at the Lewickis, a music-loving house where regular amateur concerts were held. The duo's contribution was Hummel's *La Sentinelle*, and Frycek's cello *Polonaise Brillante* to which he had now added an introduction.

On Maundy Thursday, April 8, Kostuś, who had been at Sanniki, returned to Marszałkowska Street. The next day, Good Friday, Frycek went as usual to the Pruszaks to give Olesia her lesson, and stayed to lunch. Present was a Mr Mleczko, who had asked a horrified Marianna Pruszak, while grovelling tearfully on the floor, for permission to marry Olesia. As Mr Mleczko was, in Frycek's words, 'getting on a bit', and Olesia was very young, there had been a scene. Frycek, as a friend of the family, was made privy to the matter, and the sparse Good Friday lunch of pickled herrings and soured cream was a very strained and tearful affair; finally it was resolved that Olesia should wait with her answer until her next birthday. In fact, she married Mleczko eventually. After lunch, in keeping with Polish custom, everyone went visiting graves. Frycek went with Kostuś, and together they drove from one end of the city to the other, exchanging news and recounting tales of their respective travels.

On Easter Sunday Frycek went to Dionizy Minasowicz's *Święcony*, a formal Easter feast, blessed by a priest, at which ham and *babka* cake were served on a table strewn with brightly painted eggs. Minasowicz was a poet, translator of libretti and co-editor with Kurpiński of the *Musical Weekly*. Frycek was hoping to discuss with Kurpiński the *Warsaw Gazette* article, but only pianist Maurycy Ernemann was present from the music set. Ernemann had heard the opening Allegro of Frycek's second Concerto, and had pronounced it even better than the first.

Easter Monday saw the usual custom of *Śmigus* in full swing. All the young bloods, their springtime fancies having turned to love in the traditional manner, prowled the streets of Warsaw, armed with perfumed water, looking for girls to drench. This harmless custom was lost on Frycek, for his thoughts were still elevated to his silent love for Konstancja.

He sublimated his passion for this unattainable ideal with emotional substitutes; he channelled his love and sense of sharing towards Tytus, while he disguised his true feelings for feminine company by being seen constantly with Moriolka, who was very fond of him. Their relationship was very close but basically platonic, if a little flirtatious; they had grown up together, got into childish scrapes together, had few secrets from each other and were very good friends. Most people, including his family, considered them an established pair, and Frycek was happy to maintain this illusion.

Konstancja was living at the conservatory, and had now been with Soliwa for four years. Frycek acted as accompanist for her and her friend, Anna Wołków. The two girls were Soliwa's highfliers for whom brilliant futures were predicted. From his piano stool Frycek adored Konstancja as she sang. Soliwa pursued a policy of allowing outsiders to sing duets with his pupils – a way of introducing opera to the public by participation. This inevitably resulted in young bloods coming along whose interest was in the singer rather than the song, especially as the young sopranos were generally very pretty. A sudden interest in opera by young Russian officers from the Belvedere Palace was attributed to the girls' looks rather than their coloratura skills, and every time the dashing young lieutenants Bezobrazov and Pisarevsky, resplendent in their uniforms, came for a session, Konstancja showed every sign of enjoying their company as much as their singing. Frycek used to go home after these sessions, frustrated and angry, cursing all things Russian.

Count Mostowski, who the previous year had declined to 'waste public money' on Frycek's trip to Vienna, saw fit to sanction Konstancja and Anna in forthcoming operatic roles. Konstancja was offered the title role in Ferdinando Paër's *Aniela* (Agnese), due to be given at the end of July; Anna Wołków's role was in Rossini's *Il Turco in Italia*. Frycek accompanied their rehearsals.

In late spring Tsar Nicholas arrived in Warsaw for the opening of the Seym on May 28. He criticized everything, which did not go down well. As at his coronation, his welcome was politely deferential but cold, and undercurrents of dissent were never far away. The aristocracy had migrated to the capital for the occasion, and Frycek hoped that Tytus would come too.

A concert was arranged in the Tsar's honour, but Frycek was not invited to take part. The reason was not clear. He had no love for the Russians, but did not make a point of putting his views about in the cafés. Most of the artists were foreign imports, almost as if home grown musicians were not good enough. The Tsar may have been advised on a new phenomenon that was germinating in parts of Europe: nationalism in music. This new concept, with its roots in Weber's vision of an essential German opera, became a major political force in the second half of the century, when Dvorak, Smetana, Sibelius and Wagner used the folk culture of their lands to establish their nationhood. By elevating the mazurka, the polonaise and the *krakowiak* to the concert platform, Frycek had unwittingly promoted this as yet nameless movement. The Tsar could be forgiven for fearing that a Chopin concert might spark off a surge of Polish feeling which could get out of hand.

The summer session of the Seym was an excuse for an enriched social season, with lots of balls, dinners, excursions and concerts by local as well as visiting foreign artists. Among the latter was Henrietta Sontag. At twenty-four, she was considered the greatest soprano of her day, and dented Frycek's adoration of Konstancja. He was totally overcome by her clear, bell-like voice ('she charms everyone with her voice, which is not very big, but highly cultivated'), her stage charisma ('it seems as if she breathed the perfumes of the freshest flowers into the hall, she caresses, she strokes, she enraptures'), her true pitching ('her diminuendi are non plus ultra, her portamenti lovely, and especially her ascending chromatic scales are exquisite'), her character ('she is incredibly good-natured'), and her looks ('she is not beautiful, but extraordinarily pretty').

Frycek met her socially through Prince Antoni Radziwiłł. 'You have missed five of Miss Sontag's concerts,' wrote Frycek to Tytus, reproaching him for not coming to Warsaw for the Seym. 'You cannot imagine how marvellous it was to meet her intimately, at home, on a sofa. We think about nothing except this messenger of God, as some enthusiasts call her.' Henrietta Sontag was the mainstay of the concert in the Tsar's honour.

General Józef Sowiński and his wife Katarzyna heard Sontag in concert. When Frycek visited their house, her performance of *Der Schweizerbub* was discussed. As Mrs Sowińska loved the song, Frycek sat down and wrote a set of variations on it. He gave one copy to Mrs Sowińska, and sent another to Haslinger's in Vienna.

Other visitors to Warsaw included Sigismund Wörlitzer, sixteen-year-old pianist to the Prussian Court, and French-born but Vienna-based Anne de Belleville. Her repertoire included, to Frycek's delight, his 'Là ci darem la mano' Variations, which testified to their publication at last by Haslinger. Leopoldine Blahetka wanted to come if Frycek would arrange a concert for her, but Frycek was not willing to take the financial responsibility, and discouraged her.

On June 22 Henrietta Sontag left Warsaw for St Petersburg after having conquered Warsaw with eight concerts. A week later the Seym was wound up, and the King of Poland also left. Warsaw was depleted as the aristocracy returned to their estates, and the early travellers set off for foreign parts, among them Kostuś Pruszak and history professor Romuald Hube, who were going to Italy. With his closest friend in Warsaw gone, Frycek decided that if Tytus would not come to Warsaw, then he would go to Tytus. But first there was the matter of his still unfinished second concerto. He had kept Tytus constantly informed on its progress, and was again pleased with the slow movement, even with the scoring. 'The Adagio of the new concerto is in E,' he wrote. 'It is a quiet, melancholy romance; it should convey gazing tenderly at a place of a thousand cherished memories. It is a kind of meditation in beautiful spring weather, only by moonlight. That is why I have muted accompaniment. Mutes are little combs which violinists place across the strings to deaden them, and give them a nasal, silvery tone.' Initial reactions to the first two movements had been very good, and everyone thought the new concerto better than the first. But he needed to play it to Tytus – it was his approval that Frycek sought above all others. Over the next few days he busied himself with finishing the Rondo.

Barbara Majerowa, who sang at both of Frycek's March concerts, was giving a concert of her own at the National Theatre on July 8, and asked him if he would participate. Frycek was pleased to return the compliment, as it would be an excellent opportunity to publicize the newly published 'Là ci darem la mano' Variations. The concert featured two of Warsaw's finest artists on excellent form, but it was not a success. By then Warsaw, empty and suffering from a surfeit of culture, society, the Seym, and with Henrietta Sontag's voice still echoing in thousands of ears, stayed away.

A few days later, with the Rondo finished, Frycek packed his brand new Piano Concerto in E minor, bade goodbye to his family, and set off on the Lwów diligence, out of Warsaw past the Belvedere Palace, and onto the three-hundred-kilometre journey to Poturzyn. Today the post road is the Route 723 out of Warsaw. The post stages were at Piaseczno, Góra Kalwaria, Czersk, Magnuszew, Kozienice, then on to Route 738 to Gniewoszów, then on to Route 44 over the River Vistula to Pulawy, Garbów, Lublin, then on to Route 17 to Piaski, Krasnystaw, Izbica, Zamość and Tomaszów Lubielski, the last town in Poland before the Austrian border at Belzec.

From Tomaszów to the remote Woyciechowski estate, situated almost at the very meeting point of Poland, Russia and Austria, was about fifty kilometres across woods and fields. The estate consisted of a large, elegant, stone manor house with stables and outhouses, all set among interconnected lakes at different levels. These emptied into one of the numerous tributaries of the River Bug, which partly formed the Polish eastern border, as it does today, and eventually flowed into the Vistula north of Warsaw. This was convenient for Tytus to send his wheat directly to Gdańsk by river for export. He grew sugar beet and rye, had a distillery and a mill, and kept sheep. He was making tentative plans to establish a sugar factory on his estate in order to become his own middle-man for his beet crop, but it was several years before this plan materialized.

Frycek loved Poturzyn. Harvest time had not yet come, so Tytus was able to spend many hours at the piano with him. Music was a feature at Poturzyn, and players came from the whole region to make music in the drawing-room. Other guests were Łączyński, a cousin of Nicolas Chopin's first permanent employer, and judge Baron Malsdorf, who played the cello. Frycek played Tytus all his latest works, including both the concertos, and Tytus tried them out too, as well as playing Frycek some of his own compositions. Frycek's love life was less well received. Tytus listened patiently but with increasing exasperation to his friend's tales of unrequited love, his exaggerated love language towards him, and told him that Konstancja was a girl, not an 'ideal', and should be treated as such and removed from the pedestal.

When the weather was good, Frycek and Tytus went for long walks among the ripening wheatfields, armed with a crossbow – with which they must have had enough fun to warrant Frycek's mention in a future letter: 'I had a sort of homesickness for your fields. . . . And that crossbow – so romantic.' The villages were few, tiny and far between, and in each one a different language was heard, for this had been for centuries Polish and Ukrainian frontier country. In typical fashion of the time, the two nations lived apart, each in its own villages, and contact between them was limited. Both Roman and Orthodox churches served the communities separately, and the differing music of the two liturgies was heard over the fields during two Christmases and two Easters. The Jews in their communities made up a sizeable minority, and worshipped in their synagogues, adding to the melting pot that never melted.

Every so often the mutual distrust flared into violence, the most recent being in 1944, when, in the wake of the Russian westward thrust the Ukrainians laid Poturzyn waste, massacred the inhabitants and razed the Woyciechowski manor, and burnt all its furniture, treasures, books and records. Today the frontier with Ukraine is only a few kilometres away, there is a sugar factory nearby, built in more recent times, and the local school is named after Fryderyk

Chopin. All that remains of Tytus's estate are the lakes and the original stables, of which Frycek wrote on his return to Warsaw: 'You'll have to employ me at Poturzyn as a clerk, and I could live above the stable.'

After a fortnight at Poturzyn Frycek went back to Warsaw in the company of Baron Malsdorf, who was returning to his judicial duties. He had cut short his visit in order to attend Konstancja's operatic debut in Paër's *Aniela*, scheduled at the National Theatre for July 24 in a production by Soliwa. Mindful of Tytus's reproaches, Frycek tried to be coldly objective in his assessment of his 'ideal's' performance. 'Gładkowska', he wrote, 'is better on stage than in the concert hall. Apart from the tragedy acting, one can only say it was splendid; one could not ask for better singing of its kind. Her phrasing would delight you; she shades gorgeously, and though at first her voice shook a little, afterwards she sang with confidence.'

At the time it was customary to tamper with performances, and this *Aniela* was no exception. It was abridged, perhaps rightly, as it was not considered one of Paër's better works; but in Act II, Soliwa had inserted an extra aria of his own composition, a romance by Konstancja singing with a harp. To effect this, Maurycy Ernemann played the piano backstage. 'I knew that Soliwa's air would produce an effect,' wrote Frycek, 'but I did not expect such a huge one.' The critics praised the performance highly, and Konstancja received honours both for her singing and her acting ability. Her future success was assured, because plans were already in the pipeline for her to sing in Rossini's *The Thieving Magpie* in the autumn, with Spontini's *La Vestale* to follow.

Frycek's parents and sisters had gone to Żelazowa Wola, and after having seen *Aniela* twice, he went to join them. While he was there he heard rumours of unrest in Paris. Censorship prevented details coming through, but the overall story was one of Revolution. Any thoughts of going to Paris were shelved. Frycek stayed at Żelazowa Wola for three weeks before returning to Warsaw on August 17 to compose and plan for the future, to rumours of student arrests in Warsaw.

He involved himself in chamber-music sessions, and went to hear Anna Wołków captivating her audience in Rossini's *Il Turco in Italia*. During the last week of August Frycek, at the instigation of General Piotr Szembek, paid a visit – his second – to

Szembek's Garrison at Sochaczew, near Żelazowa Wola. The General was a fine violinist of the Paganini persuasion, and a music lover. Frycek duly played the piano for him and his officers. 'He was most impressed with the Adagio,' he wrote. Frycek then heard the military band in action, and commented that he had

> heard some amazing things. It is all played on a type of bugle, and you would not believe they can do chromatic scales extremely fast, and diminuendo ascending. I had to praise the soloist; poor fellow, he won't last long, he looks so consumptive. I was greatly impressed with the cavatina from 'The Mute Girl of Portici', played on these trumpets with complete accuracy and delicacy of shading.

The Garrison was situated on the eastern banks of the River Bzura, which flows through Sochachew.

The approaching autumn plunged Frycek into depression, resulting in a sense of indolence and indecision. He had been planning to return to Vienna for months, but was unable to summon up the will to do anything about it. He was constantly tired, and at the back of his mind the spectres of Jasio Białobłocki and Emilka returned to visit him in the night. He was tormented by a sense of dread and premonition, and wrote of death: 'I do not have the strength to decide on a departure date, because I think I shall leave to forget my home for ever; I feel as if I would go away to die; and how miserable it must be to die where one has not lived.... How awful it would be to see by my deathbed a cold doctor or servant instead of my own family.' Konstancja was still on her pedestal, untouchable as ever, yet because of Moriolka's constant presence no one suspected his true feelings.

The July Revolution in France sparked off unrest throughout Europe. After fifteen years the tenuous peace of the Congress of Vienna was becoming frayed at the seams. There was trouble all over Germany, in Vienna arguments about flour had ignited more politically motivated disturbances, and there were riots in Italy. All this decided Frycek that this was not the right time to seek fame and fortune in Europe, and he concentrated on correcting his second concerto.

During the second half of September Frycek had two rehearsals, one with a quartet, and the second with full orchestra, this time conducted by Karol Soliwa. As before, the latter was a dress-rehearsal-cum-performance for the benefit of 'a numerous gathering of artists and music lovers', among them, Maurycy Ernemann, Karol Kurpiński, Józef Elsner, Ignacy Dobrzyński (who had forgiven Frycek for not having included his symphony in the March concerts) and the cellists Baron Malsdorf and Józef Kaczyński. 'This is a work of genius', wrote the *Universal National Daily*.

On the strength of similar reviews and comments, it was decided to première the Concerto at the National Theatre on Monday, October 11, and Frycek and Soliwa worked out the programme. Dispensing with the established practice of interspersing the movements with wind items, Frycek wanted arias by Konstancja and Anna. Soliwa agreed, but permission had to be sought from Count Mostowski, the girls' sponsor; this was granted. A Streicher piano was installed.

On the night of the concert the National Theatre was packed. A symphony by K. Goerner opened the programme. This was followed by the first movement of the Concerto, which was received with loud applause. Frycek's nerves were well under control, he enjoyed himself with confidence, and felt as if he were playing at home. The Allegro was followed by an Aria with chorus, written by Soliwa and sung by Anna Wołków, wearing a coquettish, elfin-like blue dress. This was followed by the Adagio, with its silvery muted strings, and the Rondo. Such was the impact of the Concerto that at the interval Frycek was beset by admirers congratulating him on the stage. The second half opened with Rossini's *Wilhelm Tell* Overture, which was followed by Konstancja, looking ravishing in a white dress and a rose in her hair, singing the cavatina from Rossini's *La donna del lago*. Secretly fired by this vision of beauty, Frycek played his heart out with his *Fantasia on Polish Airs*, which was the most liked of all; he commented that at last he had established a full rapport with the orchestra.

Although the concert was a major success, there was a feeling of *déjà vu* about it as far as the critics were concerned. Those write-ups that followed used the same language as after the March concerts, and the casual observer might have come away from Warsaw with a sense of 'heard one Chopin concerto, heard them all'.

Warsaw had been tense since the Seym, and Tsar Nicholas's

name was whispered with contempt. Dissenting talk in the cafés had been louder, simmering resentments had been brought to the boil, students had become more radical, and the unwise had been arrested. Perhaps in this climate the readers of the *Warsaw Courier* and the *Universal National Daily* had other things on their minds.

Frycek galvanized himself into making a decision about Vienna. November 2, All Souls' Day, was settled for the departure, and he would go for at least two months. He bought a new trunk, into which he packed his music, including the orchestral score of the *Krakowiak*, which had to be further corrected by Soliwa. Grand Duke Constantine gave him a letter of introduction to the Russian ambassador in Vienna. He sorted out his passport and went round Warsaw saying goodbye to everyone: the Pruszaks, the Wodzińskis, the Lindes (that year baby Aleksandra had now brought the total female offspring to six), the de Moriolles, the Skarbeks, the Kolbergs, the Elsners, Julian Fontana, Jan Matuszyński, Karol Soliwa, Karol Kurpiński and Anna Wołków. Józef Reinschmidt and Dominik Magnuszewski arranged a farewell dinner. To Frycek's delight Tytus had also decided to go to Vienna; the two friends would travel together, and they agreed to meet at Kalisz, at the house of Dr Helbich.

Before he left, encouraged by Ludka, Izabela and Jan Matuszyński, Frycek finally declared his love to Konstancja in the Botanic Gardens. She was very touched by his devotion, and gave him a lock of her hair, which Ludka fashioned into a ring for him. Jan was appointed go-between in their correspondence. In case any letter of Frycek's got into the wrong hands, he would write to Jan, enclosing letters and cryptic allusions for her.

On 2 November 1830, Frycek left Warsaw by the Wola tollgate, the same one by which he had entered as a six-month-old baby twenty years previously. Elsner was there, with a choir singing a farewell cantata that he had written for the occasion. The road continued westwards along the familiar route to Wrocław and Vienna.

On the road he had time to reflect on his achievements to date. With the composition and performance of both his piano concertos, by the age of twenty Frycek had become the complete musician. His brilliant technique and distinctive pianistic style was established and was never compromised. As a composer he had tried his hand at all the forms, culminating in the ultimate expression in pianism, the concerto. Frycek had a particular love for the human voice, especially in the dramatic context of opera. There were spasmodic suggestions, which he never dismissed, that he should write one himself. He even discussed the possibilities of collaborating with Fryderyk Skarbek as librettist, but ultimately the idea came to nought. His vocal output consisted of seventeen songs, published together in 1855 as Op. 74. Henceforth he would consolidate his musicianship and spend his maturity in perfecting those forms that he excelled in.

His Romanticism was expressed within his own, essentially classical parameters of form. Except for his songs, his compositions bore no titles other than formal ones. He would have despised such appendages as 'Raindrop' Prelude, 'Military' Polonaise and 'Revolutionary' Etude, even though the inspiration behind them might well have attracted these labels through the passage of time. A prelude was a prelude to Frycek, as much as a fugue was a fugue to Bach and a minuet was a minuet to Mozart. Apart from the *Grande Polonaise brillante* in E flat, which he was now working on, he abandoned the orchestra. He had tried it, come up with some remarkable effects, but decided it had no further place in his art. Neither had chamber music, apart from an understanding of the cello, the result of close association with Prince Radziwiłł, Kaczyński and Baron Malsdorf. The raw materials of Fryderyk Chopin's ultimate legacy – the fusion of Classicism and Romanticism – were firmly in place on the road to Kalisz in November 1830.

At Kalisz Frycek left the diligence, which dropped him off outside Dr Helbich's house, where he awaited Tytus's arrival from Poturzyn. With time on his hands, he was asked to give a concert. Not keen on the idea, he went to hear the local orchestra practising out of politeness, found it excruciating, and came up with all sorts of excuses, such as the time factor, not to play. Fortunately, Tytus arrived two days later. Without further ado, the two friends hired a carriage to take them to Wrocław for twelve thalers, and they continued on their way. At Biskupice, ten kilometres from Kalisz, they came to the frontier. Frycek and Tytus presented their passports to the authorities and crossed into Prussia.

Frycek had left his Poland for ever.

TWELVE
Exile

On the afternoon of Saturday 6 November 1830 Frycek and Tytus booked into the Golden Goose in Wrocław, and went to see Rosek von Raiter's *The Alpine King*.

On Sunday, they went to the Cathedral of St John the Baptist to see kapellmeister Josef Schnabel, whom Frycek had met previously on Elsner's recommendation. Schnabel invited the two friends to a rehearsal on Monday for a concert he was mounting at the Resource on Tuesday. At dinner, Frycek and Tytus met Herr Scharff, an amiable German merchant, and found they had mutual friends in Warsaw. Scharff took them on a sightseeing trip of the city in a buggy, before getting them tickets for a musical evening at the Resource. That night they saw Auber's *The Miller and the Locksmith* at the opera.

On Monday at the rehearsal Frycek wrote 'some amateur by the name of Hellwig was preparing to play Moscheles's Piano Concerto in E flat'. During a break in the rehearsal, Frycek was persuaded to try the piano, and played the Adagio and the Rondo from his E minor Concerto. This produced a mixed reception from the orchestra. Remarks heard by Tytus were 'What a light touch he has', and 'He can play, but he can't compose'. He succumbed to Schnabel's entreaties, and agreed to perform the last two movements of his E minor Concerto at the concert instead of the hapless Herr Hellwig.

On Tuesday evening, Scharff found, to his astonishment, that he had obtained free tickets for the star of the concert. As a compromise, Hellwig sang Figaro's air from Rossini's *The Barber of Seville.* 'Wretchedly', wrote Frycek. He performed his concerto, then improvised on themes from Auber's *The Mute Girl of Portici* to loud applause. He wrote that Josef Schnabel 'kept taking me under the chin and hugging me every moment. I'm glad to have given pleasure to the old man'. At 9 o'clock, when the dancing began, Frycek and Tytus departed to catch the end of Winter's *Das Unterbrochene Opferfest.*

The Resource building is still in the Plac Teatralny. A plaque on the wall commemorates Chopin's concert.

On Wednesday, November 10, Frycek and Tytus continued their journey, crossed into Saxony and arrived at Dresden on Friday November 12. That evening, instead of going to an eagerly anticipated performance of Auber's *The Mute Girl of Portici*, they went to hear Antonina Pechwell. Frycek explained that she was Dresden's best pianist, whom he had met the previous year, and that he should go. It would be a chance to hear Plazzesi, Dresden Opera's highly rated new soprano. Frycek decided to turn up in style. He put on his best clothes, and sent for a sedan chair to take him to Kreissig's house, where the soirée was to take place. He was bemused by the experience. 'I laughed at myself all the way,' he wrote, 'being borne by these liveried bearers. I was very tempted to kick the bottom out, but thought better of it. The contraption took me right up the steps.'

Climbing out, he sent his name to Fraulein Pechwell; Herr Kreissig emerged, and after much bowing and scraping, conducted Frycek into a large hall where a host of ladies were seated at eight tables, knitting. The clicking of the needless was interrupted by the sound of music. An orchestra at the other end of the hall burst into the Overture to Auber's *Fra Diavolo*. After that Plazzesi sang. 'Not bad,' wrote Frycek. Then Antonina Pechwell played. When the music had finished, Frycek mingled, chatted to Plazzesi and Pechwell, met various luminaries, and was offered letters of introduction. After a polite interval, he excused himself and rushed off to see the last act of *The Mute Girl of Portici.*

On Saturday, Frycek visited August Klengel, who was so pleased to see him that he gave him a bear hug. He wanted Frycek to give a concert in Dresden, but Frycek was determined to remain deaf to all entreaties. They agreed to meet the following Monday. That evening he and Tytus went to Rossini's *Tancredi,* a new production attended by King Anton with his entourage. 'It was badly done,' wrote Frycek.

On Sunday morning the friends went to High Mass, which was also attended by the King. The choral mass was by Baron Miltitz, a local aristocrat and composer. Afterwards Frycek attended a Polish dinner.

On Monday Frycek went to Klengel's as arranged, and spent the whole morning with him. 'I like to talk to him,' he wrote, 'because one can really learn something from him.' Frycek played him his new concerto, and Klengel listened carefully. 'It reminds me of Field,' he said. 'You have a rare touch. I have heard a great deal about you, but I never expected to find you such a virtuoso. This is no idle compliment. I hate to flatter people, or to have to praise them.'

The rest of the week was spent at the opera, at dinners, collecting letters of introduction, and a second visit to the art gallery.

On Friday, November 19, Frycek and Tytus left Dresden for Vienna, by way of Prague where they stayed only long enough for Frycek to send a letter home. The coach reached Vienna at 9 o'clock on a cold morning on Tuesday, November 23, and they booked into the Stadt London Hotel off the Postgasse.

Frycek reported to the *Comptoir* with his passport, bank statements, letters of introduction and all the rest of the paperwork demanded by the Viennese authorities from visitors seeking a residence permit. He then called on Tobias Haslinger, who received Frycek amiably enough, but had done nothing about the Sonata in C minor and the *Schweizerbub* Variations. His current programme, he explained, did not include publishing any further works of Frycek's for the moment, but he would still like to keep them for a more favourable time. Frycek went away with the impression that Haslinger wanted to have his compositions without having to pay. Although the 'Là ci darem la mano' Variations were selling well, Frycek got nothing out of it.

All his contacts proved disappointing. The previous year he had played for free to establish himself, and now expected to start making a living from music. But Vienna was a fickle city, and he was already yesterday's pianist. He went to see Herr Geymüller, a Jewish banker with whom Tytus had invested a large sum of money, for 'advice' on a musical career. Herr Geymüller had heard of Friedrich Chopin, but pointed out that regrettably this was not a good time for pianists as there were so many of them, and only the very biggest names could hope to succeed. Frycek read into this that he was not a good financial proposition, and left with a polite apology out loud, and an anti-Semitic oath under his breath.

Despite his legendary thrift, Count Gallenberg had gone bankrupt, and his place at the Kärntnertor Theatre was taken by Louis Dupont. Würfel called for a concert, but was too ill to do anything about it. The Blahetkas had gone to Stuttgart. Frycek went with Tomasz Nidecki to see piano maker Konrad Graff. Recalling Frycek's predilection for his pianos, Graff allowed him to practise in his showroom every afternoon, and promised him a piano when he had found lodgings. The Stadt London, where all the celebrities stayed, was expensive, so Frycek and Tytus moved to the Golden Lamb in Leopoldstadt, the Jewish quarter over the Danube Canal by the Schwedenbrücke, while they looked for a suitable apartment. They found just what they were looking for. The landlady was the attractive young Prussian Baroness Lachmanowicz, who had lived in Poland, liked Poles, disliked Austrians, and had heard of Fryderyk Chopin. The apartment consisted of 'three delightful, splendid, elegantly furnished rooms on the third floor' at No. 9 Kohlmarkt. The two friends settled in to life in Vienna. They ate at the Wilde Mann, where the strudels were, in Frycek's opinion, out of this world. They spent much time – and money – at the opera: Rossini's *Otello* and *Guillaume Tell*, Auber's *Fra Diavolo* and *The Mute Girl of Portici* and Mozart's *La Clemenza di Tito*.

The peaceful legacy of the Congress of Vienna had crumbled further, and its effects were felt all over Europe, not least in Warsaw; a rage against the Russians and Tsar Nicholas in particular was beginning to emerge. Revolution in Belgium had expelled the House of Orange-Nassau, and an independent state was proclaimed. Tsar Nicholas, pledged to uphold what his late brother had achieved in Vienna fifteen years previously, prepared to send Polish troops to suppress both the Belgian and the French Revolutions and re-establish the Houses of Orange-Nassau and Bourbon.

As the Polish army would never fight to re-establish a reactionary order, an officer, Piotr Wysocki, hatched a plot to sabotage the plan. On November 29, a week after Frycek's arrival in the Congress city, a small rebel group under Ludwik Nabielak stormed the Belvedere Palace to assassinate the Grand Duke, while Piotr

Wysocki marched on the Russian Garrisons in the Łazienki Park. Everything happened so quickly that Warsaw, the Russians, the Polish army and even the insurrectionists were taken unawares. Everything went wrong: both Constantine and the Russian Army survived. The Grand Duke escaped in his night-shirt and hid in his wife's bedroom, while the Governor Lubovitzky and General Gendre were killed in error. The Arsenal in the city centre was stormed, but both Polish and Russian armies stayed in barracks, the former waiting for credible orders, the latter in some trepidation knowing what a roused Polish insurrection can do. Over the next few days Warsaw's young radicals and students saw their chance and took to the streets taunting and beating up Russians. Prince Franciszek Lubecki, the Finance Minister, showed a cool head by grabbing the initiative, and enlisting a number of prominent figures, including Prince Czartoryski, to form a National Council pledged to restore order as an internal Polish matter, to be dealt with under the Polish Constitution, rather than a revolt against the rule of the Tsar. On December 5, a week after the storming of the Belvedere Palace, General Chłopicki was proclaimed Dictator, and put in charge of the Polish army.

An uneasy truce ensued. General Chłopicki offered Grand Duke Constantine, his court, his army units, his prisoners and his spies safe conduct out of Warsaw. He then sent Prince Lubecki to St Petersburg to talk to the Tsar, who refused to speak to him, and raged that nothing short of total capitulation from the Poles would get him to talk. His attitude inflamed the Poles, who were now baying loudly for Russian blood. General Chłopicki, no longer able to control the situation, resigned. The National Council took over the Seym and officially acknowledged the state of Insurrection. On 25 January 1831 the Seym voted for the deposition of Tsar Nicholas as King of Poland, and the proclamation of a new government under Prince Czartoryski, with Prince Michał Radziwiłł, the younger brother of Prince Antoni, as Commander-in-Chief of the Polish army.

Poland seceded from Russia, and proclaimed independence.

When the news of the assault on the Belvedere Palace first reached Kohlmarkt 9, Frycek and Tytus sat up all night trying to decide what to do. They discussed joining the army to fight the Russians. But Frycek received a letter from his father advising him against returning to Warsaw, saying that he could best help Poland abroad with his art, rather than at home with a gun in his hand. This plunged Frycek into an agony of indecision: to return to a potentially horrific war situation, to be reunited with his family and fatherland at a time of need, or to abandon them to their fate. He had not known insurrection, but his father had, with tales of atrocities to tell. Tytus decided to return to Poland to fight, but advised Frycek to listen to his father and stay away. Frycek reluctantly agreed, and Tytus set off back for Poland. Frycek suddenly changed his mind, and two hours after Tytus's departure he packed in haste, and hired a carriage, hoping to catch up with him. As he watched the monochrome, wintry Austrian countryside flashing past, he realized the futility of what he was doing. Yet he felt as if he were betraying his family when, after several stages, he ordered the carriage to return to Vienna.

His apartment was still available, but he now moved upstairs to the fourth floor, to a smaller one-man apartment which was just as comfortable but much cheaper. He was pleased with his new lodgings and settled into a semi-indolent lifestyle. He was right in the centre; the street was smart, with the Graben just round the corner. His neighbours were music publishers Pietro Mechetti and Haslingers, and the Artaria art shop, with the theatre just behind. His room was spacious, elegantly furnished, with three windows from which he could see what was happening below. Graff had now lent him a piano. He was woken in the mornings by 'an unbelievably stupid servant', after which coffee and breakfast arrived. At nine his teacher came for his German lesson, then, still in his dressing-gown, he played until Tomasz arrived to practise Frycek's concertos. Also among his visitors was Eugen Hummel, artist son of the composer and pianist, who sketched Frycek's room for the benefit of his parents, and did an aquarelle portrait of him. In the afternoons he would go for a walk with friends before eating at the Bohemian Kitchen, the haunt of students, artists and academics. After supper came a round of visits, and by dark he was back in his lodgings to curl his hair and change his shoes before going out on the town. 'About ten, eleven or twelve – never later –,' he wrote, 'I come back, play, weep, read, look, laugh, go to bed, put the light out. . . .'

His plans for a concert were more talk than action.

His chances of a career were now slimmer still, as the insurrection developed, and Viennese opinion went against the Poles. Frycek overheard, in a restaurant, a snippet of conversation that summed it up: 'The Good Lord made a mistake when he created Poles.' 'There's nothing to be got out of Poland.' It was feared that the rising could spread to Galicia, and it was a bad time for a Polish artist to make headway in the capital of one of the three partitioning powers. Despite the hostile atmosphere, Frycek knew that his circle rose above petty politics, and he continued to pursue his social and musical life. 'I get dressed, comb my hair, put my shoes on; in the drawing-room I pretend to be calm, but when I get back I vent my rage on the piano.' His socializing kept his mind off his troubles, and he made every effort to enjoy himself. When at a loose end, he would sit in his rooms, worry about his family, play with the ringed lock of Konstancja's hair, and wonder whether he would see his family or his ideal again. His emotional fluctuations were great, with social gaiety alternating with deep depression.

His innermost thoughts were now directed to Jan Matuszyński, and his letters were full of cryptic allusions to his love for Konstancja. He even expressed his love for 'her' – the closest he got to writing her name was 'Konst–, no, I am not worthy to write it' – through his letters to Jan, as if he were an intermediary of the kind found in many operatic plots:

> Tell her that as long as my strength lasts, till death and even after, my ashes will be scattered under her feet. But everything you say will still not be enough. . . . If by any chance my letter should fall into a stranger's hands, her reputation might be compromised, so it's better that you should be my spokesman.

Jan's medical studies at Warsaw University were interrupted by the insurrection, and he joined the Polish army as a surgeon. Also Julian Fontana had graduated in law at the university, and joined the army, as did Wiluś Kolberg and Tytus.

Now that Jan Matuszyński had gone, Frycek saw his last ties with Konstancja severed, and he felt as though his whole world were collapsing around him. But he was not without moral support. Dr Johann Malfatti was physician to the Imperial family and to the late Beethoven; the great composer had once wooed the doctor's teenaged niece Thérèse. His wife was the daughter of Polish senator Count Tomasz Ostrowski. The Malfattis were at the hub of Vienna's artistic life. The doctor took Frycek under his wing, and fattened him up. 'I've put on weight,' wrote Frycek, 'things are going well for me, and I trust that by the grace of God and Malfatti, the incomparable Malfatti, they will go better still.' His career may have ground to a standstill, but he was enjoying Viennese life. He could afford to be patient, and refused to perform for free, in which he was supported by Dr Malfatti and Würfel.

He became friendly with a number of Viennese musicians. He re-established contact with Czerny, who was working on some arrangements for eight pianos and sixteen pianists. At Würfel's he met the young violinist Józef Sławik, to whom Paganini had said 'When you play the world trembles', and who could do ninety-six staccatos in one bow. He also met the remarkable Josef Merk, who had been a violinist until his arm was savaged by a dog. Unable to hold a violin, he took up the cello, which he mastered to the same degree as the violin. Sławik, Merk and Frycek made vague plans to form a piano trio, but the idea came to nothing beyond a few sessions together. Frycek was in regular touch with Hummel, whose new A flat Piano Concerto was currently popular. He befriended publisher Pietro Mechetti, and they often dined together, and in 1833 Mechetti published Frycek's *Introduction and Polonaise Brillante* for cello and piano, which was dedicated to Merk, as his Op. 3. The musicologist Franz Kandler also showed Frycek friendship and support. He met nineteen-year-old pianist Sigismund Thalberg. Frycek and Thalberg were at opposite poles of piano playing; Thalberg grew into the very personification of the *donner-und-blitzen* school. 'Thalberg plays famously,' wrote Frycek, 'but he is not my man.' Despite their differences they went together to an organ recital by Adolf Hesse at the Evangelical church in the Dorotheergasse.

Christmas 1830 was a lonely affair for Frycek. He spent Christmas Eve dining with Konstancja Beyer, a Polish lady whose conversation Frycek enjoyed. At table was Józef Sławik, who left early to play at midnight at the Imperial Chapel in the Hofburg. Frycek strolled into St Stephen's Cathedral. It was empty, except for a sacristan lighting candles, his footsteps the only sound in that deafening, echoing silence. The towering, Gothic enormity of the building affected Frycek deeply. 'I can't describe the greatness, the magnificence of those huge arches,' he wrote. 'I never felt my loneliness so clearly.' Standing in the darkest corner at the foot of a pillar, Frycek reflected on merrier Christmas Eves past, when he broke unleavened bread and dined off carp and poppy-seed cake with family and friends at Żelazowa Wola, before driving on through crisp snow to Midnight Mass at Brochów. A piece of music germinated in Frycek's mind; one that was to become his greatest expression of patriotic fervour: the Scherzo in B minor, Op 20. In contrast to its dramatic turbulence, the gentle trio goes straight to the heart of Polish sensitivities with its evocative treatment of the best loved of all Polish Christmas carols, 'Lulajże Jezuniu'. The Scherzo was not completed till later the following year, and its fate was to be banned in later decades in Poland as subversive, and was consequently defiantly played at concerts.

Coming out of his reverie, Frycek left and joined the merry but sleepy throng at the Imperial Chapel in the Hofburg for Midnight Mass to listen to Józef Sławik. Christmas Day saw Frycek seated at his table, alone, in a dressing-gown, gnawing at his ring while writing a very long letter to Jan Matuszyński, with an enclosure for Konstancja.

The winter of 1830–1 was exceptionally severe. In the opening weeks of 1831, Poland tried to consolidate its position as an independent state. In February a Russian army of 115,000 troops, under General Diebitsch, marched on Warsaw from the east. The 30,000-strong Polish army under General Jan Skrzyniecki, was poised in the frozen fortification in Praga, the traditional venue for bloody confrontation with the Russians. The two armies met on February 25 at Grochów, just outside Praga, and Skrzyniecki blocked Diebitsch's advance for a month. By the end of March the winter had retreated eastwards, and Skrzyniecki optimistically gave the order to march on the Russians. His optimism paid off, and the Polish army defeated the Russians in three separate battles, at Wawer (now a Warsaw suburb just south of Praga), Dębe Wielkie (on the E30 just out of Warsaw) and finally at Iganie (just short of the town of Siedlice, one hundred kilometres to the east of Warsaw). The Russians withdrew to Lublin to regroup. The Guard Corps on its way to reinforce Diebitsch was unable to join up, which placed the Poles in a position of advantage.

The news from Poland was encouraging, and the Polish community in Vienna was optimistic. Jan Matuszyński even asked

Frycek to write a battle song, but Frycek could not find a suitable poem to set to music.

The Viennese music scene was now beginning to get on Frycek's nerves. Johann Strauss and Josef Lanner had started a new fashion with the swirl of the waltz, usually played by enormous orchestras of up to two hundred players. Barrel organs churned out waltzes by the hour. Vienna, noted for flippancy and disregard for its greatest composers, turned its back on Mozart, Haydn, Beethoven and Schubert, and embraced the waltz with the unbridled enthusiasm of a society in decay. Frycek visited eighty-three-year-old Abbé Maximilian Stadler, Mozart's friend and first collator. The old man shook his head and lamented the passing of the old Vienna. He had no time for the new philistinism that was sweeping the city. 'Here waltzes are called works,' wrote Frycek, 'and those who play them are called Kapellmeisters.'

Vienna had become for Frycek so much dead wood, and he decided it was time to move on. His first choice, Italy, was a turbulent hive of unrest, so on the advice of Stefan Witwicki, poet and revolutionary, he decided to join him in Paris. 'You did not leave home to languish abroad,' he wrote to Frycek, 'but to develop your art and become the consolation and pride of your family and fatherland.'

Intending to travel to Paris were a number of refugees, including leading Polish comedy writer Aleksander Fredro and Norbert Kumelski. Frycek had become friendly with the latter, and they planned to travel together in the early summer. Frycek, Norbert and other displaced Poles spent a lot of time together, kicking their heels, waiting for travel permits and sightseeing. In June Frycek went, with Norbert and one Czapski, on a trip out of town.

> It was a beautiful day, and the best excursion I have ever made. From the Leopoldsberg you can see the whole of Vienna ... and the castle where Richard the Lion Heart was kept prisoner, and the whole upper Danube. After lunch we went to the Kahlenberg, where King Sobieski had his camp. I sent a leaf from it to Izabela.

In the late summer of 1683, Vienna was surrounded by Turkish hordes, poised for their final thrust into the heart of Christian .

Europe, and the Austrian armies were in disarray. The day was saved by the arrival of the Polish Hussars, with the larger-than-life King Jan Sobieski at their head. On September 12 the King served at mass at the Camaldolese Monastery on the Kahlenberg, dubbed his son Jakub a knight, and led his Hussars into battle. Despite heavy losses, the Polish army put the Turks to flight, and the Habsburg Empire was saved. The irony of history was not lost on Frycek, as he considered his current position as a displaced person in an unfriendly land.

Then Kumelski fell ill, so travel plans had to be shelved. But Frycek, having now made up his mind, began to make travel arrangements, starting with retrieving his passport from the *comptoir*. This was no easy feat, and at every turn he was thwarted by bureaucracy – mostly plain harrassment of a Pole by the Austrian authorities. First they 'lost' his passport, and announced that it was not worth looking for it, as he might as well get a new one. This meant approaching the Russian Embassy, not, under the circumstances, an encouraging prospect. He decided to wait and see if his lost passport turned up.

He was also running out of money, and had to write home to ask his father to sell the diamond ring he got from Tsar Alexander.

The Polish government called on the international community for support. The governments of France and Britain made noises of encouragement, and mercenaries flocked to Warsaw from Italy, Hungary, Britain, even the United States. Napoleon's veterans joined up in droves, as did younger fighters, and Lithuanians joined with Polish forces in the north. The Polish army grew to some 200,000. There was sympathy for the Poles everywhere, even in Prussia, where *Polenlieder* became very popular. Poles were welcomed in Paris and London, and refugees were treated like heroes. Skrzyniĕcki, surprised at the ease with which the Russians had been defeated, was afraid to finish the job, and sat on his heels as the Russian Guard Corps marched to join Diebitsch's depleted forces. Instead of attacking them on the march, he let them regroup. This mistake led to the two armies meeting at the village of Ostrołĕka, to the north-east of Warsaw on May 22. The battle was fierce, but the Russians won the day, and the Polish army was in disarray. Some rushed to Lithuania, where the partisan war in the forests was having greater success, others retreated to Warsaw for what was generally accepted would be the last stand.

But there was one invincible winner at the battle: the cholera pandemic which had spread from the east. Many Russian soldiers had died from it, including General Diebitsch, and now the disease had spread to the Poles. The cholera reached Vienna, and with it the beginnings of panic. Fyrcek knew he was only marking time and would be leaving soon.

After four months of dithering, Frycek finally made a public appearance on April 4 at the Redoutensaal. It was a matinée given by singer Madame Garcia-Vestris. The programme included the Wild brothers, who were singers, as were the sisters Sabine and Klara Heinefetter. Franz Wild was the leading tenor in Vienna at this time, and Sabine Heinefetter was the star of the Vienna opera, and much admired by Frycek. There was a horn duet by the Levy brothers, Böhm and Helmesberger played violins, and there was a cello solo by Josef Merk. Frycek played his Piano Concerto in E minor. Although the artists were top class, the hall was by no means full. But he did not care: his heart was not in it. He had no illusions about the final Russian drive on Warsaw, and he was worried about what would happen to his family. He had visions of his friends, Tytus, Wiluś, Jan, and many more, falling in battle to Russian bayonets. He managed to play, and the reviews, which he sent to Warsaw, were favourable. Franz Kandler wrote in the *German Musical Journal*:

> Also taking part was M. Chopin, who had proved himself during his visit last year as a pianist of the first rank. About the performance of his new Concerto in E minor, written in a serious style, we will reiterate what we have written before: whoever expresses his art with such nobility of purpose deserves the greatest admiration.

On June 11 Frycek played his E minor concerto again at a benefit concert at the Kärntnertor Theatre.

As the weather grew warmer, Dr Malfatti repaired to his summer residence in the Wienerwald. June 24 was St John's Day, and Pietro Mechetti gave Johann Malfatti a surprise name-day party there. Several singers, including Franz Wild, were invited to provide a musical soirée after dinner, along with Frycek as accompanist. The house was perched on top of a hill; from one side there was a view of Vienna, and on the other a high wall, beyond which could be seen scattered villages and monasteries. It was an idyllic evening: the geniality of the host, the elegance, the easy atmosphere, the lively company, the wit over an exquisite supper that went on for a very long time, and finally the music. 'A crowd of strangers listened to the music on the terrace,' wrote Frycek. 'The moon shone, the fountains played, and a divine scent wafted from the open orangery – a magnificent night in a most enchanting place. Huge French windows were flung open to their full extent leading to a terrace from where you can see the whole of Vienna.' It was past midnight when Frycek's carriage took him back to the Kohlmarkt.

While waiting, Frycek had been composing. The Scherzo in B minor, with the Christmas carol trio section, was now complete, as was his Ballade in G minor, Op. 23. He was augmenting his set of 'Exercises'. He found that through these technical studies he was able to express his innermost feelings in a new way, and he became increasingly absorbed in them.

By the middle of July his passport had turned up and Kumelski had recovered. Frycek had stamped on his passport 'London via Paris', by the French Embassy, but when he went to the Russian Embassy for stamping, it was the Russians' turn to hassle. They kept the passport for two days, and then only authorized it as far as Munich. Frycek decided he would worry about it when he got to Munich. A final hiccup was the necessity of a health certificate. The cholera had taken hold in Vienna, to the consternation of Austria's neighbours. With all their papers finally in order, Kumelski and Frycek left Vienna on July 20 along the road to Salzburg. After Salzburg was the frontier with the Kingdom of Bavaria, where the frontier with Germany is today. The road continued through Wasserburg and into King Ludwig I's capital, Munich.

Frycek quickly integrated into Munich's musical set. He met several musicians and singers, including Peter von Lindpaintner, with whom he became friendly. They persuaded him to give a concert, and offered to help with arrangements. The venue was the Munich Philharmonic Society Hall; the date was August 28. A number of other Bavarian musicians and singers took part. Herr Stunz conducted the orchestra as Frycek played his E minor Concerto and, for the fatherland, the *Fantasy on Polish Airs*. The performance was warmly applauded and the reviews were favourable; but Frycek's mind was on other things. The image of Konstancja, so far away and getting further all the time, tormented him mercilessly, and he could not stop thinking about her, nor about events in Poland. The money from the sale of Tsar Alexander's ring arrived, as he had requested, in Munich, which alleviated his situation. His depression had become suicidal, and he began to write down his feelings in a diary. 'I wish I were dead,' he wrote.

In Poland the Russian General Pashkievitch set in motion his plan to settle the insurrection for once and for all. Instead of attacking Warsaw from the east through Praga in the time honoured way, he decided to skirt Warsaw to the south and take it from the less fortified west. Skrzyniecki, instead of attacking the Russians, created diversions to lure them into a trap, but Pashkievitch was not duped. He took up positions along Warsaw's western flanks, centred round the suburb of Wola. On September 6 he attacked Warsaw.

It was about this time that Frycek moved on. He left Munich by the Augsburg road, and reached the Kingdom of Württemberg at Ulm, on a smaller, younger Danube than he had known so well in Vienna. His arrival in Stuttgart, King Wilhelm I's capital, coincided with the fall of Warsaw on September 8.

The Poles fought to the death for every every inch of ground. The battle lasted two days, and the devastation of western Warsaw was total. General Sowiński, in whose house Frycek had written the *Schweizerbub* Variations for his wife Katarzyna only a few months previously, was killed in action. The new Commander-in-Chief, General Krukowiecki, had no choice but to capitulate. Dark days of terror, retribution and barbarism followed. People were deported to the wastes of Siberia in an endless stream of carts. Prisons were full, and more commandeered. Russian officials moved in swiftly and took over, and in their wake secret police, interrogators and torturers. The sound of gunfire was constant, as executions were summarily carried out. Refugees turned westwards, and many found a welcome in Prussia, Paris, London and Edinburgh. The Polish army was still out in the field, now scattered meaninglessly at no longer strategic points. Capture by the Russians was the worst of all evils; escape was only possible by crossing into Prussia and surrendering their arms.

Frycek only stopped over in Stuttgart for a couple of days because von Lindpaintner had asked him to call on his friends. Frycek did so, and found a warm welcome at the home of pianist and composer Johann Peter Pixis (1788–1874), the younger brother of the director of the Prague Conservatory, whom Frycek had met two years previously. The news of Warsaw's fall reached him a couple of days later. His rage was terrible, his depression profound, and he walked as if in a daze. He could only express this rage in music, and it was at this time that he wrote the last of his 'Exercises' an angry rhapsody in C minor, the key Beethoven had used to depict tragedy. His anger was expressed in the *perpetuum mobile* runs in the left hand. The 'Exercises' became known as the *Études*, and the first set of twelve, published later as Op. 10, was now complete. No. 12 has gained the subtitle of 'Revolutionary' by tradition, as Frycek never gave names to his works.

Before turning his eyes westwards, he wrote in his notebook:

The suburbs have been destroyed, burned down. Jaś. Wiluś. Have they died on the fortifications? Sowiński, beloved man, in the hands of those bandits. O God, you exist, but you don't avenge. Haven't you had enough of Moscow's crimes? Or are you a Muscovite? My poor father. Dearest man, starving without a *grosz* to buy bread for Mother. My sisters. Have they fallen to the fury of Moscow's beasts unbound? Pashkievitch, that hound of Mohilev, conquering the seat of Europe's first kings. A Muscovite ruling the world. Dear father, such pleasures await you in your old age. Mother, dear, suffering Mother, you survived your daughter only to see the Muscovites trample on her bones as they come to oppress you. Powązki. Have they respected her grave? The city burned. Why can't I kill just one Muscovite? Oh, Tytus, Tytus.

* * * * *

In January 1850 Mrs Ludwika Jędrzejewicz crossed into Poland and travelled on to Warsaw, carrying a casket. In this casket was the heart of her brother, Fryderyk Chopin, removed at the autopsy following the composer's death in Paris the previous year. His body was laid to rest at the Père Lachaise cemetery in Paris. She took the casket to the Church of the Holy Cross, in the Krakowskie Przedmieście, where Fryderyk Chopin's heart was entombed in one of the columns. A plaque marks the column which today is always bedecked with flowers.

Józio's Journey

from Warsaw to the Silesian Spas
as written by himself

by Ludwika Chopin (J. Wecki, Warsaw, 1830)
Translated and abridged by
Iwo and Pamela Zaluski

I
Departure from Warsaw

Thank God we have set off at last, because Mama and Papa [Prakseda & Fryderyk Skarbek] have long promised to go to the Spas and take me, Józio [Józef Skarbek], with them; every day I thought the day had come, but the day refused to come. At night I dreamt that I was on my way and that I was looking at the lovely countryside, but when I woke all I saw was the same old room.

It's a pity that our coach isn't as big as I'd have liked; they didn't let me take all my things with me, and my toys were left behind. They only let me take stories and writing books. I took with me MORAL TALES and ENTERTAINMENTS FOR CHILDREN by the authoress of RECOLLECTIONS OF A GOOD MOTHER [Klementyna Tańska]. My teacher gave me a book with blank pages, and told me to write in it everything that happens on the way, all the things I see, those things that I like and those I don't, so that I remember everything better. He also advised me to write down my thoughts, and even how I behaved, and how many times I've been naughty; but I will not write this, as it won't happen to Józio. I promised to do as he says, and promises must be kept, as I have been taught not to make false promises. So, to begin:

II
Łowicz

That morning we all got up early. I was first, and by five o'clock I was dressed, but it wasn't until nine o'clock that we set off from Warsaw. How long it seemed; from five till nine I counted the hours, but it was only four, and yet it seemed like all day. I was so happy that I would see many new things on the way, and we drove till nightfall. Passing through Sochachew we reached Łowicz in time for dinner. It was my first visit to Łowicz, and I preferred it to Sochachew; there were beautiful houses, similar to those in Warsaw, and the streets were wider and cleaner. There were three churches, but I only saw the Parish Church [the Collegiate Church still there]. Papa showed me round the whole church; it is very lovely and as grand as the churches in Warsaw. He also took me to see the Chapel of St Wiktoria to show me the curtain of marble. 'Look well, Józio, at this chapel,' he said, 'and remember that the body of Prince Józef was brought here from Germany, and lay here for two weeks. Do you remember who Prince Józef [Poniatowski] was? What have you read about him?'

'I remember everything,' I replied, 'and I shall never forget about Prince Józef, for he was such a good man. He loved Poles, so he must have loved me, as my name is also Józef.'

Papa smiled, and added, 'If he had known you, he would surely have loved you just as other Poles.'

I recalled that on 19 October 1813, before I was born, this beloved Prince died. From the church we went to the cemetery. It was very pleasant there, not as pretty as the Saxon Gardens, but I quite liked it; there were no straight streets, only winding and pretty pathways. There were many flowers, as beautiful as in any botanical garden. I also saw a tower [the tower of the church is separate], similar to a church tower, with very pretty little rooms inside, but we did not have time to visit them. It is a pity I could not see inside, as I did not like the outside very much. The tower had only recently been built, but seemed like a hundred years old. Although Papa explained to me that the older it seems the finer it is, I thought that if this belonged to me I would put a nicely decorated green house there, instead of this cluttered tower. In front of the gardens there is a big lawn; poplar-lined walkways lead from each of the four sides. It was a lovely place to run around.

After lunch we left Łowicz along the newly paved road, the coach bumping along like a cart. We arrived at a tavern in Plecka Dąbrowa, where we were met by women with berries. I was very grateful, because I love berries, but I wondered how they get to grow in the forest, where no one sows the seeds. I always thought that the earth must be tilled to make things grow, and yet they grow there without any care and effort, and are far nicer than groats and peas, for which the earth must be dug hard. Papa said that God often makes Man get down to hard work, else even God might forget about him.

After a tasty tea, we climbed back into the carriage, so as to reach Kutno by nightfall. When we arrived, I thought the Palace of the Lord of Kutno, which we saw from a distance, was very beautiful. But the town was not as nice as Łowicz, although the inn was good, the people helpful, and the cooking was tasty. I was only curious as to where we would sleep.

III
The Hill Beside Koło

I slept well, but Papa woke me early, because Mama and Papa wanted to make an early start, and I had been taught that children's first duty was always to obey their parents and elders. The first town after Kutno was Krośniewice. Nowhere along the road from Warsaw have I seen such a beautiful inn, or such a fine house. We drove along a straight road to the town of Kłodawa for lunch, but I saw nothing there. It was raining so hard that I could not go out into the town, and I could not even see the Market Place through the window. We had to wait a long time for it to stop, and soon after midday we continued.

I was bored by the endless straight road, and I wanted it to be full of bends. When I complained to Papa he replied, 'You complain about the straight road, but if it weren't straight we would not have got this far. Let this be a lesson for you, and remember that in life you must always keep to the straight road.'

'What do you mean, a straight road?' I asked. 'When I come to left and right turns, must I always continue straight?'

'That is not how to understand it, darling,' said Papa. 'To go along a straight road is always to tell the truth and to do as you say, and treat everyone the same to their faces as behind their backs, and to fulfil all your obligations diligently.'

'I shall write it down in my notebook,' I replied.

That day we were in Koło, a fine town in lovely surroundings. Beyond Koło were turf steps up to a stone monument in the shape of a pyramid. Papa said that the monument had been erected to commemorate the completion of the new road. We stopped and went up to the monument. On one side was a Latin inscription which I did not understand, because I have not started learning Latin yet, and on the other, in Polish, the date on which the Kalisz Road was completed. On the other side of the road, opposite the monument, there is a bench where the late King Alexander was supposed to have sat and gazed at the beautiful view. I also sat on the bench, and enjoyed it so much that I had a feeling that I was someone grander than just Józio. When I get home I shall tell everyone that I sat where the King had sat.

We reached Turek before eight. I did not want to go there, having often heard Mama reading the *Courier* about the war with the Greeks, and I don't like the Turks for always oppressing the poor Greeks. They should listen to the story of Tadeusz, and that would shame them into changing their ways. But this Turek, which we drove through, is not as bad as I had imagined, and the landlord of the inn also gave us a lovely, clean little room, with windows giving on to the Market Place. In front of the house there were steps with little benches – oh, how nice it was just to sit there, and how cool, but Mama and Papa made me go to bed early.

IV

The Frontier

This time I did not sleep well. By seven we were on the road again, so we were in Kalisz in good time. Oh, what a fine town is Kalisz, completely different to all the other towns I had seen. It was more like Warsaw; what houses, palaces, broad streets, people. If I had not known that I'd left Warsaw, I would have thought I was coming into it, but by a different road. Papa told me that the town has not long been built, and a few years ago was very grubby. 'All this has been achieved by hard work,' said Papa, 'because the more people worked, the more work accumulated; as the saying goes, drop by drop makes up a measure; and so brick by brick you get a house, houses make a road, and roads make up a town.'

'But how do people work to build a town?' I asked Papa. 'I could work all year and not make one brick. Were all the people here masons and carpenters?'

'No, darling,' replied Papa, 'people earn a living in different ways. A baker can earn enough money by baking bread to pay a mason and a carpenter to build him a house,'

'But why do people spend all their money on houses? Couldn't they spend it on something better? Why do people build such tall houses of stone? Can't people live just as comfortably in a low house, such as our one in the country, as in a tall one?'

Papa smiled and continued, 'The town is different from the country; in a town whoever has a large house can live in it himself, and let part of it to someone else, and so he will benefit from it twice over; he has his own home, and also an income from it.'

We were only in Kalisz for a couple of hours, but Mama wanted to show me some fine places in the town. We stopped at the Church of St Joseph [still there], where I knelt down and asked God for good health for Mama, Papa, Granny and everybody, and I did not forget me, too, saying the prayer I say every day with Mama.

From the church we went to the park. But why is it called a park? It cannot be called a garden as it's not fenced in. Our Saxon Garden in Warsaw is surrounded by latticed wrought iron, and here there are no flowers or fruit, and these things should be in a garden. Whether it's a park or a garden, it does not matter, it's always nice here, with the babbling stream, the bridge over it, quite a few trees, and room to run about out of the sun, because Mama does not like me to run in the sun. We left the park and returned to the inn for dinner and set off straight after, because Mama wanted to stop at Auntie's before nightfall.

I was curious about the frontier. I thought it would be something I'd never seen – as I've never been abroad before. Arriving at the frontier at the village of Biskupice, if Mama had not told me we had passed the frontier I would not have guessed it. There was a shabby hut on one side of the road, and on the other a post painted black and white, opposite another one painted red and white. The black and white one was ugly; ours was much nicer because it was red and had two eagles facing each other standing on top of it. I did not feel like travelling any further on the sandy road, on which horses go slowly. If only there were something nice to look at, other than endless fields. What a difference; after our fine road, here it is boring sand. If it goes on like this I do not know when we shall get to Kudowa, which is still very far away.

It was not until ten o'clock that we arrived at Auntie's [Anna Wiesiołowska], although she lives only three miles [1 old Polish mile = approximately 5 kilometres] past Kalisz. We found neither Auntie nor Uncle [Stefan Wiesiołowski] at home – they had gone to some neighbours. Ludwisia and Romanek were asleep, so I could not see them. I wanted to wait up for Auntie, but was not allowed to. 'You must go to bed and sleep, Józio, because it's late.' But I was not at all sleepy. I managed to persuade Mama to let me write up my diary. Oh, how happy I was to be at Auntie's. And tomorrow I shall play with my cousins.

V

Grandad's Grave

I dreamt about Ludwisia and Romanek, running about with them round the garden; I also dreamt about Auntie, but I only really saw her this morning; as I opened my eyes there she was, standing by my bed. Auntie gave me a hug, and when I asked about Ludwisia and Romanek, she told me they were still asleep. When Auntie had left, I dressed quickly and went out into the yard, thinking that they might come running out. Auntie came out and said, 'The children are just getting up, so why don't you come in and play with us?' Taking me by the hand, she led me into the playroom, which led from the bedroom. I could hear Ludwisia, who had learned from the maid that we had arrived, and was shrieking happily, 'What? Has Józio arrived?' Soon she was running towards us and hugged me saying, 'How are you, dear little cousin, I haven't seen you for a long time; you've grown – you're already wearing a frock coat. I'm not all that small either; I can read already, and I'll soon be able to read Helenka's book which your Papa had sent. And you should see all the new toys I got from Mama for being good. Come and see.' I was about to run after her when we were all called to breakfast. Ludwisia and I sat together at her little table, and what fun we had, laughing so loudly that Mama called to us, 'Quiet, children.'

We quietened down a little, but soon we were as noisy as before, because the maid came in with Romanek. Ludwisia ran over to kiss his hand good morning, as she had not seen him yet. I also gave him a hug, but it was not the Romanek I imagined, the one I dreamt about running around the garden with me – he could not even walk yet, and had to be carried by the nurse. Although I kissed and cuddled him, instead of doing the same to me, he pulled a cross face and turned away. 'Leave him alone, Józio, or he'll burst into tears,' cried Mama. I walked away, took Ludwisia by the hand, and asked if we could go into the garden. For a long time we ran around the garden together; then Uncle came to play with us, picked some delicious cherries for us and let us pick strawberries and raspberries ourselves, warning us not to eat those with worms in them. After we had eaten a few good strawberries and raspberries – without worms — we picked some more for Mama and for Auntie, and went back indoors. Mama and Auntie were very pleased and thanked us, and told us not to go out again, but to play indoors, because dinner was soon to be served, and we had hardly rested when the maid came in and said that it was already on the table. Dear God, I thought, it's two o'clock already and I will not be with Auntie for much longer, as tomorrow we must be on our way, and it's only a few hours until night-time.

At table I sat opposite a wall with old paintings hanging on it. I asked Papa about the people in the paintings, and Papa answered, 'Don't you recognize Grandad and Granny [Count Kacper and Countess Ludwika Skarbek], Józio?'

'No,' I replied. 'I don't have a Granny like that. Mine's completely different. She doesn't have a wig like that, only a bonnet; and my Grandad did not have his hair in a plait, and did not wear a frock coat like that. This one here looks like a German, and my Grandad was Polish. No, it's not my Grandad.'

'Ah, but you see, Józio, this portrait was painted a long time ago, and in those days Granny and Grandad used to dress like that.' I was surprised at the fashions of long ago; I looked at the paintings carefully, but I could not recognize my grandparents.

After dinner we went to see Grandad's grave at the parish church. Mama, Papa, Auntie and Uncle went together, and I took Ludwisia's hand, and we ran on ahead, because, although the road was lined with trees, we were still very hot in the sunshine. Reaching the village where Grandad was buried [Kotłów], we met the parish priest, Uncle's good friend; when he learned where we were going, he invited us to call on him for a rest. It was the first time I had been to a priest's house. It was very nice, simple, with pretty rooms; he does not have a lot of furniture, but everything is neat and tidy. He offered us some delicious cherries. When we were rested, the priest took us to Grandad's grave. Dear God, this is where Grandad is lying, I thought to myself, seeing the gravestone surrounded with trees, and I was so sad that I burst into tears. Dear Grandad! Dear God! I was only very little when he died, but I remember how much he loved me, how he used to play with me, and now I shall never see him again, now all I can do is to pray to God for him. I knelt down beside the grave and said a little prayer for him. As I finished I heard Mama's voice calling to me. I ran quickly to join them and Mama asked me where I had been; I replied that I was finishing my prayer. She hugged me as tears came into her eyes, and began to whisper to Auntie – in French.

Meanwhile Ludwisia was running around the cemetery, gathering flowers. 'Come here, Józio,' she called, 'come and help me pick these pretty flowers.'

'No,' I replied, 'you should not pick them, Ludwisia, and throw away the ones you've got in your hand, for those flowers are for the dead.' My little cousin scattered her bouquet on the fresh graves; then she took me by the hand and together we ran ahead.

Back at the house, tea was waiting for us on Ludwisia's table, which was laid in the garden. When it began to get dark, we came indoors and Auntie played for us on the piano, while Ludwisia and I danced the *kozak*, the mazurka and some other dances. So we passed the time till supper. Soon after it was time for me to say goodbye to my cousin, because Auntie said she had to go to bed at the usual time, even though she wanted to play a little longer.

VI
The Storm

It was sad leaving Auntie. I got up early to spend more time with my cousins, and we left at nine. Uncle came with us for a few miles, and we passed through Mikstat, a village that came to my mind because I had heard the saying 'From which date? From Mikstat'. So I thought it would be a famous place. But there were just a few newly built stone houses. Papa told me that the village had burnt down a few years ago, and they are rebuilding it; but even before the fire it was very shabby. Uncle came with us as far as Ostrzeszów, where he said goodbye. I have not seen an uglier village on this journey than Ostrzeszów. It was good that we did not have to stay there, because I do not know where we would have put up. There was no inn to be seen, only houses, each uglier than the other; only one in the whole village stood out, a synagogue. In the past bands of outlaws used to invade the village, and to protect themselves, the villagers built a tall tower in the middle of the village [still there] on top of which a guard was posted to warn the inhabitants of danger. From this word *ostrzegać* (to warn), they called the village Ostrzeszów, or Schildberg in German.

We continued on sandy roads towards Sycew. The road was boring, and I fell asleep, and I was still asleep when we arrived at Sycew. It was reckoned to be a nice little town, but I did not see much of it. Mama and Papa went out into the town and said that I should not be woken until their return. I woke up when it was time for dinner. So I missed seeing my first real Silesian town, but as we left I noticed a long, pretty road, lined with poplars, leading to a large and fine palace, which Papa said belonged to the Princes Byron. It has a famous pheasantry. 'A pheasantry', said Papa, 'is a place where birds called pheasants are bred; they are released into the woods in summer, and in winter they are lured indoors, where they are fed. Keeping these birds is very expensive, which is why pheasantries are not very common, but we can boast of a similar one at Skierniewice, though it's not as fine as this one. In some houses in Warsaw they keep pheasants for curiosity. Pheasants are beautiful, with dark green and red feathers. They are delicious to eat, and you might just happen to eat pheasant during this trip.' I said to Papa that they should not kill such beautiful birds for us to eat.

Oh, I will not forget the fright that I had on the road to Sycew. A terrible storm burst, the rain began to pour, lightning flashed and thunder roared without stopping. I did not know what to do. I cuddled up to Mama and Papa, and I shook all over. 'Why are you so afraid?' asked Mama. 'This storm will soon be over, and the rain, too, will not last very long, the sky will brighten, and the road will improve. You will be able to see the countryside better.'

'But before the storm passes,' I said to Mama, 'we might be struck by lightning. I remember a story about a little boy who once went for a walk with his father; when a storm broke he wanted to shelter under a tree, but his father said it is dangerous at such times to go under trees, because there is a chance of the lightning striking there. It was true, because no sooner had the little boy walked a few steps away than lightning struck the tree.'

'But we're not sheltering under trees, my child,' said Papa.

'No,' I said, 'but our coach is made of wood, so we could be struck.'

'Trees and timber are different; trees have trunks which flow with sap, and are alive, but timber has been cut down and sawed up; it is dead and has no moisture, and does not attract lightning as trees do. When you are older, you will understand better the thunder and lightning that frighten you today.'

Also, we must trust in God,' added Mama, 'and give ourselves over to Him, so that nothing bad happens to us. So calm yourself, my child.' I did calm down a little, but I was still glad when the storm passed and the thunder and lightning disappeared into the distance; only the rain continued endlessly, and we could not reach Oleśnica by nightfall, but stopped at the village before.

VII
The First Mountain

It was a bad lodging, and Mama and Papa could not sleep, because of all the Germans drinking beer and smoking tobacco which made the whole inn dark. But I took no notice, and slept well. The following day was fresh after the rain, and it promised to be a pleasant journey, especially as the boring sand had come to an end. The road became harder, but still not as good as our paved ones. After a while I saw some tall towers ahead which made me think there was a great city ahead. 'That is Oleśnica,' said Papa. 'It's not a great city, as you'll see.' Shortly we were driving into a narrow but clean street, then to the left and to the right, and finally into the Market Place. What cherries there were! And what enormous strawberries! It was a lovely town, but all I remember were the cherries and strawberries, because as soon as I had eaten some of both, the coach set off again, and soon we were out of town. From Oleśnica we found ourselves on a fine long road lined with trees, till we came to another little town. I wondered what this town was called. 'Hundsfeld,' said Papa.

'Hundsfeld? You mean Psiepole ["Dogfield"]? Where Krzywousty beat the Germans in 1109? Oh, I'm so happy to be where that brave King once came with the Polish army.'

'You see, Józio,' said Papa, 'how good it is to learn carefully and willingly, because not only will we always profit from it, but it can also give us great pleasure. This place interests you now because you know what happened here long ago. If you hadn't known this, you might have passed through the town without even asking where its name came from.'

After leaving Psiepole, Papa asked, 'Can you see the mountain, Józio?' I looked in every direction, but there was no mountain to be seen, just the flat plain. 'Look ahead, far away to the left, rising up, level with that grey-blue cloud. Look closely and you will see it doesn't change shape, which means it's a mountain, and not a cloud.'

'What? A blue mountain? Our Denassauski Mountains near Warsaw are green, not blue.'

'This one is also green, and when we get closer you'll see it'll be similar to our Denassauski, only bigger and different in shape. But because we are very far from it, it seems to be purple.'

'I don't understand,' I said, 'Are all the mountains we shall be going through like that one? How shall we climb so high? There might be an accident.'

'Don't be afraid,' said Papa. 'We will not be going through high mountains, and even so, everyone takes great care about travelling safely.'

'What is that mountain called?'

'Zottenberg [Sobótka]. Write the name in your notebook, and also what we have been talking about. You will laugh about it one day when you read it.' I should like to know what there will be to laugh at myself about – after all there was nothing funny about it. But I wrote about it in my notebook, because Papa had told me to.

At two o'clock in the afternoon we arrived at Wrocław. I don't know how to begin describing this city. I sat till dusk in the window, looking at everything. There were lots of people, just like in Warsaw, only mostly Germans, and carriages, but not as nice as the ones in Warsaw. There were stalls, buildings and tents. There was a market, and houses in every direction; and an enormous Town Hall. It was hard to take it all in. Now evening had come, and it was impossible to see the street. Everything is so jumbled in my head.

VIII
Wrocław

We have just returned from a walk, and I am so tired that my legs ache. We are staying in the Market Square itself, and the inn has a golden tree as its sign. Opposite is the Town Hall, old and dirty, and yet they say it's very beautiful. Beneath my window there are stalls with merchants who have come to the market. It was fun watching the people bustling about and going in and out of the shops. I saw some lovely toys, little ponies, ninepins, soldiers and dolls. I asked Mama if she would buy me something, but Papa said, 'No, there's no room in the coach for anything else.' I nearly cried when Papa added, 'Józio, you should know better than to be unreasonable about filling the coach with toys.

When we reach our destination, then we can think about toys, but in the meantime, you must be a good boy.' Mama called out, 'Get your cap, Józio, we're going into the town.'

We went to the shops because Mama had something to buy. That is when I learned that you should be able to speak German here. In the shops and in the street they only speak German, and I cannot understand anything. Mama went into a shop to buy me a new cap. I thought the merchant did not want to take the money that Mama offered. I was afraid Mama would give up trying, but in the end Mama bought the cap. I jumped with joy and threw off my old cap and asked if I could wear the new one; but when I went out into the narrow alleys between the stalls, there was a big crowd, and I was afraid for myself and for my cap; so I held on to Mama's skirt with one hand in case I got lost, and with the other I held my cap tightly in case it got knocked off.

After dinner we went out for a walk where there were no crowds, where smartly dressed people were strolling. This was a lovely walk over the River Odra, which flows through Wrocław. I was told that here, long ago, there were fortifications and ramparts; but it is better that they made them into a garden, that they turned the ditches into gravelled walkways along which I could run among the lawns, flowers and the shady trees. And there was music, which was so nice to listen to that I wished we could also have music playing in the Saxon Gardens and alleys.

Papa became thirsty, because it was very hot, and we went into a garden beside a wide walkway, which was full of stools and little tables, all painted white. 'Here we can get anything,' said Papa. 'I'm going to order a bottle of beer, because I'm very thirsty, and we can sit down and have a little rest.'

'Is Papa going to drink beer in this garden?' I asked. 'Will Papa get a beer here? And won't Papa be ashamed to drink beer in front of other people?'

'Why should I be ashamed?' said Papa.

'In Warsaw, whenever I ask Papa if we can go into one of those gardens, Papa always refuses, saying that one shouldn't go into those places, even though Papa and I are both thirsty, and yet here Papa doesn't care if people will snigger or not, and wants to sit down with a bottle of beer?'

'It's not the same, my child. Here the custom is accepted, and no one will hold it against me, while in Warsaw it is frowned upon.'

'Can't they bring this custom to us? It would be very convenient; there are so many things brought to us from abroad, they should bring in this one too.'

'Perhaps it will come to that one day.' The garden began to fill up, and soon there were very few tables free. Not only gentlemen, but also well-dressed ladies sat drinking beer. Everyone brought their own pipes and cigars to smoke, which suprised me, for I had never seen this in Warsaw. Papa often retired to his room with a pipe whenever ladies called on Mama, because he said that it is impolite to smoke tobacco in front of ladies. Here no one takes any notice, and all these ladies have to sit surrounded by smoke. Again I asked Papa why they do this in this city, and again Papa replied, 'It is the custom.'

After a little rest we continued our walk. New paths led us to a hill from which I saw the mountain that Papa had showed me on the road. It could be seen clearly, and even though it was grey I would still have recognized it as a mountain. I ran up to the bridge, which was not very pretty, but I do so like to go on bridges, and at last I found one in this garden. I must not forget to write about it in my diary, especially as I stood on it for a long time, looking at the swans swimming past. Soon we returned to our lodgings along a different path, meeting many people who were just setting out to take the air. No doubt they were going to the garden, I thought enviously, as it was so nice there, and so jolly with the music. I will remember that garden for a very long time.

IX
The Name Day

When we went out into the street this morning, I was amazed at the number of flowers for sale. Would they be throwing garlands into the water, just like the garlands of cornflowers that boys and girls carry about in their baskets on St John's Day back home? I wondered what these garlands were for. We met a gentleman, an old friend of Papa's. He asked whether we might call on him, as he lived very close by, and it was his wife's name day, and she would be delighted to see us, so we all went off together.

Entering the house, I was surprised to see the stairs bedecked with flowers, and above them a sign saying 'WILLKOMMEN' in large letters. I could read this because it was written in Polish letters, but I did not understand what it meant. Papa explained it was a greeting to guests.

'And why is it written in Polish letters, as everyone speaks German here, and nobody understands Polish?'

'These are not Polish letters, Józio, they are Roman. The Poles, like many European nations, have adopted the Roman alphabet, and the Germans are also beginning to use it. There are already many German books written in Roman letters.' The doors leading to the rooms were bedecked with flowers; there was an inscription above every one, and there were different garlands everywhere.

Then the lady herself appeared, and with much bowing, talked to Mama for a long time in German, while her husband went to fetch the children, two little boys and two little girls, all beautifully dressed. The older boy, Henryś, had on a brand new sailor-suit, because the buttons shone brightly. Karolinka, the older daughter, wore a lovely white dress with a pink ribbon round the waist. The younger children were also dressed in white, and wore wreaths of flowers on their heads. The children went up to their mother; the two eldest placed a garland of roses round her shoulders, and the youngest two put flowers from baskets at her feet. Then they took off the garlands and presented them to their mother for plaiting, and then everyone began to kiss and hug her, and tears of joy came to their eyes. Now I know why there were all those flowers for sale. I shall have to make such garlands for Mama; I'm always sad that I cannot do anything for Mama on her name day, as I have not yet started to learn to draw or to play music; Papa said that next year I will have a teacher for drawing and music. Mama's name day will be soon, and I shall make her a pretty garland, so I shall try to find some nice flowers. It is a pity I have not got a sister, so I shall have to make it on my own. But I do not know what to do about Papa's name day; it is in winter, when it is difficult to find flowers, but I am sure Mama will buy me some from a hothouse.

Then the children took me into another room, where there were lots of toys, and they each had their own special trinkets, even the oldest girl; even though she was already ten, she still dressed her doll and sewed her frocks. We played as best we could, using signs, because the children did not speak Polish, and I did not understand German. But I did understand that a rifle was for shooting, and a rocking horse was for riding. Henryś had just set up the ninepins and I was just about to roll the ball when Mama called, 'Say goodbye nicely to the young ladies and gentlemen, Józio, and get your cap because we must be on our way.' As we left, the lady give me a hug and some gingerbreads, and the children were sorry that I could not stay with them longer. It was quite late when we got back.

X
Poor Oleś

We were all sitting in our lodgings when there was a knock at the door, and in came a well-dressed man with a little boy. 'I am Polish,' said the stranger. 'I have come to speak not for myself, but for this boy. I am not related to him, but the care of this child has fallen on to my shoulders. Oleś's father, born in the Czech lands, had settled in Warsaw and gave music lessons. He married a poor but educated young lady. They lived simply but happily for a few years, their only joy being their little son. Before long, God saw fit to bestow ill-health upon his dear mother, and last year she departed from him for ever, leaving him only his father. Her long illness had exacted expenses which her husband's meagre income could scarce afford, so that he fell into debt; but God never forgets the unfortunate, and he received notification from Prague that a distant relative had left him half of his modest estate. My good friend, a citizen of Warsaw, who was setting out for the spas, wished to be of service to the music teacher, and took him and the boy along, intending to escort him to Prague, and after having concluded his affairs there, to bring them back to Warsaw. When they reached Wrocław, the father became seriously ill, and, because he had to continue his journey, my friend entrusted the care of Oleś to me. Despite the efforts of the doctors and all my efforts, the raging fever resisted all healing, and the child became an orphan. Shortly before his death the music teacher regained consciousness, took me to be his benefactor and begged me to protect his little child, while indicating the casket containing the documents connected with the Prague affair. As I did not know what to do, having neither the time nor the money to go to Prague, I decided to contact any fellow-countrymen on their way to the waters, to see if one might be prepared to do for the child the kindness of taking him to Prague and looking after his interests there.'

We were moved by the stranger's tale, and Papa took the boy into his care, and Papa and the stranger left to arrange getting the money in Prague. 'Why are you crying, Józio?' asked Mama when we were alone.

I replied, 'I am crying for the poor little boy. Dear God, he is so unlucky. He doesn't have a mama or a papa any more; and if it hadn't been for that good man, I wonder what would have happened to him?'

'He doesn't understand yet what death is,' said Mama. 'The man said that he is always asking about his father, always looking for him, thinking that he has gone off somewhere and crying because he did not take him along too. Poor Oleś.'

'Oh, Mama, he will be so much better off now, with us; I will do everything I can to cheer him up. Oh, it will be so good, Mama, that together we will get to know him; I will learn to love him, I will never hold anything against him, and will always give way to him, because he is smaller than me, and he has no mama and papa.'

XI
Old Maids

Oleś slept soundly, did not cry, his eyes were bright, and he even smiled. The following morning, before packing, we played together until ten o'clock, when we left Wrocław.

The road from Wrocław to Frankenstein [Ząbkowice Śląskie]

was very beautiful; whichever way I looked there were lovely views. The ride was good, because the road was paved, and lined with fruit trees, with lovely cherries ripening, which we were not allowed to pick except off the ground. We saw many women carrying baskets of fruit into town, so we stopped several times, and Mama bought cherries which she shared between Oleś and me. We passed several villages, and the horses were tired; although it was too early to stop, Papa ordered a halt so that the horses could have some hay. Oleś soon fell asleep. He woke suddenly when the coach stopped, opened his eyes, and cried, 'What's happening? What are those big buildings?'

'That's a mountain,' replied Papa. 'Do you remember, Józio, the mountain we saw from the other side of Wrocław? This is the same one, Zottenberg. Now we're closer to it, you can see for yourself.'

'Oh, Papa, let's climb the mountain while the horses are eating their hay. I'd love to know what there is up there. It's very close, because I can see houses and villages beneath it, and trees on top.'

'It's an illusion,' said Papa. 'From here it's over a mile. The houses you can see beneath it are the town.' So I had to stop thinking about climbing the mountain, and we went on our way.

A few miles further on we stopped at a village called Jordansmühle [Jordanów Śląski]. We went into an inn where two old women were sitting. One sat shivering by the stove, the other was seated at a table, knitting stockings. They were the ugliest women I have ever seen; the one by the stove was so frightful that Oleś burst into tears when she looked at him and said something in German in a grating voice to the landlady, who was so old, ugly and skinny, that I put my hand over my eyes so as not to see her. As soon as we had calmed Oleś down, I was wiping his eyes, and looking at the old hag out of the corner of my eye while edging towards the door. 'I can see that Józio is being silly,' said Mama, 'and cannot see that this old lady will not do him any harm; she is the landlady's mother, and loves children; look how she's kissing her grandchildren, who have just come from school with their satchels.'

We were shown rooms upstairs, and told that it would be quieter, because at this time all sorts of people like to come to rest or to have a drink. Up a few more stairs was our room, with a view of the church and the village; the sun was shining and it was very bright. Oleś and I chased one another round the room for fun, after which we stood at the window. 'Oh, Mama,' I called, 'look, there's another old hag. Look, Mama, she limps and pulls horrible faces and bows and jumps and claps her hands. Oh, Mama, she's coming this way. Dear God, why did we have to stop here?'

'That woman is confused,' said Mama, 'but there is nothing to be afraid of.' Mama took Oleś on her knee and cuddled him, because he had started crying again. I did not dare to go to the window, but hid behind the curtain and peered out at the old woman, who, seeing there was no one at the window, sat on a boulder. Papa told us about these women who had frightened us so much. He said that the old one who had been sitting by the stove, the landlady's mother, was the best woman in the whole world. She had worked hard all her life, and had bought this house, which now belongs to her daughter. God has also blessed her with grandchildren, who study hard at school and are well behaved. But the one sitting on that boulder lost her only son in the wars, which caused her to lose her mind. She thinks he will come back one day, and every day she runs out with open arms into the road to the place where she had said goodbye to him. 'So you see, children,' said Mama, 'that you should never judge people by appearances; it is always better to say too many good things about people than even just a few bad things. You must never let a deformed face or a shabby dress cloud your judgement of people. Behind a crooked face or dirty rags there is often a kindlier soul than behind a beautiful face and fine clothes.'

After dinner, learning that there was a little garden not far from the house, we all went there. Coming out of the house I met the mad woman in the doorway. I did not run away from her because I knew now that she was a good but unfortunate woman. What a garden it was, just a lawn with some apple trees. Oleś and I ran from tree to tree, holding hands. Papa found games for us to play, and even joined in himself. A short distance from Jordansmühle, we came to the town of Nimpsch [Niemcza], full of tight, badly paved roads going up and down, making the coach sway this way and that. There were many people, and there were signs hanging from every house, mostly painted shoes. Oleś liked the signs, and pointed to them, saying, 'Józio, look at those nice yellow shoes,' or 'What a pretty pony with a saddle, how real it looks, even if it is small,' or 'What a lovely little tree, with a man sitting under it, drinking beer'. It was all true, but I did not see any fine houses, coaches and gentlemen, because all I could see in front of the houses were women knitting stockings; they must have been maidservants. 'Papa, wouldn't it be so much nicer to see more gentlemen in fine coaches rather than all these shoe-makers, saddlers and other traders?'

'They need one another; why would these craftsmen work if there were no one to buy their wares? We all live for one another; the poor work for the rich, and so become richer themselves. Hard work and thrift bring wealth and respect.'

XII
The Unfortunate Father

The landlady prepared some good *kasza* [buckwheat], but it was too hot and I burnt my tongue. Mama scolded me for being care-less, pointing out how Oleś, although younger, ate slowly, and waited for the *kasza* to cool before putting it into his mouth.

This morning we were getting ready to continue our journey when we found there was no Papa. We looked for him here, there and everywhere, but there was no sign of him. In the main room of the inn there were lots of people, but no Papa, neither the landlord nor the landlady, who might know where he was. 'Oh, what a lovely little garden,' cried Oleś. The door was open and I could see the green grass and flowers outside.

'It looks very nice, Mama, can we run along and see it?' Mama said yes, and we jumped over the doorstep straight into the gar-den. 'Oh, Mama, it was just as well we came here,' I cried, be-cause there was Papa walking towards us with the landlord. The landlord was talking to Mama and Papa, leading them towards the cemetery which was separated from the garden by a fence. He pointed to some graves, and spoke with a trembling voice. When Mama and Papa had said goodbye to him, I asked why the man was crying.

'He is an unfortunate father,' said Papa. 'He once had a son, and lived only for him. This young man died while caring for his friend, who was mortally ill. He is buried in that cemetery, where his parents visit his grave every day. The unfortunate father took me there, and his grief made me forget that you might be looking for me.'

XIII
The Wedding

Approaching Glatz [Kłodzko] I saw from a distance great walls on the mountains. 'That's a fortress,' said Papa. I remembered my teacher telling me that a fortress was a town in which an army defended its land from enemy attack.

It was only four miles to Reinertz [Duszniki] and two more to Kudowa, so we should be there soon. I was glad, but sorry that we had to stay in Glatz. 'Why can't we go on? Why do the horses have to eat just when we are in a hurry to go on?'

'Because the poor horses are very tired, going up and down the mountains; they need rest and food. Also our brakes were damaged, and there is a big mountain ahead that we shall have to cross.' I never knew that when travelling in the mountains they put a piece of iron, like a shoe, under the wheel to stop the coach going too fast, as this could cause an accident. While dinner was being prepared, the brake was being mended and the horses fed, rested and harnessed.

I sat down to write up my diary when I was distracted by the sound of noisy music outside the window. I put down my pen, and rushed up with Oleś to see what was happening. There was a long procession that took up the whole street. Every coach driver wore a striped ribbon and a green twig in his hat. The coaches stopped in a line outside a house opposite, and beautifully dressed guests stepped out of them. I had never seen such strange costumes before. One of the gentlemen had blue stockings with red stripes, another one white with blue stripes and shoes with shining buckles, and long frock coats of many colours. There were waistcoats of coloured velvet and silk, decorated with embroidered silver flowers.

The men all had three-cornered hats on their heads or clutched to their shoulders. People held sprigs of rosemary tied with handkerchiefs, so as not to stain their silk gloves. Some women wore curious wide dresses with bodices bordered with lace, but mostly they wore skirts with embroidered aprons, and held fans. I have seen similar costumes at the theatre, worn by old 'Jegomoście and Jejmoście' [a Punch-and-Judy type slapstick] when they appeared on the scene, but I did not think people dressed like that any more. We asked what was happening, and were told that it was the wedding of a dyer's daughter. The whole guild was there, and the bride stood outside her door to welcome the arriving guests into her house. For a long time we sat staring at what was happening, and I was sorry we had to leave to continue on our way.

My mind was still full of the colourful ribbons and three-cornered hats when Papa pointed to the surrounding countryside. We had reached the top of the mountain. What a marvellous view. The near hills were covered in woods and meadows, some sown with wheat. There were rocky streams flowing past little huts. I could not sit still in the carriage and Papa let us get out, but kept hold of Oleś's and my hands, in case we fell down. Then we continued along the mountain road, and thought how tiny the houses in the valleys seemed. The man ploughing a field in the valley below looked even smaller than Oleś. While I was marvelling at this, Papa said, 'Compared to these mountains, people seem so small, so how tiny must we all be next to God, who created these mountains? Less than dust, and yet God cares for this dust, never forgets about it, grants all its needs, and observes its progress. You must love God so much, children, and always be good and obedient to your parents and to older people, that way you will become worthy of His continuing goodness. As long as you have His blessing, you will be truly happy.' I do not know if I have written Papa's words correctly, but I wrote them as best I could, so that I could remember the bits I liked best.

We drove on, and after a short while Papa said, 'We're there; Reinertz, where the waters are.'

'The waters?' I asked. 'I can't see any water.' Then we drove into a narrow street with tall houses on both sides, then along a wider street, past a church and into the Market Square.

'I only hope we will find good lodgings,' said Papa, 'because if there are a lot of people coming to the waters this year, it might be difficult to find somewhere.'

'But where are these waters?' I asked, 'I still can't see any waters.' I did hear the sound of rushing water at the big house that we had just passed on the left, near the church. I wondered if that was where they take the water from to drink? And what sort of water is it anyway? Why travel such a long way when we've got water in Warsaw from the well or the river? I was disappointed in the ugly town and its waters, and blamed everyone for bringing me here.

XIV
The Waters

Waking up this morning, I heard music. 'Is that music I can hear, Papa?' I asked, not believing my ears.

'Yes,' replied Papa.

I jumped out of bed and rushed over to the window; I saw several people with wind instruments playing lovely waltzes. 'Why are they playing under our window, Papa? Are we going to have this music every morning?'

'No, only today, my child. The local musicians have heard that there were newly arrived guests here, and they're playing a welcome. We must return the compliment and thank them.' When I began to bow to them from the window, Papa smiled, and sent down some money. Ah, that sort of thanks, I thought to myself, and went away from the window, because the music had stopped. Now I understand what these waters are. They're not like the springs I have often seen, from which water is poured straight into a glass from a little pipe. It is a nice, round room with a well in the middle, surrounded by railings in case any one falls in by accident, surely put there because of disobedient children going too close. There is a door and some steps from which women draw the water and serve the drinkers.

'Why have they got such long sticks?' I asked Papa. 'Is it because they can't reach the water with their hands?'

'Yes,' replied Papa, 'firstly because the well is very deep, and secondly, leaning into the well can be harmful; these waters contain certain elements which could even kill people who might breathe them in. Not long ago, there was an accident where the father of a large family leaned over too far, and was overcome by the vapours, and collapsed, and lay still.' I was horrified by what Papa had said, and did not even dare to go up to the railings.

'Are you going to drink these waters, Mama?' I asked. 'Isn't it going to harm you, if even the smell is so unhealthy?'

'Everything can be used to advantage,' said Papa, 'if taken in moderation, and according to need; that which is good for you in measured amounts can have terrible consequences if taken to excess.' Mama drank the water, and gave me a little to taste. I did not like it; it tasted like ink, and I much preferred the gingerbread biscuit that Mama gave me to nibble afterwards. Here they give those people who find the water unpleasant a gingerbread biscuit to cover the taste.

We have to walk a great deal here, and there are crowds of people walking and children running about. It is just like the Saxon Gardens; there is a big road lined with lime trees and paths going off in different directions. There is also another road which is covered, where people can shelter when it rains. But today it was not raining; it was a lovely day, the sun was shining, which is why everyone was strolling in the gardens full of lovely flowers, roses and mallows. I enjoyed the music, although Papa was cross because they played out of tune; but I did not know the difference, and listened to the merry mazurkas and waltzes with pleasure. They must enjoy playing, sitting in such a pretty place in the middle of the garden, under the lime trees, surrounded by all those people. Everywhere there are little tables, chairs and benches. Ladies bring their work, and sit there doing it while listening to the music. I could not run about until all the people out walking went away, and the walkways and roads were clear. I wish some other little boys had stayed to play; and why is Oleś sleeping so long? And there was something else I saw. Papa said it was called a waterfall; how beautiful – the water falling from high up, spraying and roaring, and tumbling down over the stones. I especially liked the little flowers growing out from the water. How lovely they were, and how fresh. They will never wither, because they will always be watered. But how did they get there in the first place?

Were they always growing there? Apparently not, because Papa said that the waterfall can be stopped, pots of flowers carefully put in place, and then the waterfall released again.

XV
Where King Casimir Slept

Never before have we lived so well; even out in the country is not as pleasant as it is here, where we have a garden with flowers in it, meadows, woods, mountains and a little river; there are lots of people, and there are fine views in all directions. We have enough neighbours, because there are several families living in this house as well as ourselves; I saw some children too, little boys and girls; it will be fun to play together once we get to know one another. Today I have spent all day out in the fresh air. Papa took me to see one of his friends who is staying in the Market Square at 'U Niedźwiedzia' [Bear Inn]. While I was playing with the man's little son, Papa pointed to a plaque fixed to the wall, on which was written, 'A. 1669 DEN 17 AUGUST IST JOH: CASIMIRUS GEWESENET KOENIG IN POLEN BEY MIR UEBER NACHT GELEGEN'. Papa said that this meant 'In the year 1669, on August 17, Jan Casimir, then King of Poland, spent the night here in my house'. I immediately had to tell Papa everything that I remember from my history lessons about this king, who after twenty years of unhappy rule gave up the crown, and by doing so he put a stop to internal squabbles and returned the nation to peace. I was sure he was not king any more when he slept here, because it would not have been as comfortable as the Palace in Warsaw that bears his name, now the school which many of my friends attend [Casimir Palace].

At about six o'clock, when Mama had finished drinking the waters, a large crowd of us went for a walk, but we stopped at the shops near the spring selling all sorts of things, and we did not go much further. 'Let's go in here,' said Papa, going up to a glass shop. 'Off you go, children, and choose yourselves a little glass, and I shall buy them for you, and have your names engraved on them.'

'All right,' I called to Papa. 'Go on, Oleś, a bit quicker, so we can choose our glasses.'

'I would prefer a tankard to a little glass,' said Oleś. 'My Papa always drinks beer from a tankard, and I'd like his name to be engraved on it, and when I get back home and my Papa returns after his long journey I will give it to him as a present. He will be happy with it, won't he? I hope I shall see my Papa soon, because I haven't seen him for ages, and it is a long time since he gave me a cuddle.' We were all moved by Oleś's memory of his father, and we tried to stop tears from coming to our eyes. But Papa agreed, and Oleś was overjoyed with his tankard, and was sorry he could not take it with him, because the names on my glass and Oleś's tankard had to be engraved, and they would not be ready until tomorrow morning. Oh, it was so difficult to be patient, and Oleś kept asking me every few moments if it was tomorrow yet. Oleś will now be getting up earlier. Mama went to see the doctor because he was listless and thin, and he prescribed whey from goat's milk mixed with herbs. The poor chap won't be allowed to eat fruit, and there are so many raspberries and strawberries here; but he is a good boy, and will not make a fuss. We then went into a toy shop. Mama bought Oleś some trinkets that he had chosen; I did not want anything, but when Oleś asked Mama to buy me something I chose a box of toy soldiers. As soon as we got back we put them all out on the table, divided them into two armies, and that was when war broke out. I made a fortress just like the one in Glatz from a pile of books, while Oleś made a city from the box; our soldiers then spent the rest of the evening attacking in turn the city and the fortress.

XVI
Poor Boy

After a few days I started to get bored. Every day it was the same: in the mornings I was not allowed to run because the walkways were full of guests, at midday I was not allowed to run because of the heat, after dinner I was not allowed to run because the guests were out again, drinking the water. So I do my lessons in the day and wait for the cool of the evening to go for a walk. The waters and bath-houses are in meadows that have been turned into gardens, enclosed by mountains on both sides.

I missed home, and the open spaces, and yet everyone says it is so nice here. It is true there are lovely surroundings, especially going along the banks of a sparkling stream which whispers over the stones; and going even further, coming to a little hut among the cliffs and spruce woods, called 'Zimmermann's Ruh'. Papa explained the meaning of the name; it was the place where a wise man by the name of Zimmermann liked to stop for a rest during his walks. Today we went for tea to the village of Kohlaw [Podgórze], where a lady bakes all sorts of cakes which she takes into town to sell. Her cottage is simple, with a garden and a bower beside it.

After tea Oleś and I ran on ahead, and got further away from Mama, until we reached a cottage, where we came across a little boy with a large swelling on his throat, who was sitting on a rock; he rested his tilted head and twisted neck on his arms. When we saw him we backed away from him, but the boy leapt up, and came jumping towards us; we shouted and ran off. Mama was startled, but soon realized why we were shouting when she saw the little boy, who, seeing so many people, stopped in his tracks. 'You see, children,' said Papa, 'what comes of being disobedient? I told you not to run off too far, because you might have an accident, or be bitten by a mad dog, and the slightest thing that you don't understand might upset you, and now it has. If you had stayed in front of us, such a thing would not have happened, you would not have had a fright, and we would not have been worried by your shout. Oleś is not to blame, as he is younger than you, and follows your example. So make sure, Józio, that you are always good, in case by bad example you cause harm to others. I have spoken to you before about this, and if this happens one more time, I shall not take you with me, but leave you at the lodgings with the servants.'

I felt ashamed and burst into tears. Papa told me off in front of all those people, and now they are going to laugh at me, I thought, and I didn't feel like running any more. Soon we reached the cottage, where we found that the boy was the son of a Góral [mountain man]. The poor boy has been handicapped since infancy, and lives with it, does no one any harm, but he has no sense of reason, and there's nothing anyone can do for him. 'How lucky you are, children, compared to this poor fellow, who lives to spoil his parents' lives. You must thank God that He has protected you from such a handicap.'

I asked Papa about the lump on his throat, which must hurt him a lot. I felt very sorry for the boy.

'No, children, it doesn't hurt him at all; you sometimes find these lumps among the Górals. It's the result of work and the water. You must have seen how the people here are always carting heavy things up and down the mountains; like that timber. Always having to bend weakens the body. And the mountain water contains iron and sulphur which cause these growths that are found in these parts.'

It was after sunset when we returned to our lodgings. The pleasant songs of the herdsmen leading the cattle in the mountains reached our ears. By that time I could not run about any more with Oleś, because he was exhausted, and a servant had to carry him in his arms. I picked flowers on the way, and reached our lodgings with a sweet-smelling bouquet in my hand.

XVII
The Paper Mill

'Today we should go and visit the paper mill,' Papa said this morning to Mama, 'so Józio can see how they make the paper, of which he has already wasted a lot in his life. If he sees how much work it takes to make one notebook perhaps he will try to write better, and appreciate the work of so many people.' So it was decided that we would go to the paper mill after dinner. It was not until about five o'clock that we left the house along with some other people. We took the long walkway into the town, then past the church by the stream, until my legs – as well as those of the older gentlemen – began to ache. When we came to the enormous house which was the paper mill, we sat down to have a little rest on the benches on the bridge leading to the house, and we all had some crunchy biscuits and some good milk that somebody had brought.

Then Papa asked the manager to show us round. For an hour he took us up and down, into the attic and the cellars, and I saw so many things that were new to me: stairs, wheels, frames, rags, pipes, hammers – it was all so confusing. Before they start making the paper, they buy linen and woollen rags; woollen for blotting paper and linen for writing paper and books. They buy them from poor merchants who go from village to village, collecting them after people have died. I shall not throw old rags away any more; when I have collected enough, I shall give them to a poor merchant to sell to the paper mill. These rags are brought in to women whose job it is to separate them into wool and linen, thick and thin. Then they put each load into a container, where they are soaked in water, and pounded with enormous hammers, until they are turned into one large mass. This mass is then boiled in a huge vat beside which stand two people who stretch the cooling mass finely across four-sided frames with crossed wires, like on a sieve, the size of a sheet of paper. The tightly stretched mass cools down and immediately thickens, and the water drains off through the wires. And there it is, a sheet of paper. Then the sheet is removed from the frame and placed on a cloth to take out the moisture; then the still-damp sheet is placed under the roof to dry out completely. After that it is pulled through glue, placed in another press and again dried. Then, in a different part of the house it is placed into another box, where another hammer, like an enormous wooden cube, beats it until it is smooth. This is done for every sheet of paper, and there are twenty-four sheets in a quire, twenty quires in a ream, and ten reams in a bale. Imagine the work and time needed to make the 4,800 sheets of paper which make up a bale.

I wonder what people used to write on before there was paper. Have they been making paper for a long time? Did King Popiel have paper? I asked Papa all these things, and I learned that they had paper somewhere in Asia – in China, but in Europe it has not been used for very long, and anyway, King Popiel could not write on it. The ancient Romans did not have paper; they wrote on leaves, roots, little boards and wax, not with pens but pointed instruments called chisels. Later tanned animal skins were used to write on;

and to this day they still write on donkey hides. Who would have thought that wise words could be written on the hide of a donkey?

XVIII
The Hermit

I hope it will not rain any more, as there is nowhere to play except outside. It has rained for three whole days, and I sat indoors like a prisoner, doing more lessons than usual, until I got fed up with them. The only place Oleś and I could play was in the corridors with the landlord's little boys. It is a pity they did not understand Polish, because when we're playing at soldiers or coachmen, they do the opposite to what I say. Actually they have learned a few Polish expressions, and Oleś and I some German ones, but it does not help much. Mostly we talk in signs, and because they are well behaved everything runs smoothly between us.

Today I did what I had always wanted to do. I have always wanted to see a hermit, because many times I have come across hermits in stories. Whenever I happened to be in a forest I was always looking out for a hermit's hut, hoping he would come out. But that has never happened, and I could only imagine a hermit from stories and pictures. I imagined a hermit as old, with a grey beard, wearing a dark gown, carrying a big stick in his hand, and a Jewish hat on his head. Today I saw a real hermit who lives close by. He was not old, and did not have a grey beard nor a Jewish hat. I did not believe he was a hermit, until Papa assured me that he really was one. I asked him why he was different to all the other hermits in the pictures I had seen, and he told me that even this one will have a beard one day, and that when he grows old, he will also be leaning on a stick. Still, it was a pity he was not old, because then I would have seen what is to me a real hermit. We climbed up about a hundred and fifty steps to reach him; he received us very politely, and invited us into his house. He has a nice little chapel that leads into his home, but that is not what caught my attention, because I was only interested in seeing his cell and his garden, and I was delighted when he opened the door to his cell and I went in.

It was a tiny room. Over the door was a picture of Jesus with a crown of thorns, and all the walls were covered in pictures. Instead of a bed he had a plank covered in a dark cloth, and a leather pillow. It must be hard to sleep on it. Beside his cot was a table and a prie-dieu. On the table were some books, a cross and a skull, which was not nice to look at. Opposite was a fireplace and a window giving on to the garden, and a small door leading into it. Beside the house stands a little bench that he had built, and flowers that he had planted, pretty pink carnations, white stocks and beautiful mallows decorating the patch of ground, and beside them for his needs I saw carrots and cabbage among the flowers. Over to the left a wall, lined with bushes and a row of wooden crosses. The hermit said they were the graves of his predecessors, that there are several buried there, and that his own cross would be there one day.

In 1679 a plague had been raging in the whole county of Glatz. The children, seeing the danger, climbed up the hill in a crowd to pray, and to give themselves over to God's protection. Behind them went a number of old people, and their warm prayers healed them. God looked kindly on the region, and the town of Reinertz was protected from disease. Nineteen years later this little chapel was built in remembrance of those children who had made the pilgrimage and offered their prayers to God; and the hermit now holds services there for the people. The present hermit has been there for several years; in summer he is very happy, the surroundings are pretty and people come to see him, but in winter not even a bird comes to him. It must be very dreary here when the snows come; the cottages in the valley are snowed in, and the poor people who live in them cannot leave their homes for several weeks. The people are used to this, and stock up with food and fuel in good time. My God, I thought, how unlucky they must be not to see other people or even daylight, or to breathe fresh air. How they must be glad when spring comes.

The hermit offered me a bunch of freshly cut flowers, which I shall dry as a memento. Then he brought out a large book in which he wrote all our names and the date of our visit; when my turn came I wanted to write my name beautifully, but could not because the pen was bad.

XIX
Devout People

Yesterday evening we went to Kudowa; I will never forget the short, interesting mile and a half trip. Just past Reinertz we came to a very high mountain. To make it easier for the horses, we got out and walked along the edge of a pine forest, which covered the whole mountain. While Oleś and I picked flowers and looked for wild strawberries, we heard the sound of singing in the distance, but could not see where it was coming from because of the winding road. Then, turning a corner, we saw coming down from the mountain a crowd of smartly dressed men and women, led by a serious-looking old man. Papa told me that these were devout Czechs going all together to mass, led by the oldest man. Even when we had reached the top, we could still hear the hymns of these devout people; we stood and listened until their singing faded into the distance. It was only when I turned to look at the pretty countryside that I saw a round, tufted hill completely covered in dark forest, and next to it another, long and low, without a single tree on it. On the first I saw ruins of an old wall. What could this be? What is that beautiful mountain called? Papa did not know, but a beggar sitting under a tree replied, 'That mountain is called Hummel, in Czech Gomol, that is, a lump [*gomolka*], because that's what it looks like: those little Czech cheeses that are named after it. The wall is all that remains of a castle where brigands used to live in olden times. They say that underneath there were tunnels leading to the nearest town, where these wicked people hid.'

We continued down the mountain along a rocky road into the town of Lewin. The sun was just setting, the Angelus was ringing, and everyone in the streets knelt where they were and prayed. What a lovely sight. What good and devout people. How is it that in olden times there could be robbers among them? 'In olden times,' said Papa, 'people were rougher and cruder than today. Can you see the other mountain, how well it is kept, and how wheat grows on it? In the olden days it was covered in shrubs and trees, and inhabited only by wild animals. But hard working farmers cut down the trees and exposed the fertile soil to the sun and the dew, and today it yields fine wheat.'

Leaving this good town we found ourselves on a level road,

lined with trees; on the left there were houses and a babbling brook right beside the road, and on the right a large plain. 'What is that white field' I asked.

'It's linen spread out on the grass to whiten,' replied Papa, 'because in this region they make linen, and this is where they whiten it.'

'But won't it get green from the grass or burnt by the sun?'

'No, because it is the sun which whitens it. The sun takes away the colours from wool, cloth and other coloured materials. Look at your nankeen trousers, can you see how they have faded where the sun has shone on them? It's the same with the linen. When it comes off the looms it is greyish; it is spread on the grass and soaked in water. As the sun dries it, the grey disappears, and that is how linen is blanched. People find ways of doing things and even things that damage can be useful.'

XX
Kudowa

The sun had set when we arrived at Kudowa. It was a pleasant evening, and we went out into a garden for a walk in the fresh air. Coming back to the house through the village, we met two people with packs on their backs, who greeted us politely, drew near and began to speak. It seemed that they were talking in Polish; but after a while I realized that they could not be Poles, because I could not understand them, even though they spoke very clearly. 'Who are these people, Papa?' I asked.

'They are merchants from a nearby town,' replied Papa, 'asking if we want any linen.'

'Are they Polish?'

'No, they are Czechs.'

'Czechs? But why don't they speak their own language, instead of spoiling ours? Haven't they got their own language?'

'Yes they have, and they are speaking it. What you have heard that sounded to you a little like Polish is Czech. They are similar because both languages come from the ancient Slav, which today has branched out into many languages. A quarter of a mile from here is the Czech frontier, and Kudowa used to be in the Czech lands; soon I will be visiting their capital with Oleś.' It's a great pity that I won't be going to Prague, but I am happy to have seen so many lands, because I now know so many towns and mountains that I only knew from descriptions and maps.

Oleś has gone. Papa has taken him to Prague. I was sad to part from him, because I had got used to him and he was like a younger brother to me; but he was glad to be going because he thought he was going to his Papa. Now I haven't got anyone to run with, to hide, laugh and play with. Only Mama is left, and I can't muck about with Mama as I could with Oleś. Everyone is complaining that Kudowa is boring, but I would love it, if only I had someone to play with. This isn't a town like Reinertz, but at least we are staying in a house with a garden, like in the country. No one comes to see me because I don't know anyone. If I go out to chase butterflies on the lawn, even if I catch one, I haven't got anyone to show it to. Thousands of roses, all of different colours, gave me a lot of pleasure for a couple of days, but now as I wander among the flower groves, the flowers bore me.

The high mountains that surround Kudowa can be seen in the distance; I could see Schnee Koppe, the highest of the mountains and capped with snow, ten miles away, from my window. The view is beautiful, and it is a pity that I cannot draw, because I would make pictures of all the things that I liked, which perhaps I shall never see again. It would be nice to take back to Warsaw more permanent mementoes than just memories. Papa promised me that on our return he will get me a teacher for drawing and painting; and I shall have a lovely paint box.

Very early, when I am still asleep, the guests go for walks, and by the time I get up and go into the garden, everyone is gone. I know every corner of the garden, there is no little boy of my age to play with, and I'm bored. When I complained to Mama, she said, 'You must learn from an early age, Józio, that things do not always happen as we would want them to, and to accept changes that we don't like. The best remedy for this is patience, as you will soon learn for yourself. Be patient, and you will bear upsets; divide your time well between study and play, and you will not be bored.' I listened to Mama, and I spent more time on my studies now than on the whole of the journey put together; and having spent a couple of hours with my books and my writing, I enjoyed going out for a walk all the more. But I have nothing to write in my diary. I will rewrite it neatly for my teacher.

Select Bibliography

BAUER, W.A., and O.E. DEUTSCH   *Mozart – Briefe und Aufzeichnungen*, Bärenreiter Kassel, Basel, 1975

BELZA, IGOR   *Michał Kleofas Ogiński*, Moscow, 1965

BIENIECKI, RYSZARD   *Pałac Myśliwski*, WDK Kalisz, 1985

BINENTAL, LEOPOLD   *Chopin*, Breitkopf & Hartel, Leipzig, 1932

BORAS, ZYGMUNT, ZBYGNIEW DWORECKI and JÓZEF MORZY   *Sulechów i Okolice*, Mickiewicz University, Poznań, 1985

BOURNIQUEL, CAMILLE   *Chopin*, Evergreen, London, 1960

BUKOWSKI, ANDRZEJ   'Czy Chopin był w Sopocie?', *Rocznik Sopocki Sopot*, 1985–6

BURGER, ERNST   *Frédéric Chopin*, Hirmer Verlag, Munich, 1990

CLAVIER, ANDRÉ   *A l'immortelle memoire d'Emilia Chopin*, Narodowiec, Ets Kwiatkowski, Lens, 1975

   Dans l'entourage de Chopin, Narodowiec, Ets Kwiatkowski, Lens, 1984

   'Duszniki: Epizod Rodziny Chopinów', Duszniki

CHOTOMSKA, WANDA   *Tam Gdzie Był Chopin*, PTTK 'Kraj' Warsaw, 1990

CZARTORYSKI, PRINCE ADAM   *Memoirs*, London, 1888

CZERWIŃSKA, TERESA   'Chopin Museums in Poland', FCSW Agpol, Warsaw, 1990

DAVIES, NORMAN   *God's Playground: A History of Poland*, Clarendon Press, Oxford, 1981

EIGELDINGER, JEAN-JACQUES   *Chopin: Pianist and Teacher*, CUP, Cambridge, 1990

GANCHE, EDOUARD   *Frédéric Chopin: sa vie et ses oeuvres*,

Mercure de France, Paris, 1921
GANCHE EDOUARD   *Dans le Souvenir de Frédéric Chopin*,
Mercure de France, Paris, 1925
    Voyages avec Frédéric Chopin, Mercure de France, Paris, 1934
GUERQUIN, BOHDAN   *Zamki w Polsce*, Arkady, Warsaw, 1984
HARASOWSKI, ADAM   *Skein of Legends around Chopin*, Da
Capo Press, Glasgow, 1967
HEDLEY, ARTHUR   *Chopin*, JM Dent & Sons, London, 1947
    Chopin: Selected Correspondence, Heinemann, London, 1962
HOESICK, FERDYNAND   *Chopin: His Life and Work*, PWM,
Kraków, 1962
HOLMES, EDWARD   *A Ramble Among Music and Musical Pro-
fessors in Germany*, Hunt & Clarke, London, 1828
HUGHES, ROSEMARY   *A Mozart Pilgrimage*, Eulenburg Books,
London, 1975
JEŻEWSKA, ZOFIA   *Fryderyk Chopin*, PTTK 'Kraj', Warsaw, 1985
KAŃSKI, JÓZEF   *Chopin and the Land of his Birth*, Interpress,
Poland, 1981
KARASOWSKI, MORITZ   *Life and Letters of Chopin*, W. Reeves,
London, 1879
KNAPTON, E.J. and T.K. DERRY   *Europe 1815–1914*, John
Murray, London, 1965
KOBYLAŃSKA, KRYSTYNA   *Chopin in his own Land*, PWM,
Kraków, 1956
KWIATKOWSKA, MARIA   *Kościół Ewangelicko-Augsburgski*,
PWN, Warsaw, 1982
LORAINE, PETRIE F.   *Napoleon's Campaigns in Poland 1806–7*,
Sampson Low Marston & Co, London, 1901
MAINE, BASIL   *Chopin*, Duckworth, London, 1933
MIRSKA, MARIA   *Szlakiem Chopina*, Warsaw, 1949
MIZWA, S.P.   *Frédéric Chopin*, Greenwood Press, London, 1949
MURDOCH, WILLIAM   *Chopin: His Life*, John Murray, Lon-
don, 1938
NIECKS, FREDERICK   *Frederick Chopin as Man and Musician*,
Novello, London, 1888
NORMINGTON, SUSAN   *Napoleon's Children*, Bath Press, Bath,
1993
NOWACZYŃSKI, ADOLF   *Młodość Chopina*, Czytelnik, Kraków,
1948
OPIEŃSKI, HENRYK   *Chopin*, H. Altenberga, Lvov, 1909
    Chopin's Letters, Dover Publications, New York, 1988

PALÉOLOGUE, G.M.   *The Enigmatic Tsar*, London, 1938
SCHONBERG, HAROLD C.   *The Great Pianists*, Gollancz, London, 1964
SIWKOWSKA, JANINA   *Pan Chopin Opuszcza Warszawę*, Książka i Wiedza, Warsaw, 1958
SKARBEK, COUNT FRYDERYK   *Pamiętniki*, Poznań, 1878
STRAKHOVSKY, LEONID I.   *Alexander I of Russia*, Williams & Norgate Ltd, London, 1949
SUTHERLAND, CHRISTINE   *Maria Walewska*, London, 1986
SYDÓW, EDOUARD (in collaboration with Suzanne & Denise Chainaye)   *Correspondence de Frédéric Chopin*, Państwowy Instytut Wydawniczy, Paris, 1953
SZULC, M.A.   *Fryderyk Chopin*, Jan Konstanty Żupański, Poznań, 1873
TARNOWSKI, COUNT STANISŁAW   *Chopin As Revealed From Extracts From His Diary*, William Reeves, London, 1899
TROYAT, HENRI   *Catherine the Great*, Aidan Ellis Ltd, Henley-on-Thames, 1978
TULARD, JEAN   *Napoleon: The Myth of the Saviour*, Libraire Arthème, France, 1985
WIERZYŃSKI, CASIMIR   *The Life and Death of Chopin*, Cassell, London, 1951
ZAŁUSKI, ANDRZEJ   'Researches into Michał Kleofas Ogiński', 1994
ZAMOYSKI, ADAM   *Chopin*, Collins, London, 1979
    The Polish Way, John Murray, London, 1987

AUTHORS' NOTE: The entries above are in some cases incomplete, but we have supplied all the information available to us.

Contemporary Newspapers

Bluszcz, Warsaw, 1882
Gazeta Korespondenta Warszawskiego i Zagranicznego, Warsaw, 1818
Gazeta Warszawska (dodatek), Warsaw, 1818–19
Gazeta Polska, Warsaw, 1829
Kurier dla Płci Pięknej, Warsaw, 1823
Kurier Warszawski, Warsaw, 1821–30
Powszechny Dziennik Krajowy, Warsaw, 1830
Poland Illustrated Magazine, No 6 (130), Warsaw, 1965

Index